The System of Nature, or, the Laws of the Moral and Physical World.

(Volume 1)

baron d' Paul Henri Thiry Holbach

Alpha Editions

This edition published in 2024

ISBN : 9789366385938

Design and Setting By
Alpha Editions
www.alphaedis.com
Email - info@alphaedis.com

As per information held with us this book is in Public Domain.
This book is a reproduction of an important historical work. Alpha Editions uses the best technology to reproduce historical work in the same manner it was first published to preserve its original nature. Any marks or number seen are left intentionally to preserve its true form.

Contents

INTRODUCTION ....- 1 -

PREFACE ....- 3 -

PART I. ....- 7 -

    LAWS OF NATURE—OF MAN—
    THE FACULTIES OF THE SOUL—
    DOCTRINE OF IMMORTALITY—
    ON HAPPINESS. ....- 7 -

CHAP. I. ....- 9 -

    Nature and her Laws. ....- 9 -

CHAP. II. ....- 18 -

    Of Motion, and its Origin..- 18 -

CHAP. III. ....- 30 -

CHAP. IV ....- 36 -

CHAP. V. ....- 46 -

    Order and Confusion.—Intelligence.—
    Chance...- 46 -

CHAP. VI. ....- 55 -

Moral and Physical Distinctions of Man.—His Origin. .... - 55 -

CHAP. VII. .... - 67 -

The Soul and the Spiritual System. .... - 67 -

CHAP. VIII. .... - 77 -

The Intellectual Faculties derived from the Faculty of Feeling. .... - 77 -

CHAP. IX. .... - 87 -

CHAP. X. .... - 112 -

CHAP. XI. .... - 131 -

Of the System of Man's free agency. .... - 131 -

CHAP. XII. .... - 154 -

CHAP. XIII. .... - 176 -

CHAP. XIV. .... - 198 -

CHAP. XV. .... - 211 -

CHAP. XVI. .... - 227 -

CHAP. XVII. .... - 240 -

CONCLUSION. .... - 246 -

INTRODUCTION

Paul Henri Thiery, Baron d'Holbach (1723-1789), was the center of the radical wing of the *philosophes*. He was friend, host, and patron to a wide circle that included Diderot, D'Alembert, Helvetius, and Hume. Holbach wrote, translated, edited, and issued a stream of books and pamphlets, often under other names, that has made him the despair of bibliographers but has connected his name, by innuendo, gossip, and association, with most of what was written in defense of atheistic materialism in late eighteenth-century France.

Holbach is best known for *The System of Nature* (1770) and deservedly, since it is a clear and reasonably systematic exposition of his main ideas. His initial position determines all the rest of his argument. "There is not, there can be nothing out of that Nature which includes all beings." Conceiving of nature as strictly limited to matter and motion, both of which have always existed, he flatly denies that there is any such thing as spirit or a supernatural. Mythology began, Holbach claims, when men were still in a state of nature and at the point when wise, strong, and for the most part benign men were arising as leaders and lawgivers. These leaders "formed discourses by which they spoke to the imaginations of their willing auditors," using the medium of poetry, because it "seem{ed} best adapted to strike the mind." Through poetry, then, and by means of "its images, its fictions, its numbers, its rhyme, its harmony... the entire of nature, as well as all its parts, was personified, by its beautiful allegories." Thus mythology is given an essentially political origin. These early poets are literally legislators of mankind. "The first institutors of nations, and their immediate successors in authority, only spoke to the people by fables, allegories, enigmas, of which they reserved to themselves the right of giving an explanation." Holbach is rather condescending about the process, but since mythology is a representation of nature itself, he is far more tolerant of mythology than he is of the next step. "Natural philosophers and poets were transformed by leisure into metaphysicians and theologians," and at this point a fatal error was introduced: the theologians made a distinction between the power of nature and nature itself, separated the two, made the power of nature prior to nature, and called it God. Thus man was left with an abstract and chimerical being on one side and a despoiled inert nature, destitute of power, on the other. In Holbach's critique the point at which theology split off from mythology marks the moment of nature's alienation from itself and paves the way for man's alienation from nature.

Holbach is thus significant for Romantic interest in myth in two ways. First, he provides a clear statement of what can be loosely called the antimythic position, that rationalist condescension and derogation of all myth and all religion that was never far from the surface during the Romantic era. Holbach was and is a reminder that the Romantic affirmation of myth was never easy, uncritical, or unopposed. Any new endorsement of myth had to be made in the teeth of Holbach and the other skeptics. The very vigor of the Holbachian critique of myth impelled the Romantics to think more deeply and defend more carefully any new claim for myth. Secondly, although Holbach's argument generally drove against myth and religion both, he did make an important, indeed a saving distinction between mythology and theology. Mythology is the more or less harmless personification of the power in and of nature; theology concerns itself with what for Holbach was the nonexistent power beyond or behind nature. By exploiting this distinction it would become possible for a Shelley, for example, to take a strong antitheological—even an anti-Christian—position without having to abandon myth.

Holbach was one of William Godwin's major sources for his ideas about political justice, and Shelley, who discussed Holbach with Godwin, quotes extensively from *The System of Nature* in *Queen Mab*. Furthermore, Volney's *Ruins*, another important book for Shelley, is directly descended from *The System of Nature*. On the other side, Holbach was a standing challenge to such writers as Coleridge and Goethe and was reprinted and retranslated extensively in America, where his work was well known to the rationalist circle around Jefferson and Barlow.

Issued in 1770 as though by Jean Baptiste de Mirabaud (a former perpetual secretary to the Académie française who had died ten years before), *La Système de la nature* was translated and reprinted frequently. The Samuel Wilkinson translation we have chosen to reprint was the most often reprinted or pirated version in English. A useful starting point for Holbach's work is Jerome Vercruysse, *Bibliographie descriptive des écrits du baron d'Holbach* (Paris, 1971). The difficult subject of the essentially clandestine evolution of biblical criticism as an anti-Christian and antimyth critique in the early part of the eighteenth century, before the well-documented era of the biblical critic Eichhorn in Germany, is illuminated in Ira Wade, *The Clandestine Organization and Diffusion of Philosophic Ideas in France from 1700-1750* (Princeton Univ. Press, 1938).

Robert D. Richardson, Jr.

University of Denver

{Illustration: Parke sculp't M. DE MIRABAUD}

PREFACE

The source of man's unhappiness is his ignorance of Nature. The pertinacity with which he clings to blind opinions imbibed in his infancy, which interweave themselves with his existence, the consequent prejudice that warps his mind, that prevents its expansion, that renders him the slave of fiction, appears to doom him to continual error. He resembles a child destitute of experience, full of ideal notions: a dangerous leaven mixes itself with all his knowledge: it is of necessity obscure, it is vacillating and false:—He takes the tone of his ideas on the authority of others, who are themselves in error, or else have an interest in deceiving him. To remove this Cimmerian darkness, these barriers to the improvement of his condition; to disentangle him from the clouds of error that envelope him; to guide him out of this Cretan labyrinth, requires the clue of Ariadne, with all the love she could bestow on Theseus. It exacts more than common exertion; it needs a most determined, a most undaunted courage—it is never effected but by a persevering resolution to act, to think for himself; to examine with rigour and impartiality the opinions he has adopted. He will find that the most noxious weeds have sprung up beside beautiful flowers; entwined themselves around their stems, overshadowed them with an exuberance of foliage, choaked the ground, enfeebled their growth, diminished their petals; dimmed the brilliancy of their colours; that deceived by their apparent freshness of their verdure, by the rapidity of their exfoliation, he has given them cultivation, watered them, nurtured them, when he ought to have plucked out their very roots.

Man seeks to range out of his sphere: notwithstanding the reiterated checks his ambitious folly experiences, he still attempts the impossible; strives to carry his researches beyond the visible world; and hunts out misery in imaginary regions. He would be a metaphysician before he has become a practical philosopher. He quits the contemplation of realities to meditate on chimeras. He neglects experience to feed on conjecture, to indulge in hypothesis. He dares not cultivate his reason, because from his earliest days he has been taught to consider it criminal. He pretends to know his date in the indistinct abodes of another life, before he has considered of the means by which he is to render himself happy in the world he inhabits: in short, man disdains the study of Nature, except it be partially: he pursues phantoms that resemble an ignis-fatuus, *which at once dazzle, bewilders, and affright: like the benighted traveller led astray by these deceptive exhalations of a swampy soil, he frequently quits the plain, the simple road of truth, by pursuing of which, he can alone ever reasonably hope to reach the goal of happiness.*

The most important of our duties, then, is to seek means by which we may destroy delusions that can never do more than mislead us. The remedies for these evils must be sought for in Nature herself; it is only in the abundance of her resources, that we can rationally expect to find antidotes to the mischiefs brought upon us by an ill directed, by an overpowering enthusiasm. It is time these remedies were sought; it is time to look the evil boldly in the face, to examine its foundations, to scrutinize its superstructure: reason, with its faithful guide experience, must attack in their entrenchments those prejudices, to which the human race has but too long been the victim. For this purpose reason must be restored to its proper rank,—it must be rescued from the evil company with which it is associated. It has been too long degraded—too long neglected—cowardice has rendered it subservient to delirium, the slave to falsehood. It must no longer be held down by the massive claims of ignorant prejudice.

Truth is invariable—it is requisite to man—it can never harm him—his very necessities, sooner or later, make him sensible of this; oblige him to acknowledge it. Let us then discover it to mortals—let us exhibit its charms—let us shed it effulgence over the darkened road; it is the only mode by which man can become disgusted with that disgraceful superstition which leads him into error, and which but too often usurps his homage by treacherously covering itself with the mask of truth—its lustre can wound none but those enemies to the human race whose power is bottomed solely on the ignorance, on the darkness in which they have in almost every claimed contrived to involve the mind of man.

Truth speaks not to those perverse beings:—her voice can only be heard by generous souls accustomed to reflection, whose sensibilities make them lament the numberless calamities showered on the earth by political and religious tyranny—whose enlightened minds contemplate with horror the immensity, the ponderosity of that series of misfortunes which error has in all ages overwhelmed mankind.

To error must be attributed those insupportable chains which tyrants, which priests have forged for most nations. To error must be equally attributed that abject slavery into which the people of almost every country have fallen. Nature designed they should pursue their happiness by the most perfect freedom.—To error must be attributed those religious terrors which, in almost every climate, have either petrified man with fear, or caused him to destroy himself for coarse or fanciful beings. To error must be attributed those inveterate hatreds, those barbarous persecutions, those numerous massacres, those dreadful tragedies, of which, under pretext of serving the interests of heaven, the earth has been but too frequently made the theatre. It is error consecrated by religious enthusiasm, which produces that ignorance, that uncertainty in which man ever finds himself with regard to his most evident duties, his clearest rights, the most demonstrable truths. In short, man is almost everywhere a poor degraded captive, devoid of greatness of soul, of reason, or of virtue, whom his inhuman gaolers have never permitted to see the light of day.

Let us then endeavour to disperse those clouds of ignorance, those mists of darkness, which impede man on his journey, which obscure his progress, which prevent his marching through life with a firm, with a steady grip. Let us try to inspire him with courage—with respect for his reason—with an inextinguishable love for truth—with a remembrance of Gallileo—to the end that he may learn to know himself—to know his legitimate rights—that he may learn to consult his experience, and no longer be the dupe of an imagination led astray by authority—that he may renounce the prejudices of his childhood—that he may learn to found his morals on his nature, on his wants, on the real advantage of society—that he may dare to love himself—that he may learn to pursue his true happiness by promoting that of others—in short, that he may no longer occupy himself with reveries either useless or dangerous—that he may become a virtuous, a rational being, in which case he cannot fail to become happy.

If he must have his chimeras, let him at least learn to permit others to form theirs after their own fashion; since nothing can be more immaterial than the manner of men's thinking on subjects not accessible to reason, provided those thoughts be not suffered to embody themselves into actions injurious to others: above all, let him be fully persuaded that it is of the utmost importance to the inhabitants of this world to be JUST, KIND, and PEACEABLE.

Far from injuring the cause of virtue, an impartial examination of the principles of this work will shew that its object is to restore truth to its proper temple, to build up an altar whose foundations shall be consolidated by morality, reason, and justice: from this sacred pane, virtue guarded by truth, clothed with experience, shall shed forth her radiance on delighted mortals; whose homage flowing consecutively shall open to the world a new aera, by rendering general the belief that happiness, the true end of man's existence, can never be attained but BY PROMOTING THAT OF HIS FELLOW CREATURE.

In short, man should learn to know, that happiness is simply an emanative quality formed by reflection; that each individual ought to be the sun of his own system, continually shedding around him his genial rays; that these, re-acting, will keep his own existence constantly supplied with the requisite heat to enable him to put forth kindly fruit.

PART I.

LAWS OF NATURE—OF MAN—THE FACULTIES OF THE SOUL—DOCTRINE OF IMMORTALITY—ON HAPPINESS.

CHAP. I.

Nature and her Laws.

Man has always deceived himself when he abandoned experience to follow imaginary systems.—He is the work of nature.—He exists in Nature.—He is submitted to the laws of Nature.—He cannot deliver himself from them:—cannot step beyond them even in thought. It is in vain his mind would spring forward beyond the visible world: direful and imperious necessity ever compels his return—being formed by Nature, he is circumscribed by her laws; there exists nothing beyond the great whole of which he forms a part, of which he experiences the influence. The beings his fancy pictures as above nature, or distinguished from her, are always chimeras formed after that which he has already seen, but of which it is utterly impossible he should ever form any finished idea, either as to the place they occupy, or their manner of acting—for him there is not, there can be nothing out of that Nature which includes all beings.

Therefore, instead of seeking out of the world he inhabits for beings who can procure him a happiness denied to him by Nature, let him study this Nature, learn her laws, contemplate her energies, observe the immutable rules by which she acts.—Let him apply these discoveries to his own felicity, and submit in silence to her precepts, which nothing can alter.—Let him cheerfully consent to be ignorant of causes hid from him under the most impenetrable veil.—Let him yield to the decrees of a universal power, which can never be brought within his comprehension, nor ever emancipate him from those laws imposed on him by his essence.

The distinction which has been so often made between the *physical* and the *moral* being, is evidently an abuse of terms. Man is a being purely physical: the moral man is nothing more than this physical being considered under a certain point of view; that is to say, with relation to some of his modes of action, arising out of his individual organization. But is not this organization itself the work of Nature? The motion or impulse to action, of which he is susceptible, is that not physical? His visible actions, as well as the invisible motion interiorly excited by his will or his thoughts, are equally the natural effects, the necessary consequences, of his peculiar construction, and the impulse he receives from those beings by whom he is always surrounded. All that the human mind has successively invented, with a view to change or perfect his being, to render himself happy, was never more than the necessary consequence of man's peculiar essence, and that of the beings who act upon him. The object of all his institutions, all his reflections, all his knowledge, is only to procure that happiness toward which he is continually impelled by the peculiarity of his nature. All that he does, all that he thinks, all that he is, all that he will be, is nothing more than what Universal Nature has made him. His ideas, his actions, his will, are the necessary effects of those properties infused into him by Nature, and of those circumstances in which she has placed him. In short, art is nothing but Nature acting with the tools she has furnished.

Nature sends man naked and destitute into this world which is to be his abode: he quickly learns to cover his nakedness—to shelter himself from the inclemencies of the weather, first with artlessly constructed huts, and the skins of the beasts of the forest; by degrees he mends their appearance, renders them more convenient: he establishes manufactories to supply his immediate wants; he digs clay, gold, and other fossils from the bowels of the earth; converts them into bricks for his house, into vessels for his use, gradually improves their shape, and augments their beauty. To a being exalted above our terrestrial globe, man would not appear less subjected to the laws of Nature when naked in the forest painfully seeking his sustenance, than when living in civilized society surrounded with ease, or enriched with greater experience, plunged in luxury, where he every day invents a thousand new wants and discovers a thousand new modes of supplying them. All the steps taken by man to regulate his existence, ought only to be considered as a long succession of causes and effects, which are nothing more than the development of the first impulse given him by nature.

The same animal, by virtue of his organization, passes successively from the most simple to the most complicated wants; it is nevertheless the consequence of his nature. The butterfly whose beauty we admire, whose colours are so rich, whose appearance is so brilliant, commences as an inanimate unattractive egg; from this, heat produces a worm, this becomes a chrysalis, then changes into that beautiful insect adorned with the most vivid tints: arrived at this stage he reproduces, he generates; at last despoiled of his ornaments, he is obliged to disappear, having fulfilled the task imposed on him by Nature, having performed the circle of transformation marked out for beings of his order.

The same course, the same change takes place in the vegetable world. It is by a series of combinations originally interwoven with the energies of the aloe, that this plant is insensibly regulated, gradually expanded, and at the end of a number of years produces those flowers which announce its dissolution.

It is equally so with man, who in all his motion, all the changes he undergoes, never acts but according to the laws peculiar to his organization, and to the matter of which he is composed.

The *physical man*, is he who acts by the causes our faculties make us understand.

The *moral man*, is he who acts by physical causes, with which our prejudices preclude us from becoming perfectly acquainted.

The *wild man* is a child destitute of experience, incapable of proceeding in his happiness, because he has not learnt how to oppose resistance to the impulses he receives from those beings by whom he is surrounded.

The *civilized man*, is he whom experience and sociality have enabled to draw from nature the means of his own happiness, because he has learned to oppose resistance to those impulses he receives from exterior beings, when experience has taught him they would be destructive to his welfare.

The *enlightened man* is man in his maturity, in his perfection; who is capable of advancing his own felicity, because he has learned to examine, to think for himself, and not to take that for truth upon the authority of others, which experience has taught him a critical disquisition will frequently prove erroneous.

The *happy man* is he who knows how to enjoy the benefits bestowed upon him by nature: in other words, he who thinks for himself; who is thankful for the good he possesses; who does not envy the welfare of others, nor sigh after imaginary benefits always beyond his grasp.

The *unhappy man* is he who is incapacitated to enjoy the benefits of nature; that is, he who suffers others to think for him; who neglects the absolute good he possesses, in a fruitless search after ideal benefits; who vainly sighs after that which ever eludes his pursuit.

It necessarily results, that man in his enquiry ought always to contemplate experience, and natural philosophy: These are what he should consult in his religion,—in his morals,—in his legislation,—in his political government,—in the arts,—in the sciences,—in his pleasures,—above all, in his misfortunes. Experience teaches that Nature acts by simple, regular, and invariable laws. It is by his senses, man is bound to this universal Nature; it is by his perception he must penetrate her secrets; it is from his senses he must draw experience of her laws. Therefore, whenever he neglects to acquire experience or quits its path, he stumbles into an abyss; his imagination leads him astray.

All the errors of man are physical: he never deceives himself but when he neglects to return back to nature, to consult her laws, to call practical knowledge to his aid. It is for want of practical knowledge he forms such imperfect ideas of matter, of its properties, of its combinations, of its power, of its mode of action, and of the energies which spring from its essence. Wanting this experience, the whole universe, to him, is but one vast scene of error. The most ordinary results appear to him the most astonishing phenomena; he wonders at every thing, understands nothing, and yields the guidance of his actions to those interested in betraying his interests. He is ignorant of Nature, and he has mistaken her laws; he has not contemplated the necessary routine which she has marked out for every thing she holds. Mistaken the laws of Nature, did I say? He has mistaken himself: the consequence is, that all his systems, all his conjectures, all his reasonings, from which he has banished experience, are nothing more than a tissue of errors, a long chain of inconsistencies.

Error is always prejudicial to man: it is by deceiving himself, the human race is plunged into misery. He neglected Nature; he did not comprehend her laws; he formed gods of the most preposterous and ridiculous kinds: these became the sole objects of his hope, and the creatures of his fear: he was unhappy, he trembled under these visionary deities; under the supposed influence of visionary beings created by himself; under the terror inspired by blocks of stone; by logs of wood; by flying fish; or the frowns of men, mortal as himself, whom his disturbed fancy had elevated above that Nature of which alone he is capable of forming any idea. His very posterity laughs at his folly, because experience has convinced them of the absurdity of his groundless fears—of his misplaced worship. Thus has passed away the ancient mythology, with all the trifling and nonsensical attributes attached to it by ignorance.

Not understanding that Nature, equal in her distributions, entirely destitute of malice, follows only necessary and immutable laws, when she either produces beings or destroys them, when she causes those to suffer, whose construction creates sensibility; when she scatters among them good and evil; when she subjects them to incessant change—he did not perceive it was in the breast of Nature herself, that it was in her exuberance he ought to seek to satisfy his deficiencies; for remedies against his pains; for the means of rendering himself happy: he expected to derive these benefits from fantastic beings, whom he supposed to be above Nature; whom he mistakingly imagined to be the authors of his pleasures, and the cause of his misfortunes. From hence it appears that to his ignorance of Nature, man owes the creation of those illusive powers; under which he has so long trembled with fear; that superstitious worship, which has been the source of all his misery, and the evils entailed upon posterity.

For want of clearly comprehending his own peculiar nature, his proper course, his wants, and his rights, man has fallen in society, from

FREEDOM into SLAVERY. He had forgotten the purpose of his existence, or else he believed himself obliged to suppress the natural desires of his heart, to sacrifice his welfare to the caprice of chiefs, either elected by himself, or submitted to without examination. He was ignorant of the true policy of association—of the object of government; he disdained to listen to the voice of Nature, which loudly proclaimed the price of all submission to be protection and happiness: the end of all government is the benefit of the governed, not the exclusive advantage of the governors. He gave himself up without enquiry to men like himself, whom his prejudices induced him to contemplate as beings of a superior order, as Gods upon earth, they profited by his ignorance, took advantage of his prejudices, corrupted him, rendered him vicious, enslaved him, and made him miserable. Thus man, intended by Nature for the full enjoyment of liberty, to patiently search out her laws, to investigate her secrets, to cling to his experience; has, from a neglect of her salutary admonitions, from an inexcusable ignorance of his own peculiar essence, fallen into servility: has been wickedly governed.

Having mistaken himself, he has remained ignorant of the indispensable affinity that subsists between him, and the beings of his own species: having mistaken his duty to himself, it consequently follows, he has mistaken his duty to others. He made a calculation in error of what his happiness required; he did not perceive, what he owed to himself, the excesses he ought to avoid, the desires he ought to resist, the impulses he ought to follow, in order to consolidate his felicity, to promote his comfort, and to further his advantage. In short, he was ignorant of his true interests; hence his irregularities, his excesses, his shameful extravagance, with that long train of vices, to which he has abandoned himself, at the expense of his preservation, at the hazard of his permanent prosperity.

It is, therefore, ignorance of himself that has hindered man from enlightening his morals. The corrupt authorities to which he had submitted, felt an interest in obstructing the practice of his duties, even when he knew them. Time, with the influence of ignorance, aided by his corruption, gave them a strength not to be resisted by his enfeebled voice. His duties continued unperformed, and he fell into contempt both with himself and with others.

The ignorance of Man has endured so long, he has taken such slow, such irresolute steps to ameliorate his condition, only because he has neglected to study Nature, to scrutinize her laws, to search out her expedients, to discover her properties, that his sluggishness finds its account, in permitting himself to be guided by example, rather than to follow experience, which demands activity; to be led by routine, rather than by his reason, which enjoins reflection; to take that for truth upon the authority of others, which would require a diligent and patient investigation. From hence may be traced the hatred man betrays for every thing that deviates from those rules to which he has been accustomed; hence his stupid, his scrupulous respect for antiquity, for the most silly, the most absurd and ridiculous institutions of his fathers: hence those fears that seize him, when the most beneficial changes are proposed to him, or the most likely attempts are made to better his condition. He dreads to examine, because he has been taught to hold it irreverent of something immediately connected with his welfare; his credulity suffers him to believe the interested advice, and spurns at those who wish to show him the danger of the road he is travelling.

This is the reason why nations linger on in the most shameful lethargy, suffering under abuses handed down from century to century, trembling at the very idea of that which alone can repair their calamities.

It is for want of energy, for want of consulting experience, that medicine, natural philosophy, agriculture, painting, in fact, all the useful sciences, have so long remained under the fetters of authority, have progressed so little: those who profess these sciences, prefer treading the beaten paths, however imperfect, rather than strike out new ones,—they prefer the phrensy of their imagination, their voluntary conjectures, to that laboured experience which alone can extract her secrets from Nature.

Man, in short, whether from sloth or from terror, having abnegated the evidence of his senses, has been guided in all his actions, in all his enterprizes, by imagination, by enthusiasm, by habit, by preconceived opinions, but above all, by the influence of authority, which knew well how to deceive him, to turn his ignorance to esteem, his sloth to advantage. Thus imaginary, unsubstantial systems, have supplied the place of experience—of mature reflection—of reason. Man, petrified with his fears, intoxicated with the marvellous, stupified with sloth, surrendered his experience: guided by his credulity, he was unable to fall back upon it; he became consequently inexperienced; from thence he gave birth to the most ridiculous opinions, or else adopted all those vague chimeras, all those idle notions offered to him by men whose interest it was to continue him in that lamentable state of ignorance.

Thus the human race has continued so long in a state of infancy, because man has been inattentive to Nature; has neglected her ways, because he has disdained experience—because he has thrown by his reason—because he has been enraptured with the marvellous and the supernatural,—because he has unnecessarily TREMBLED. These are the reasons there is so much trouble in conducting him from this state of childhood to that of manhood. He has had nothing but the most trifling hypotheses, of which he has never dared to examine either the principles or the proofs, because he has been accustomed to hold them sacred, to consider them as the most perfect truths, and which he is not permitted to doubt, even for an instant. His ignorance made him credulous; his curiosity made him swallow the wonderful: time confirmed him in his opinions, and he passed his conjectures from race to race for realities; a tyrannical power maintained him in his notions, because by those alone could society be enslaved. It was in vain that some faint glimmerings of Nature occasionally attempted the recall of his reason—that slight corruscations of experience sometimes threw his darkness into light, the interest of the few was founded on his enthusiasm; their pre-eminence depended on his love of the marvellous; their very existence rested on the firmness of his ignorance; they consequently suffered no opportunity to escape, of smothering even the transient flame of intelligence. The many were thus first deceived into credulity, then forced into submission. At length the whole science of man became a confused mass of darkness, falsehood, and contradictions, with here and there a feeble ray of truth, furnished by that Nature, of which he can never entirely divest himself; because, without his perception, his necessities are continually bringing him back to her resources.

Let us then, if possible, raise ourselves above these clouds of prepossession! Let us quit the heavy atmosphere in which we are enucleated; let us in a more unsullied medium—in a more elastic current, contemplate the opinions of men, and observe their various systems. Let us learn to distrust a disordered conception; let us take that faithful monitor, experience, for our guide; let us consult Nature, examine her laws, dive into her stores; let us draw from herself, our ideas of the beings she contains; let us recover our senses, which interested error has taught us to suspect; let us consult that reason, which, for the vilest purposes has been so infamously calumniated, so cruelly dishonoured; let us examine with attention the visible world; let us try, if it will not enable us to form a supportable judgment of the invisible territory of the intellectual world: perhaps it may be found there has been no sufficient reason for distinguishing them—that it is not without motives, well worthy our enquiry, that two empires have been separated, which are equally the inheritance of nature.

The universe, that vast assemblage of every thing that exists, presents only matter and motion: the whole offers to our contemplation, nothing but an immense, an uninterrupted succession of causes and effects; some of these causes are known to us, because they either strike immediately on our senses, or have been brought under their cognizance, by the examination of long experience; others are unknown to us, because they act upon us by effects, frequently very remote from their primary cause. An immense variety of matter, combined under an infinity of forms, incessantly communicates, unceasingly receives a diversity of impulses. The different qualities of this matter, its innumerable combinations, its various methods of action, which are the necessary consequence of these associations, constitute for man what he calls the ESSENCE of beings: it is from these varied essences that spring the orders, the classes, or the systems, which these beings respectively possess, of which the sum total makes up that which is known by the term *nature*.

Nature, therefore, in its most significant meaning, is the great whole that results from the collection of matter, under its various combinations, with that contrariety of motion, which the universe presents to our view. Nature, in a less extended sense, or considered in each individual, is the whole that results from its essence; that is to say, the peculiar qualities, the combination, the impulse, and the various modes of action, by which it is discriminated from other beings. It is thus that MAN is, as a whole, or in his nature, the result of a certain combination of matter, endowed with peculiar properties, competent to give, capable of receiving, certain impulses, the arrangement of which is called *organization*; of which the essence is, to feel, to think, to act, to move, after a manner distinguished from other beings, with which he can be compared. Man, therefore, ranks in an order, in a system, in a class by himself, which differs from that of other animals, in whom we do not perceive those properties of which he is possessed. The different systems of beings, or if they will, their *particular natures*, depend on the general system of the great whole, or that Universal Nature, of which they form a part; to which every thing that exists is necessarily submitted and attached.

Having described the proper definition that should be applied to the word NATURE, I must advise the reader, once for all, that whenever in the course of this work the expression occurs, that "Nature produces such or such an effect," there is no intention of personifying that nature which is purely an abstract being; it merely indicates that the effect spoken of necessarily springs from the peculiar properties of those beings which compose the mighty macrocosm. When, therefore, it is said, *Nature demands that man should pursue his own happiness*, it is to prevent circumlocution—to avoid tautology; it is to be understood, that it is the property of a being that feels, that thinks, that acts, to labour to its own happiness; in short, that is called *natural*, which is conformable to the essence of things, or to the laws, which Nature prescribes to the beings she contains, in the different orders they occupy, under the various circumstances through which they are obliged to pass. Thus health is *natural* to man in a certain state; disease is *natural* to him under other circumstances; dissolution, or if they will, death, is a *natural* state for a body, deprived of some of those things, necessary to maintain the existence of the animal, &c. By ESSENCE is to be understood, that which constitutes a being, such as it is; the whole of the properties or qualities by which it acts as it does. Thus, when it is said, it is the *essence* of a stone to fall, it is the same as saying that its descent is the necessary effect of its gravity—of its density—of the cohesion of its parts—of the elements of which it is composed. In short, the *essence* of a being is its particular, its individual nature.

CHAP. II.

Of Motion, and its Origin.

Motion is an effect by which a body either changes, or has a tendency to change, its position: that is to say, by which it successively corresponds with different parts of space, or changes its relative distance to other bodies. It is motion alone that establishes the relation between our senses and exterior or interior beings: it is only by motion that these beings are impressed upon us—that we know their existence—that we judge of their properties—that we distinguish the one from the other—that we distribute them into classes.

The beings, the substances, or the various bodies of which Nature is the assemblage, are themselves effects of certain combinations or causes which become causes in their turn. A CAUSE is a being which puts another in motion, or which produces some change in it. The EFFECT is the change produced in one body, by the motion or presence of another.

Each being, by its essence, by its peculiar nature, has the faculty of producing, is capable of receiving, has the power of communicating, a variety of motion. Thus some beings are proper to strike our organs; these organs are competent to receiving the impression, are adequate to undergoing changes by their presence. Those which cannot act on any of our organs, either immediately and by themselves, or immediately by the intervention of other bodies, exist not for us; since they can neither move us, nor consequently furnish us with ideas: they can neither be known to us, nor of course be judged of by us. To know an object, is to have felt it; to feel it, it is requisite to have been moved by it. To see, is to have been moved, by something acting on the visual organs; to hear, is to have been struck, by something on our auditory nerves. In short, in whatever mode a body may act upon us, whatever impulse we may receive from it, we can have no other knowledge of it than by the change it produces in us.

Nature, as we have already said, is the assemblage of all the beings, consequently of all the motion of which we have a knowledge, as well as of many others of which we know nothing, because they have not yet become accessible to our senses. From the continual action and re-action of these beings, result a series of causes and effects; or a chain of motion guided by the constant and invariable laws peculiar to each being; which are necessary or inherent to its particular nature—which make it always act or move after a determinate manner. The different principles of this motion are unknown to us, because we are in many instances, if not in all, ignorant of what constitutes the essence of beings. The elements of bodies escape our senses; we know them only in the mass: we are neither acquainted with their intimate combination, nor the proportion of these combinations; from whence must necessarily result their mode of action, their impulse, or their different effects.

Our senses bring us generally acquainted with two sorts of motion in the beings that surround us: the one is the motion of the mass, by which an entire body is transferred from one place to another. Of the motion of this genus we are perfectly sensible.—Thus, we see a stone fall, a ball roll, an arm move, or change its position. The other is an internal or concealed motion, which always depends on the peculiar energies of a body: that is to say, on its *essence*, or the combination, the action, and re-action of the minute—of the insensible particles of matter, of which that body is composed. This motion we do not see; we know it only by the alteration or change, which after some time we discover in these bodies or mixtures. Of this genus is that concealed motion which fermentation produces in the particles that compose flour, which, however scattered, however separated, unite, and form that mass which we call BREAD. Such also is the imperceptible motion by which we see a plant or animal enlarge, strengthen, undergo changes, and acquire new qualities, without our eyes being competent to follow its progression, or to perceive the causes which have produced these effects. Such also is the internal motion that takes place in man, which is called his INTELLECTUAL FACULTIES, his THOUGHTS, his PASSIONS, his will. Of these we have no other mode of judging, than by their action; that is, by those sensible effects which either accompany or follow them. Thus, when we see a man run away, we judge him to be interiorly actuated by the passion of fear.

Motion, whether visible or concealed, is styled ACQUIRED, when it is impressed on one body by another; either by a cause to which we are a stranger, or by an exterior agent which our senses enable us to discover. Thus we call that *acquired motion*, which the wind gives to the sails of a ship. That motion which is excited in a body, that contains within itself the causes of those changes we see it undergo, is called SPONTANEOUS. Then it is said, this body acts or moves by its own peculiar energies. Of this kind is the motion of the man who walks, who talks, who thinks. Nevertheless, if we examine the matter a little closer, we shall be convinced, that, strictly speaking, there is no such thing as spontaneous motion in any of the various bodies of Nature; seeing they are perpetually acting one upon the other; that all their changes are to be attributed to the causes, either visible or concealed, by which they are moved. The will of man is secretly moved or determined by some exterior cause that produces a change in him: we believe he moves of himself, because we neither see the cause that determined him, the mode in which it acted, nor the organ that it put in motion.

That is called SIMPLE MOTION, which is excited in a body by a single cause. COMPOUND MOTION, that which is produced by two or more different causes; whether these causes are equal or unequal, conspiring differently, acting together or in succession, known or unknown.

Let the motion of beings be of whatsoever nature it may, it is always the necessary consequence of their essence, or of the properties which compose them, and of those causes of which they experience the action. Each being can only move and act after a particular manner; that is to say, conformably to those laws which result from its peculiar essence, its particular combination, its individual nature: in short, from its specific energies, and those of the bodies from which it receives an impulse. It is this that constitutes the invariable laws of motion: I say *invariable*, because they can never change, without producing confusion in the essence of things. It is thus that a heavy body must necessarily fall, if it meets with no obstacle sufficient to arrest its descent; that a sensible body must naturally seek pleasure, and avoid pain; that fire must necessarily burn, and diffuse light.

Each being, then, has laws of motion, that are adapted to itself, and constantly acts or moves according to these laws; at least when no superior cause interrupts its action. Thus, fire ceases to burn combustible matter, as soon as sufficient water is thrown into it, to arrest its progress. Thus, a sensible being ceases to seek pleasure, as soon as he fears that pain will be the result.

The communication of motion, or the medium of action, from one body to another, also follows certain and necessary laws; one being can only communicate motion to another, by the affinity, by the resemblance, by the conformity, by the analogy, or by the point of contact, which it has with that other being. Fire can only propagate when it finds matter analogous to itself: it extinguishes when it encounters bodies which it cannot embrace; that is to say, that do not bear towards it a certain degree of relation or affinity.

Every thing in the universe is in motion: the essence of matter is to act: if we consider its parts, attentively, we shall discover there is not a particle that enjoys absolute repose. Those which appear to us to be without motion, are, in fact, only in relative or apparent rest; they experience such an imperceptible motion, and expose it so little on their surfaces, that we cannot perceive the changes they undergo. All that appears to us to be at rest, does not, however, remain one instant in the same state. All beings are continually breeding, increasing, decreasing, or dispersing, with more or less dullness or rapidity. The insect called EPHEMERON, is produced and perishes in the same day; of consequence, it experiences the greatest changes of its being very rapidly, in our eyes. Those combinations which form the most solid bodies, which appear to enjoy the most perfect repose, are nevertheless decomposed, and dissolved in the course of time. The hardest stones, by degrees, give way to the contact of air. A mass of iron, which time, and the action of the atmosphere, has gnawed into rust, must have been in motion, from the moment of its formation, in the bowels of the earth, until the instant we behold it in this state of dissolution.

Natural philosophers, for the most part, seem not to have sufficiently reflected on what they call the *nisus*; that is to say, the incessant efforts one body is making on another, but which, notwithstanding appear, to our superficial observation, to enjoy the most perfect repose. A stone of five hundred weight seems to rest quiet on the earth, nevertheless, it never ceases for an instant, to press with force upon the earth, which resists or repulses it in its turn. Will the assertion be ventured, that the stone and earth do not act? Do they wish to be undeceived? They have nothing to do but interpose their hand betwixt the earth and the stone; it will then be discovered, that notwithstanding its seeming repose, the stone has power adequate to bruise it; because the hand has not energies sufficient, within itself, to resist effectually both the stone and earth.—Action cannot exist in bodies without re-action. A body that experiences an impulse, an attraction, or a pressure of any kind, if it resists, clearly demonstrates by such resistance that it re-acts; from whence it follows, there is a concealed force, called by these philosophers *vis inertia*, that displays itself against another force; and this clearly demonstrates, that this inert force is capable of both acting and re-acting. In short, it will be found, on close investigation, that those powers which are called *dead*, and those which are termed *live* or *moving*, are powers of the same kind; which only display themselves after a different manner. Permit us to go a greater distance yet. May we not say, that in those bodies, or masses, of which their whole become evident from appearances to us to be at rest, there is notwithstanding, a continual action, and counter-action, constant efforts, uninterrupted or communicated force, and continued opposition? In short, a *nisus*, by which the constituting portions of these bodies press one upon another, mutually resisting each other, acting and re-acting incessantly? that this reciprocity of action, this simultaneous re-action, keeps them united, causes their particles to form a mass, a body, and a combination, which, viewed in its whole, has the appearance of complete rest, notwithstanding no one of its particles really ceases to be in motion for a single instant? These collective masses appear to be at rest, simply by the equality of the motion—by the responsory impulse of the powers acting in them.

Thus it appears that bodies enjoying perfect repose, really receive, whether upon their surface, or in their interior, a continual communicated force, from those bodies by which they are either surrounded or penetrated, dilated or contracted, rarified or condensed: in fact, from those which compose them; whereby their particles are incessantly acting and re-acting, or in continual motion, the effects of which are displayed by extraordinary changes. Thus heat rarifies and dilates metals, which is evidence deducible that a bar of iron, from the change of the atmosphere alone, must be in continual motion; that there is not a single particle in it that can be said to enjoy rest even for a single moment. In those hard bodies, indeed, the particles of which are in actual contact, and which are closely united, how is it possible to conceive, that air, cold, or heat, can act upon one of these particles, even exteriorly, without the motion being communicated to those which are most intimate and minute in their union? Without motion, how should we be able to comprehend the manner in which our sense of smelling is affected, by emanations escaping from the most solid bodies, of which all the particles appear to be at perfect rest? How could we, even by the assistance of a telescope, see the most distant stars, if there was not a progressive motion of light from these stars to the retina of our eye?

Observation and reflection ought to convince us, that every thing in Nature is in continual motion—that there is not a single part, however small, that enjoys repose—that Nature acts in all—that she would cease to be Nature if she did not act. Practical knowledge teaches us, that without unceasing motion, nothing could be preserved—nothing could be produced—nothing could act in this Nature. Thus the idea of Nature necessarily includes that of motion. But it will be asked, and not a little triumphantly, from whence did she derive her motion? Our reply is, we know not, neither do they—that *we* never shall, that *they* never will. It is a secret hidden from us, concealed from them, by the most impenetrable veil. We also reply, that it is fair to infer, unless they can logically prove to the contrary, that it is in herself, since she is the great whole, out of which nothing can exist. We say this motion is a manner of existence, that flows, necessarily, out of the nature of matter; that matter moves by its own peculiar energies; that its motion is to be attributed to the force which is inherent in itself; that the variety of motion, and the phenomena which result, proceed from the diversity of the properties—of the qualities—of the combinations, which are originally found in the primitive matter, of which Nature is the assemblage.

Natural philosophers, for the most part, have regarded as inanimate, or as deprived of the faculty of motion, those bodies which are only moved by the intervention of some agent or exterior cause; they have considered themselves justified in concluding, that the matter which forms these bodies is perfectly inert in its nature. They have not forsaken this error, although they must have observed, that whenever a body is left to itself, or disengaged from those obstructions which oppose themselves to its descent, it has a tendency to fall or to approach the centre of the earth, by a motion uniformly accelerated; they have rather chosen to suppose a visionary exterior cause, of which they themselves had but an imperfect idea, than admit that these bodies held their motion from their own peculiar nature.

These philosophers, also, notwithstanding they saw above them an infinite number of globes that moved with great rapidity round a common centre, still adhered to their favourite opinions; and never ceased to suppose some whimsical causes for these movements, until the immortal NEWTON clearly demonstrated that it was the effect of the gravitation of these celestial bodies towards each other. Experimental philosophers, however, and amongst them the great Newton himself, have held the cause of gravitation as inexplicable. Notwithstanding the great weight of this authority, it appears manifest that it may be deduced from the motion of matter, by which bodies are diversely determined. Gravitation is nothing more than a mode of moving—a tendency towards a centre: to speak strictly, all motion is relative gravitation; since that which falls relatively to us, rises, with relation to other bodies. From this it follows, that every motion in our microcosm is the effect of gravitation; seeing that there is not in the universe either top or bottom, nor any absolute centre. It should appear, that the weight of bodies depends on their configuration, as well external as internal, which gives them that form of action which is called gravitation. Thus, for instance, a piece of lead, spherically formed, falls quickly and direct: reduce this ball into very thin plates, it will be sustained in the air for a much longer time: apply to it the action of fire, this lead will rise in the atmosphere: here, then, the same metal, variously modified, has very different modes of action.

A very simple observation would have sufficed to make the philosophers, antecedent to Newton, feel the inadequateness of the causes they admitted to operate with such powerful effect. They had a sufficiency to convince themselves, in the collision of two bodies, which they could contemplate, and in the known laws of that motion, which these always communicate by reason of their greater or less compactness; from whence they ought to have inferred, that the density of *subtle* or *ethereal* matter, being considerably less than that of the planets, it could only communicate to them a very feeble motion, quite insufficient to produce that velocity of action, of which they could not possibly avoid being the witnesses.

If Nature had been viewed uninfluenced by prejudice, they must have been long since convinced that matter acts by its own peculiar activity; that it needs no exterior communicative force to set it in motion. They might have perceived that whenever mixed bodies were placed in a situation to act on each other, motion was instantly excited; and that these mixtures acted with a force capable of producing the most surprising results.

If particles of iron, sulphur, and water be mixed together, these bodies thus capacitated to act on each other, are heated by degrees, and ultimately produce a violent combustion. If flour be wetted with water, and the mixture closed up, it will be found, after some lapse of time, (by the aid of a microscope) to have produced organized beings that enjoy life, of which the water and the flour were believed incapable: it is thus that inanimate matter can pass into life, or animate matter, which is in itself only an assemblage of motion.

Reasoning from analogy, which the philosophers of the present day do not hold incompatible, the production of a man, independent of the ordinary means, would not be more astonishing than that of an insect with flour and water. Fermentation and putrid substances, evidently produce living animals. We have here the principle; with proper materials, principles can always be brought into action. That generation which is styled *uncertain* is only so for those who do not reflect, or who do not permit themselves, attentively, to observe the operations of Nature.

The generative of motion, and its developement, as well as the energy of matter, may be seen everywhere; more particularly in those unitions in which fire, air, and water, find themselves combined. These elements, or rather these mixed bodies, are the most volatile, the most fugitive of beings; nevertheless in the hands of Nature, they are the essential agents employed to produce the most striking phenomena. To these we must ascribe the effects of thunder, the eruption of volcanoes, earthquakes, &c. Science offers to our consideration an agent of astonishing force, in gunpowder, the instant it comes in contact with fire. In short, the most terrible effects result from the combination of matter, which is generally believed to be dead and inert.

These facts prove, beyond a doubt, that motion is produced, is augmented, is accelerated in matter, without the help of any exterior agent: therefore it is reasonable to conclude that motion is the necessary consequence of immutable laws, resulting from the essence, from the properties existing in the different elements, and the various combinations of these elements. Are we not justified, then, in concluding, from these precedents, that there may be an infinity of other combinations, with which we are unacquainted, competent to produce a great variety of motion in matter, without being under the necessity of having recourse, for the explanation, to agents who are more difficult to comprehend than even the effects which are attributed to them?

Had man but paid proper attention to what passed under his review, he would not have sought out of Nature, a power distinguished from herself, to set her in action, and without which he believes she cannot move. If, indeed, by Nature is meant a heap of dead matter, destitute of peculiar qualities purely passive, we must unquestionably seek out of this Nature the principle of her motion. But if by Nature be understood, what it really is, a whole, of which the numerous parts are endowed with various properties, which oblige them to act according to these properties; which are in a perpetual ternateness of action and reaction; which press, which gravitate towards a common center, whilst others depart from and fly off towards the periphery, or circumference; which attract and repel; which by continual approximation and constant collision, produce and decompose all the bodies we behold; then, I say, there is no necessity to have recourse to supernatural powers, to account for the formation of things, and those extraordinary appearances which are the result of motion.

Those who admit a cause exterior to matter, are obliged to believe that this cause produced all the motion by which matter is agitated in giving it existence. This belief rests on another, namely, that matter could begin to exist; an hypothesis that, until this moment, has never been satisfactorily demonstrated. To produce from nothing, or the CREATION, is a term that cannot give us the least idea of the formation of the universe; it presents no sense, upon which the mind can rely. In fact, the human mind is not adequate to conceive a moment of non-existence, or when all shall have passed away; even admitting this to be a truth, it is no truth for us, because by the very nature of our organization, we cannot admit positions as facts, of which no evidence can be adduced that has relation to our senses; we may, indeed, consent to believe it, because others say it; but will any rational being be satisfied with such an admission? Can any moral good spring from such blind assurance? Is it consistent with sound doctrine, with philosophy, or with reason? Do we, in fact, pay any respect to the intellectual powers of another, when we say to him, "I will believe this, because in all the attempts you have ventured, for the purpose of proving what you say, you have entirely failed; and have been at last obliged to acknowledge you know nothing about the matter?" What moral reliance ought we to have on such people? Hypothesis may succeed hypothesis; system may destroy system: a new set of ideas may overturn the ideas of a former day. Other Gallileos may be condemned to death—other Newtons may arise—we may reason—argue—dispute—quarrel—punish and destroy: nay, we may even exterminate those who differ from us in opinion; but when we have done all this, we shall be obliged to fall back upon our original darkness—to confess, that that which has no relation with our senses, that which cannot manifest itself to us by some of the ordinary modes by which other things are manifested, has no existence for us—is not comprehensible by us—can never entirely remove our doubt—can never seize on our stedfast belief; seeing it is that of which we cannot form even a notion; in short, that it is that, which as long as we remain what we are, must be hidden from us by a veil, which no power, no faculty, no energy we possess, is able to remove. All who are not enslaved by prejudice agree to the truth of the position, that *nothing can be made of nothing*. Many theologians have acknowledged Nature to be an active whole. Almost all the ancient philosophers were agreed to regard the world as eternal. OCELLUS LUCANUS, speaking of the universe, says, "*it has always been, and it always will be.*" VATABLE and GROTIUS assure us, that to render the Hebrew phrase in the first chapter of GENESIS correctly, we must say, "*when God made heaven and earth, matter was without form.*" If this be true, and every Hebraist can judge for himself, then the word which has been rendered *created*, means only to fashion, form, arrange. We know that the Greek words *create* and *form*, have always indicated the same thing. According to ST. JEROME, *creare* has the same meaning as *condere*, to found, to build. The Bible does not anywhere say in a clear manner, that the world was made of nothing. TERTULLIAN and the father PETAU both admit, that "*this is a truth established more by reason than by authority.*" ST. JUSTIN seems to have contemplated matter as eternal, since he commends PLATO for having said, that "*God, in the creation of the world, only gave impulse to matter, and fashioned it.*" BURNET and PYTHAGORAS were entirely of this opinion, and even our Church Service may be adduced in support; for although it admits by implication a beginning, it expressly denies an end: "*As it was in the beginning, is now, and ever shall be, world without end.*" It is easy to perceive that that which cannot cease to exist, must have always been.

Motion becomes still more obscure, when creation, or the formation of matter, is attributed to a SPIRITUAL being; that is to say, to a being which has no analogy, no point of contact, with it—to a being which has neither extent or parts, and cannot, therefore, be susceptible of motion, as we understand the term; this being only the change of one body, relatively to another body, in which the body moved presents successively different parts to different points of space. Moreover, as all the world are nearly agreed that matter can never be totally annihilated, or cease to exist; by what reasoning, I would ask, do they comprehend—how understand—that that which cannot cease to be, could ever have had a beginning?

If, therefore, it be asked, whence came matter? it is very reasonable to say it has always existed. If it be inquired, whence proceeds the motion that agitates matter? the same reasoning furnishes the answer; namely, that as motion is coeval with matter, it must have existed from all eternity, seeing that motion is the necessary consequence of its existence—of its essence—of its primitive properties, such as its extent, its gravity, its impenetrability, its figure, &c. By virtue of these essential constituent properties, inherent in all matter, and without which it is impossible to form an idea of it, the various matter of which the universe is composed must from all eternity have pressed against, each other—have gravitated towards a center—have clashed—have come in contact—have been attracted—have been repelled—have been combined—have been separated: in short, must have acted and moved according to the essence and energy peculiar to each genus, and to each of its combinations.

Existence supposes properties in the thing that exists: whenever it has properties, its mode of action must necessarily flow from those properties which constitute, its mode of being. Thus, when a body is ponderous, it must fall; when it falls, it must come in collision with the bodies it meets in its descent; when it is dense, when it is solid, it must, by reason of this density, communicate motion to the bodies with which it clashes; when it has analogy, when it has affinity with these bodies, it must be attracted, must be united with them; when it has no point of analogy with them, it must be repulsed.

From which it may be fairly inferred, that in supposing, as we are under the necessity of doing, the existence of matter, we must suppose it to have some kind of properties; from which its motion, or modes of action, must necessarily flow. To form the universe, DESCARTES asked but matter and motion: a diversity of matter sufficed for him; variety of motion was the consequence of its existence, of its essence, of its properties: its different modes of action would be the necessary consequence of its different modes of being. Matter without properties would be a mere nothing; therefore, as soon as matter exists, it must act; as soon as it is various, it must act variously; if it cannot commence to exist, it must have existed from all eternity; if it has always existed, it can never cease to be: if it can never cease to be, it can never cease to act by its own energy. Motion is a manner of being, which matter derives from its peculiar existence.

The existence, then, of matter is a fact: the existence of motion is another fact. Our visual organs point out to us matter with different essences, forming a variety of combinations, endowed with various properties that discriminate them. Indeed, it is a palpable error to believe that matter is a homogeneous body, of which the parts differ from each other only by their various modifications. Among the individuals of the same species that come under our notice, no two resemble exactly; and it is therefore evident that the difference of situation alone will, necessarily, carry a diversity more or less sensible, not only in the modifications, but also in the essence, in the properties, in the entire system of beings. This truth was well understood by the profound and subtle LEIBNITZ.

If this principle be properly digested, and experience seems always to produce evidence of its truth, we must be convinced that the matter or primitive elements which enter into the composition of bodies, are not of the same nature, and consequently, can neither have the same properties, nor the same modifications; and if so, they cannot have the same mode of moving and acting. Their activity or motion, already different, can be diversified to infinity, augmented or diminished, accelerated or retarded, according to the combinations, the proportions, the pressure, the density, the volume of the matter, that enters their composition. The endless variety to be produced, will need no further illustration than the commonest book of arithmetic furnishes us, where it will be found, that to ring all the changes that can be produced on twelve bells only, would occupy a space of more than ninety-one years. The element of fire is visibly more active and more inconstant than that of earth. This is more solid and ponderous than fire, air, or water. According to the quantity of these elements, which enter the composition of bodies, these must act diversely, and their motion must in some measure partake the motion peculiar to each of their constituent parts. Elementary fire appears to be in Nature the principle of activity; it may be compared to a fruitful leaven, that puts the mass into fermentation and gives it life. Earth appears to be the principle of solidity in bodies, from its impenetrability, and by the firm coherence of its parts. Water is a medium, to facilitate the combination of bodies, into which it enters itself, as a constituent part. Air is a fluid whose business it seems to be, to furnish the other elements with the space requisite to expand, to exercise their motion, and which is, moreover, found proper to combine with them. These elements, which our senses never discover in a pure state—which are continually and reciprocally set in motion by each other—which are always acting and re-acting, combining and separating, attracting and repelling—are sufficient to explain to us the formation of all the beings we behold. Their motion is uninterruptedly and reciprocally produced from each other; they are alternately causes and effects. Thus, they form a vast circle of generation and destruction—of combination and decomposition, which, it is quite reasonable to suppose, could never have had a beginning, and which, consequently can never have an end. In short, Nature is but an immense chain of causes and effects, which unceasingly flow from each other. The motion of particular beings depends on the general motion, which is itself maintained by individual motion. This is strengthened or weakened, accelerated or retarded, simplified or complicated, procreated or destroyed, by a variety of combinations and circumstances, which every moment change the directions, the tendency, the modes of existing, and of acting, of the different beings that receive its impulse.

If it were true, as has been asserted by some philosophers, that every thing has a tendency to form one unique or single mass, and in that unique mass the instant should arrive when all was in *nisus*, all would eternally remain in this state; to all eternity there would be no more than one Being and one effort: this would be eternal and universal death.

If we desire to go beyond this, to find the principle of action in matter, to trace the origin of things, it is for ever to fall back upon difficulties; it is absolutely to abridge the evidence of our senses; by which only we can understand, by which alone we can judge of the causes acting upon them, or the impulse by which they are set in action.

Let us, therefore, content ourselves with saying WHAT is supported by our experience, and by all the evidence we are capable of understanding; against the truth of which not a shadow of proof, such as our reason can admit, has ever been adduced—which has been maintained by philosophers in every age—which theologians themselves have not denied, but which many of them have upheld; namely, that *matter always existed; that it moves by virtue of its essence; that all the phenomena of Nature is ascribable to the diversified motion of the variety of matter she contains; and which, like the phoenix, is continually regenerating out of its own ashes.*

CHAP. III.

Of Matter.—Of its various Combinations.—Of its diversified Motion, or of the Course of Nature.

We know nothing of the elements of bodies, but we know some of their properties or qualities; and we distinguish their various matter by the effect or change produced on our senses; that is to say, by the variety of motion their presence excites in us. In consequence, we discover in them, extent, mobility, divisibility, solidity, gravity, and inert force. From these general and primitive properties flow a number of others, such as density, figure, colour, ponderosity, &c. Thus, relatively to us, matter is all that affects our senses in any manner whatever; the various properties we attribute to matter, by which we discriminate its diversity, are founded on the different impressions we receive on the changes they produce in us.

A satisfactory definition of matter has not yet been given. Man, deceived and led astray by his prejudices, formed but vague, superficial, and imperfect notions concerning it. He looked upon it as an unique being, gross and passive, incapable of either moving by itself, of forming combinations, or of producing any thing by its own energies. Instead of this unintelligible jargon, he ought to have contemplated it as a *genus* of beings, of which the individuals, although they might possess some common properties, such as extent, divisibility, figure, &c. should not, however, be all ranked in the same class, nor comprised under the same general denomination.

An example will serve more fully to explain what we have asserted, throw its correctness into light, and facilitate the application. The properties common to all matter, are extent, divisibility, impenetrability, figure, mobility, or the property of being moved in mass. FIRE, beside these general properties, common to all matter, enjoys also the peculiar property of being put into activity by a motion that produces on our organs of feeling the sensation of heat; and by another, that communicates to our visual organs the sensation of light. Iron, in common with matter in general, has extent and figure; is divisible, and moveable in mass: if fire be combined with it in a certain proportion, the iron acquires two new properties; namely, those of exciting in us similar sensations of heat and light, which were excited by the element of fire, but which the iron had not, before its combination with the igneous matter. These distinguishing properties are inseparable from matter, and the phenomena that result, may, in the strictest sense of the word, be said to result necessarily.

If we contemplate a little the paths of Nature—if, for a time, we trace the beings in this Nature, under the different states through which, by reason of their properties, they are compelled to pass; we shall discover, that it is to motion, and motion only, that is to be ascribed all the changes, all the combinations, all the forms, in short, all the various modifications of matter. That it is by motion every thing that exists is produced, experiences change, expands, and is destroyed. It is motion that alters the aspect of beings; that adds to, or takes away from their properties; which obliges each of them, by a consequence of its nature, after having occupied a certain rank or order, to quit it, to occupy another, and to contribute to the generation, maintenance, and decomposition of other beings, totally different in their bulk, rank, and essence.

In what experimental philosophers have styled the THREE ORDERS OF NATURE, that is to say, the *mineral*, the *vegetable*, and *animal* worlds, they have established, by the aid of motion, a transmigration, an exchange, a continual circulation in the particles of matter. Nature has occasion in one place, for those particles which, for a time, she has placed in another. These particles, after having, by particular combinations, constituted beings endued with peculiar essences, with specific properties, with determinate modes of action, dissolve and separate with more or less facility; and combining in a new manner, they form new beings. The attentive observer sees this law execute itself, in a manner more or less prominent, through all the beings by which he is surrounded. He sees nature full of *erratic germe*, some of which expand themselves, whilst others wait until motion has placed them in their proper situation, in suitable wombs or matrices, in the necessary circumstances, to unfold, to increase, to render them more perceptible by the addition of other substances of matter analogous to their primitive being. In all this we see nothing but the effect of motion, necessarily guided, modified, accelerated or slackened, strengthened or weakened, by reason of the various properties that beings successively acquire and lose; which, every moment, infallibly produces alterations in bodies more or less marked. Indeed, these bodies cannot be, strictly speaking, the same in any two successive moments of their existence; they must, every instant, either acquire or lose: in short, they are obliged to undergo continual variations in their essences, in their properties, in their energies, in their masses, in their qualities, in their mode of existence.

Animals, after they have been expanded in, and brought out of, the wombs that are suitable to the elements of their machine, enlarge, strengthen, acquire new properties, new energies, new faculties; either by deriving nourishment from plants analogous to their being, or by devouring other animals whose substance is suitable to their preservation; that is to say, to repair the continual deperdition or loss of some portion of their own substance, that is disengaging itself every instant. These same animals are nourished, preserved, strengthened, and enlarged, by the aid of air, water, earth, and fire. Deprived of air, or of the fluid that surrounds them, that presses on them, that penetrates them, that gives them their elasticity, they presently cease to live. Water, combined with this air, enters into their whole mechanism of which it facilitates the motion. Earth serves them for a basis, by giving solidity to their texture: it is conveyed by air and water, which carry it to those parts of the body with which it can combine. Fire itself, disguised and enveloped under an infinity of forms, continually received into the animal, procures him heat, continues him in life, renders him capable of exercising his functions. The aliments, charged with these various principles, entering into the stomach, re-establish the nervous system, and restore, by their activity, and the elements which compose them, the machine which begins to languish, to be depressed, by the loss it has sustained. Forthwith the animal experiences a change in his whole system; he has more energy, more activity; he feels more courage; displays more gaiety; he acts, he moves, he thinks, after a different manner; all his faculties are exercised with more ease. This igneous matter, so congenial to generation—so restorative in its effect—so necessary to life, was the JUPITER of the ancients: from all that has preceded, it is clear, that what are called the elements, or primitive parts of matter, variously combined, are, by the agency of motion, continually united to, and assimilated with, the substance of animals—that they visibly modify their being—have an evident influence over their actions, that is to say, upon the motion they undergo, whether visible or concealed.

The same elements, which under certain circumstances serve to nourish, to strengthen, to maintain the animal, become, under others, the principles of his weakness, the instruments of his dissolution—of his death: they work his destruction, whenever they are not in that just proportion which renders them proper to maintain his existence: thus, when water becomes too abundant in the body of the animal, it enervates him, it relaxes the fibres, and impedes the necessary action of the other elements: thus, fire admitted in excess, excites in him disorderly motion destructive of his machine: thus, air, charged with principles not analogous to his mechanism, brings upon him dangerous diseases and contagion. In fine, the aliments modified after certain modes, in the room of nourishing, destroy the animal, and conduce to his ruin: the animal is preserved no longer than these substances are analogous to his system. They ruin him when they want that just equilibrium that renders them suitable to maintain his existence.

Plants that serve to nourish and restore animals are themselves nourished by earth; they expand on its bosom, enlarge and strengthen at its expense, continually receiving into their texture, by their roots and their pores, water, air, and igneous matter: water visibly reanimates them whenever their vegetation or genus of life languishes; it conveys to them those analogous principles by which they are enabled to reach perfection: air is requisite to their expansion, and furnishes them with water, earth, and the igneous matter with which it is charged. By these means they receive more or less of the inflammable matter; the different proportions of these principles, their numerous combinations, from whence result an infinity of properties, a variety of forms, constitute the various families and classes into which botanists have distributed plants: it is thus we see the cedar and the hyssop develop their growth; the one rises to the clouds, the other creep humbly on the earth. Thus, by degrees, from an acorn springs the majestic oak, accumulating, with time, its numerous branches, and overshadowing us with its foliage. Thus, a grain of corn, after having drawn its own nourishment from the juices of the earth, serves, in its turn, for the nourishment of man, into whose system it conveys the elements or principles by which it has been itself expanded, combined, and modified in such a manner, as to render this vegetable proper to assimilate and unite with the human frame; that is to say, with the fluids and solids of which it is composed.

The same elements, the same principles, are found in the formation of minerals, as well as in their decomposition, whether natural or artificial. We find that earth, diversely modified, wrought, and combined, serves to increase their bulk, and give them more or less density and gravity. Air and water contribute to make their particles cohere; the igneous matter, or inflammable principle, tinges them with colour, and sometimes plainly indicates its presence, by the brilliant scintillation which motion elicits from them. These stones and metals, these bodies, so compact and solid, are disunited, are destroyed, by the agency of air, water, and fire; which the most ordinary analysis is sufficient to prove, as well as a multitude of experience, to which our eyes are the daily evidence.

Animals, plants, and minerals, after a lapse of time, give back to Nature; that is to say, to the general mass of things, to the universal magazine, the elements, or principles, which they have borrowed: The earth retakes that portion of the body of which it formed the basis and the solidity; the air charges itself with these parts, that are, analogous to it, and with those particles which are light and subtle; water carries off that which is suitable to liquescency; fire, bursting its chains, disengages itself, and rushes into new combinations with other bodies.

The elementary particles of the animal, being thus dissolved, disunited, and dispersed; assume new activity, and form new combinations: thus, they serve to nourish, to preserve, or destroy new beings; among others, plants, which arrived at their maturity, nourish and preserve new animals; these in their turn yielding to the same fate as the first.

Such is the constant, the invariable course, of Nature; such is the eternal circle of mutation, which all that exists is obliged to describe. It is thus motion generates, preserves for a time, and successively, destroys, one part of the universe by the other; whilst the sum of existence remains eternally the same. Nature, by its combinations, produces suns, which place themselves in the centre of so many systems: she forms planets, which, by their peculiar essence, gravitate and describe their revolutions round these suns: by degrees the motion is changed altogether, and becomes eccentric: perhaps the day may arrive when these wondrous masses will disperse, of which man, in the short space of his existence, can only have a faint and transient glimpse.

It is clear, then, that the continual motion inherent in matter, changes and destroys all beings; every instant depriving them of some of their properties, to substitute others: it is motion, which, in thus changing their actual essence, changes also their order, their direction, their tendency, and the laws which regulate their mode of acting and being: from the stone formed in the bowels of the earth, by the intimate combination and close coherence of similar and analogous particles, to the sun, that vast reservoir of igneous particles, which sheds torrents of light over the firmament; from the benumbed oyster, to the thoughtful and active man; we see an uninterrupted progression, a perpetual chain of motion and combination; from which is produced, beings that only differ from each other by the variety of their elementary matter—by the numerous combinations of these elements, from whence springs modes of action and existence, diversified to infinity. In generation, in nutrition, in preservation, we see nothing more than matter, variously combined, of which each has its peculiar motion, regulated by fixed and determinate laws, which oblige them to submit to necessary changes. We shall find, in the formation, in the growth, in the instantaneous life, of animals, vegetables, and minerals, nothing but matter; which combining, accumulating, aggregating, and expanding by degrees, forms beings, who are either feeling, living, vegetating, or else destitute of these faculties; which, having existed some time under one particular form, are obliged to contribute by their ruin to the production of other forms.

Thus, to speak strictly, nothing in Nature is either born, or dies, according to the common acceptation of those terms. This truth was felt by many of the ancient philosophers. PLATO says, that according to tradition, "the living were born of the dead, the same as the dead did come of the living; and that this is the constant routine of Nature." He adds from himself, "who knows, if to live, be not to die; and if to die, be not to live?" This was the doctrine of PYTHAGORAS, a man of great talent and no less note. EMPEDOCLES asserts, "there is neither birth nor death, for any mortal; but only a combination, and a separation of that which was combined, and that this is what amongst men they call birth, and death." Again he remarks, "those are infants, or short-sighted persons, with very contracted understandings, who imagine any thing is born, which did not exist before, or that any thing can die or perish totally."

CHAP. IV.

Laws of Motion, common to every Being of Nature.—Attraction and Repulsion.—Inert Force.—Necessity.

Man is never surprised at those effects, of which he thinks he knows the cause; he believes he does know the cause, as soon as he sees them act in an uniform and determinate manner, or when the motion excited is simple: the descent of a stone, that falls by its own peculiar weight, is an object of contemplation to the philosopher only; to whom the mode by which the most immediate causes act, and the most simple motion, are no less impenetrable mysteries than the most complex motion, and the manner by which the most complicated causes give impulse. The uninformed are seldom tempted either to examine the effects which are familiar to them, or to recur to first principles. They think they see nothing in the descent of a stone, which ought to elicit their surprise, or become the object of their research: it requires a NEWTON to feel that the descent of heavy bodies is a phenomenon, worthy his whole, his most serious attention; it requires the sagacity of a profound experimental philosopher, to discover the laws by which heavy bodies fall, by which they communicate to others their peculiar motion. In short, the mind that is most practised in philosophical observation, has frequently the chagrin to find, that the most simple and most common effects escape all his researches, and remain inexplicable to him.

When any extraordinary, any unusual, effect is produced, to which our eyes have not been accustomed; or when we are ignorant of the energies of the cause, the action of which so forcibly strikes our senses, we are tempted to meditate upon it, and take it into our consideration. The European, accustomed to the use of GUNPOWDER, passes it by, without thinking much of its extraordinary energies; the workman, who labours to manufacture it, finds nothing marvellous in its properties, because he daily handles the matter that forms its composition. The American, to whom this powder was a stranger, who had never beheld its operation, looked upon it as a divine power, and its energies as supernatural. The uninformed, who are ignorant of the true cause of THUNDER, contemplate it as the instrument of divine vengeance. The experimental philosopher considers it as the effect of the electric matter, which, nevertheless, is itself a cause which he is very far from perfectly understanding.—It required the keen, the penetrating mind of a FRANKLIN, to throw light on the nature of this subtle fluid—to develop the means by which its effects might be rendered harmless—to turn to useful purposes, a phenomenon that made the ignorant tremble—that filled their minds with terror, their hearts with dismay, as indicating the anger of the gods: impressed with this idea, they prostrated themselves, they sacrificed to JUPITER, to deprecate his wrath.

Be this as it may, whenever we see a cause act, we look upon its effect as natural: when this cause becomes familiar to the sight, when we are accustomed to it, we think we understand it, and its effects surprise us no longer. Whenever any unusual effect is perceived, without our discovering the cause, the mind sets to work, becomes uneasy; this uneasiness increases in proportion to its extent: as soon as it is believed to threaten our preservation, we become completely agitated; we seek after the cause with an earnestness proportioned to our alarm; our perplexity augments in a ratio equivalent to the persuasion we are under: how essentially requisite it is, we should become acquainted with the cause that has affected us in so lively a manner. As it frequently happens that our senses can teach us nothing respecting this cause which so deeply interests us—which we seek with so much ardour, we have recourse to our imagination; this, disturbed with alarm, enervated by fear, becomes a suspicious, a fallacious guide: we create chimeras, fictitious causes, to whom we give the credit, to whom we ascribe the honour of those phenomena by which we have been so much alarmed. It is to this disposition of the human mind that must be attributed, as will be seen in the sequel, the religious errors of man, who, despairing of the capacity to trace the natural causes of those perplexing phenomena to which he was the witness, and sometimes the victim, created in his brain (heated with terror) imaginary causes, which have become to him a source of the most extravagant folly.

In Nature, however, there can be only natural causes and effects; all motion excited in this Nature, follows constant and necessary laws: the natural operations, to the knowledge of which we are competent, of which we are in a capacity to judge, are of themselves sufficient to enable us to discover those which elude our sight; we can at least judge of them by analogy. If we study Nature with attention, the modes of action which she displays to our senses will teach us not to be disconcerted by those which she refuses to discover. Those causes which are the most remote from their effects, unquestionably act by intermediate causes; by the aid of these, we can frequently trace out the first. If in the chain of these causes we sometimes meet with obstacles that oppose themselves to our research, we ought to endeavour by patience and diligence to overcome them; when it so happens we cannot surmount the difficulties that occur, we still are never justified in concluding the chain to be broken, or that the cause which acts is SUPER-NATURAL. Let us, then, be content with an honest avowal, that Nature contains resources of which we are ignorant; but never let us substitute phantoms, fictions, or imaginary causes, senseless terms, for those causes which escape our research; because, by such means we only confirm ourselves in ignorance, impede our enquiries, and obstinately remain in error.

In spite of our ignorance with respect to the meanderings of Nature, (for of the essence of being, of their properties, their elements, their combinations, their proportions, we yet know the simple and general laws, according to which bodies move;) we see clearly, that some of these laws, common to all beings, never contradict themselves; although, on some occasions, they appear to vary, we are frequently competent to discover that the cause becoming complex, from combination with other causes, either impedes or prevents its mode of action being such as in its primitive state we had a right to expect. We know that active, igneous matter, applied to gunpowder, must necessarily cause it to explode: whenever this effect does not follow the combination of the igneous matter with the gunpowder—whenever our senses do not give us evidence of the fact, we are justified in concluding, either that the powder is damp, or that it is united with some other substance that counteracts its explosion. We know that all the actions of man have a tendency to render him happy: whenever, therefore, we see him labouring to injure or destroy himself, it is just to infer that he is moved by some cause opposed to his natural tendency; that he is deceived by some prejudice; that, for want of experience, he is blind to consequences: that he does not see whither his actions will lead him.

If the motion excited in beings was always simple; if their actions did not blend and combine with each other, it would be easy to know, and we should be assured, in the first instance, of the effect a cause would produce. I know that a stone, when descending, ought to describe a perpendicular: I also know, that if it encounters any other body which changes its course, it is obliged to take an oblique direction, but if its fall be interrupted by several contrary powers, which act upon it alternately, I am no longer competent to determine what line it will describe. It may be a parabola, an ellipsis, spiral, circular, &c. this will depend on the impulse, it receives, and the powers by which it is impelled.

The most complex motion, however, is never more than the result of simple motion combined: therefore as soon as we know the general laws of beings and their action, we have only to decompose, to analyse them, in order to discover those of which they are combined; experience teaches us the effects we are to expect. Thus it is clear, the simplest motion causes that necessary junction of different matter, of which all bodies are composed: that matter, varied in its essence, in its properties, in its combinations, has each its several modes of action or motion, peculiar to itself; the whole motion of a body is consequently the sum total of each particular motion that is combined.

Amongst the matter we behold, some is constantly disposed to unite, whilst other is incapable of union; that which is suitable to unite, forms combinations, more or less intimate, possessing more or less durability: that is to say, with more or less capacity to preserve their union, to resist dissolution. Those bodies which are called SOLIDS, receive into their composition a great number of homogeneous, similar, and analogous particles, disposed to unite themselves with energies conspiring or tending to the same point. The primitive beings, or elements of bodies, have need of supports, of props; that is to say, of the presence of each other, for the purpose of preserving themselves; of acquiring consistence or solidity: a truth, which applies with equal uniformity to what is called *physical*, as to what is termed *moral*.

It is upon this disposition in matter and bodies, with relation to each other, that is founded those modes of action which natural philosophers designate by the terms *attraction, repulsion, sympathy, antipathy, affinities, relations*; that moralists describe under the names of *love, hatred, friendship, aversion.* Man, like all the beings in nature, experiences the impulse of attraction and repulsion; the motion excited in him differing from that of other beings, only, because it is more concealed, and frequently so hidden, that neither the causes which excite it, nor their mode of action are known. This system of attraction and repulsion is very ancient, although it required a NEWTON to develop it. That love, to which the ancients attributed the unfolding, or disentanglement of chaos, appears to have been nothing more than a personification of the principle of attraction. All their allegories and fables upon chaos, evidently indicate nothing more than the accord or union that exists between analogous and homogeneous substances; from whence resulted the existence of the universe: whilst discord or repulsion, which they called SOIS, was the cause of dissolution, confusion, and disorder; there can scarcely remain a doubt, but this was the origin of the doctrines of the TWO PRINCIPLES. According to DIOGENES LAERTIUS, the philosopher, EMPEDOCLES, asserted, that "*there is a kind of affection by which the elements unite themselves; and a sort of discord, by which they separate or remove themselves.*"

However it may be, it is sufficient for us to know that by an invariable law, certain bodies are disposed to unite with more or less facility; whilst others cannot combine or unite themselves: water combines itself readily with salt, but will not blend with oil. Some combinations are very strong, cohering with great force, as metals; others are extremely feeble, their cohesion slight and easily decomposed, as in fugitive colours. Some bodies, incapable of uniting by themselves, become susceptible of union by the agency of other bodies, which serve for common bonds or MEDIUMS. Thus, oil and water, naturally heterogeneous, combine and make soap, by the intervention of alkaline salt. From matter diversely combined, in proportions varied almost to infinity, result all physical and moral bodies; the properties and qualities of which are essentially different, with modes of action more or less complex: which are either understood with facility, or difficult of comprehension, according to the elements or matter that has entered into their composition, and the various modifications this matter has undergone.

It is thus, from the reciprocity of their attraction, the primitive imperceptible particles of matter, which constitute bodies, become perceptible, form compound substances, aggregate masses; by the union of similar and analogous matter, whose essences fit them to cohere. The same bodies are dissolved, their union broken, whenever they undergo the action of matter inimical to their junction. Thus by degrees are formed, plants, metals, animals, men; each grows, expands, and increases in its own system or order; sustaining itself in its respective existence, by the continual attraction of analogous matter; to which it becomes united, and by which it is preserved and strengthened. Thus, certain aliments become fit for the sustenance of man, whilst others destroy his existence: some are pleasant to him, strengthen his habit; others are repugnant to him, weaken his system: in short, never to separate physical from moral laws, it is thus that men, mutually attracted to each other by their reciprocal wants, form those unions which we designate by the terms, MARRIAGE, FAMILIES, SOCIETIES, FRIENDSHIPS, CONNEXIONS: it is thus that virtue strengthens and consolidates them; that vice relaxes or totally dissolves them.

Of whatever nature may be the combination of beings, their motion has always one direction or tendency: without direction we could not have any idea of motion: this direction is regulated by the properties of each being; as soon as they have any given properties, they necessarily act in obedience to them: that is to say, they follow the law invariably determined by these same properties; which, of themselves, constitute the being such as he is found, and settle his mode of action, which is always the consequence of his manner of existence. But what is the general direction, or common tendency, we see in all beings? What is the visible and known end of all their motion? It is to conserve their actual existence—to preserve themselves—to strengthen their several bodies—to attract that which is favorable to them—to repel that which is injurious them—to avoid that which can harm them—to resist impulsions contrary to their manner of existence, and to their natural tendency.

To exist, is to experience the motion peculiar to a determinate essence: to conserve this existence, is to give and receive that motion from which results its maintenance:—it is to attract matter suitable to corroborate its being—to avoid that by which it may be either endangered or enfeebled. Thus, all beings of which we have any knowledge, have a tendency to conserve themselves, each after its peculiar manner: the stone, by the firm adhesion of its particles, opposes resistance to its destruction. Organized beings conserve themselves by more complicated means, but which are, nevertheless, calculated to maintain their existence against that by which it may be injured. Man, both in his physical and in his moral capacity, is a living, feeling, thinking, active being; who, every instant of his duration, strives equally to avoid that which may be injurious, and to procure that which is pleasing to him, or that which is suitable to his mode of existence; all his actions tending solely to conserve himself. ST. AUGUSTINE admits this tendency in all whether organized or not.

Conservation, then, is the common point to which all the energies, all the powers, all the faculties of beings, seem continually directed. Natural philosophers call this direction or tendency, SELF-GRAVITATION: NEWTON calls it INERT FORCE: moralists denominate it in man, SELF-LOVE which is nothing more than the tendency he has to preserve himself—a desire of happiness—a love of his own welfare—a wish for pleasure—a promptitude in seizing on every thing that appears favourable to his conservation—a marked aversion to all that either disturbs his happiness, or menaces his existence—primitive sentiments, that are common to all beings of the human species; which all their faculties are continually striving to satisfy; which all their passions, their wills, their actions, have eternally for their object and their end. This self-gravitation, then, is clearly a necessary disposition in man, and in all other beings; which, by a variety means, contribute to the preservation of the existence they have received, as long as nothing deranges the order of their machine, or its primitive tendency.

Cause always produces effect; there can be no effect without cause. Impulse is always followed by some motion, more or less sensible; by some change, more or less remarkable in the body which receives it. But motion, and its various modes of displaying itself, is, as has been already shewn, determined by the nature, the essence, the properties, the combinations of the beings acting. It must, then, be concluded that motion, or the modes by which beings act, arises from some cause; that as this cause is not able to move or act, but in conformity with the manner of its being or its essential properties, it must equally be concluded, that all the phenomena we perceive are necessary; that every being in Nature, under the circumstances in which it is placed, and with the given properties it possesses, cannot act otherwise than it does.

Necessity is the constant and infallible relation of causes with their effects. Fire consumes, of necessity, combustible matter plated within its circuit of action: man, by fatality, desires either that which really is, or appears to be serviceable to his welfare. Nature, in all the extraordinary appearances she exhibits, necessarily acts after her own peculiar essence: all the beings she contains, necessarily act each after its own a individual nature: it is by motion that the whole has relation with its parts; and these parts with the whole: it is thus that in the general system every thing is connected: it is itself but an immense chain of causes and effects, which flow without ceasing, one from the other. If we reflect, we shall be obliged to acknowledge that every thing we see is necessary; that it cannot be otherwise than it is; that all the beings we behold, as well as those which escape our sight, act by invariable laws. According to these laws, heavy bodies fall—light bodies ascend—analogous substances attract each other—beings tend to preserve themselves—man cherishes himself; loves that which he thinks advantageous—detests that which he has an idea may prove unfavourable to him.—In fine, we are obliged to admit, there can be no perfectly independent energy—no separated cause—no detached action, in a nature where all the beings are in a reciprocity of action—who, without interruption, mutually impel and resist each other—who is herself nothing more than an eternal circle of motion, given and received according to necessary laws; which under the same given incidents, invariably produce the same effect.

Two examples will serve to throw the principle here laid down, into light—one shall be taken from physics, the other from morals.

In a whirlwind of dust, raised by elemental force, confused as it appears to our eyes, in the most frightful tempest excited by contrary winds, when the waves roll high as mountains, there is not a single particle of dust, or drop of water, that has been placed by CHANCE, that has not a cause for occupying the place where it is found; that does not, in the most rigorous sense of the word, act after the manner in which it ought to act; that is, according to its own peculiar essence, and that of the beings from whom it receives this communicated force. A geometrician exactly knew the different energies acting in each case, with the properties of the particles moved, could demonstrate that after the causes given, each particle acted precisely as it ought to act, and that it could not have acted otherwise than it did.

In those terrible convulsions that sometimes agitate political societies, shake their foundations, and frequently produce the overthrow of an empire; there is not a single action, a single word, a single thought, a single will, a single passion in the agents, whether they act as destroyers, or as victims, that is not the necessary result of the causes operating; that does not act, as, of necessity, it must act, from the peculiar essence of the beings who give the impulse, and that of the agents who receive it, according to the situation these agents fill in the moral whirlwind. This could be evidently proved by an understanding capacitated to rate all the action and re-action, of the minds and bodies of those who contributed to the revolution.

In fact, if all be connected in Nature, if all motion be produced, the one from the other, notwithstanding their secret communications frequently elude our sight; we ought to feel convinced of this truth, that there is no cause, however minute, however remote, that does not sometimes produce the greatest and most immediate effects on man. It may, perhaps, be in the parched plains of Lybia, that are amassed the first elements of a storm or tempest, which, borne by the winds, approach our climate, render our atmosphere dense, and thus operating on the temperament, may influence the passions of a man, whose circumstances shall have capacitated him to influence many others, who shall decide after his will the fate of many nations.

Man, in fact, finds himself in Nature, and makes a part of it: he acts according to laws, which are appropriate to him; he receives in a manner more or less distinct, the action and impulse of the beings who surround him; who themselves act after laws that are peculiar to their essence. Thus he is variously modified; but his actions are always the result of his own energy, and that of the beings who act upon him, and by whom he is modified. This is what gives such variety to his determinations—what generally produces such contradiction in his thoughts, his opinions, his will, his actions; in short, in that motion, whether concealed or visible, by which he is agitated. We shall have occasion, in the sequel, to place this truth, at present so much contested, in a clearer light: it will be sufficient for our purpose at present to prove, generally, that every thing in Nature is necessary—that nothing to be found in it can act otherwise than it does.

Motion, alternately communicated and received, establishes the connection or relation between the different orders of beings: when they are in the sphere of reciprocal action, attraction approximates them; repulsion dissolves and separates them; the one strengthens and preserves them; the other enfeebles and destroys them. Once combined, they have a tendency to conserve themselves in that mode of existence, by virtue of their *inert force*; in this they cannot succeed, because they are exposed to the continual influence of all other beings, who perpetually and successively act upon them; their change of form, their dissolution, is requisite to the preservation of Nature herself: this is the sole end we are able to assign her—to which we see her tend without intermission—which she follows without interruption, by the destruction and reproduction of all subordinate beings, who are obliged to submit to her laws—to concur, by their mode of action, to the maintenance of her active existence, so essentially requisite to the GREAT WHOLE.

It is thus each being is an individual, who, in the great family, performs his necessary portion of the general labour—who executes the unavoidable task assigned to him. All bodies act according to laws, inherent in their peculiar essence, without the capability to swerve, even for a single instant, from those according to which Nature herself acts. This is the central power, to which all other powers, essences, and energies, are submitted: she regulates the motions of beings, by the necessity of her own peculiar essence: she makes them concur by various modes to the general plan: this appears to be nothing more than the life, action, and maintenance of the whole, by the continual change of its parts. This object she obtains, in removing them, one by the other; by that which establishes, and by that which destroys, the relation subsisting between them; by that which gives them, and that which deprives them of, their forms, combinations, proportions, and qualities, according to which they act for a time, after a given mode; these are afterwards taken from them, to make them act after a different manner. It is thus that Nature makes them expand and change, grow and decline, augment and diminish, approximate and remove, forms and destroys them, according as she finds it requisite to maintain the whole; towards the conservation which this Nature is herself essentially necessitated to have a tendency.

This irresistible power, this universal necessity, this general energy, then, is only a consequence of the nature of things; by virtue of which every thing acts, without intermission, after constant and immutable laws: these laws not varying more for the whole than for the beings of which it is composed. Nature is an active living whole, to which all its parts necessarily concur; of which, without their own knowledge, they maintain the activity, the life, and the existence. Nature acts and exists necessarily: all that she contains, necessarily conspires to perpetuate her active existence. This is the decided opinion of PLATO, when he says, "*matter and necessity are the same thing; this necessity is the mother of the world.*" In point of fact, we cannot go beyond this aphorism, MATTER ACTS, BECAUSE IT EXISTS; AND EXISTS, TO ACT. If it be enquired how, or for why, matter exists? We answer, we know not: but reasoning by analogy, of what we do not know by that which we do, we should be of opinion it exists necessarily, or because it contains within itself a sufficient reason for its existence. In supposing it to be created or produced by a being distinguished from it, or less known than itself, (which it may be, for any thing we know to the contrary,) we must still admit, that this being is necessary, and includes a sufficient reason for his own existence. We have not then removed any of the difficulty, we have not thrown a clearer light upon the subject, we have not advanced a single step; we have simply laid aside a being, of which we know some few of the properties, but of which we are still extremely ignorant, to have recourse to a power, of which it is utterly impossible we can, as long as we are men, form any distinct idea; of which, notwithstanding it may be a truth, we cannot, by any means we possess, demonstrate the existence. As, therefore, these must be at best but speculative points of belief, which each individual, by reason of its obscurity, may contemplate with different optics, under various aspects, they surely ought to be left free for each to judge after his own fashion: the Hindoo can have no just cause of enmity against the Christian for his faith: this has no moral right to question the Mussulman upon his; the numerous sects of each of the various persuasions spread over the face of the earth, ought to make it a creed to look with an eye of complacency on the deviation of the others; and rest upon that great moral axiom, which is strictly conformable to Nature, which contains the whole of man's happiness—"*Do not unto another, that which do you not wish another should do unto you;*" for it is evident, according to their own doctrines, out of all the variety of systems, one only can be right.

We shall see in the sequel, how much man's imagination labours to form an idea, of the energies of that Nature he has personified, and distinguished from herself: in short, we shall examine some of the ridiculous and pernicious inventions, which, for want of understanding Nature, have been imagined to impede her course, to suspend her eternal laws, to place obstacles to the necessity of things.

CHAP. V.

Order and Confusion.—Intelligence.—Chance.

The observation of the necessary, regular, and periodical motion in the universe, generated in the mind of man the idea of ORDER; this term, in its original signification, represents nothing more than a mode of considering, a facility of perceiving, together and separately, the different relations of a whole; in which is discovered, by its manner of existing and acting, a certain affinity or conformity with his own. Man, in extending this idea to the universe, carried with him those methods of considering things which are peculiar to himself: he has consequently supposed there really existed in Nature affinities and relations, which he classed under the name of ORDER; and others which appeared to him not to conform to those, which he has ranked under the term of CONFUSION.

It is easy to comprehend, that this idea of order and confusion can have no absolute existence in Nature, where every thing is necessary; where the whole follows constant and invariable laws, which oblige each being, in every moment of its duration, to submit to other laws, which flow from its own peculiar mode of existence. Therefore it is in his imagination, only, man finds a model of that which he terms order or confusion; which, like all his abstract, metaphysical ideas, supposes nothing beyond his reach. Order, however, is never more than the faculty of conforming himself with the beings by whom he is environed, or with the whole of which he forms a part.

Nevertheless, if the idea of order be applied to Nature, it will be found to be nothing but a series of action or motion, which he judges to conspire to one common end. Thus, in a body that moves, order is the chain of action, the series of motion, proper to constitute it what it is, and to maintain it in its actual state. Order, relatively to the whole of Nature, is the concatenation of causes and effects, necessary to her *active* existence—to maintaining her constantly together; but, as it has been proved in the chapter preceding, every individual being is obliged to concur to this end, in the different ranks they occupy; from whence it is a necessary deduction, that what is called the ORDER OF NATURE, can never be more than a certain manner of considering the necessity of things, to which all, of which man has any knowledge, is submitted. That which is styled CONFUSION, is only a relative term, used to designate that series of necessary action, that chain of requisite motion, by which an individual being is necessarily changed or disturbed in its mode of existence—by which it is instantaneously obliged to alter its manner of action; but no one of these actions, no part of this motion is capable, even for a single instant, of contradicting or deranging the general order of Nature; from which all beings derive their existence, their properties, the motion appropriate to each.

What is termed confusion in a being, is nothing more than its passage into a new class, a new mode of existence; which necessarily carries with it a new series of action, a new chain of motion, different from that of which this being found itself susceptible in the preceding rank it occupied. That which is called order, in Nature, is a mode of existence, or a disposition of its particles, strictly *necessary*. In every other assemblage of causes and effects, of worlds, as well as in that which we inhabit, some sort of arrangement, some kind of order would necessarily be established. Suppose the most incongruous, the most heterogeneous substances were put into activity, and assembled by a concatenation of extraordinary circumstances; they would form amongst themselves, a complete order, a perfect arrangement. This is the true notion of a property, which may be defined, an aptitude to constitute a being, such as it is actually found, such as it is with respect to the whole of which it makes a part.

Order, then, is nothing but necessity, considered relatively to the series of actions, or the connected chain of causes and effects, that it produces in the universe. What is the motion in our planetary system; but a series of phenomena, operated upon according to necessary laws, that regulate the bodies of which it is composed? In conformity to these laws, the sun occupies the centre; the planets gravitate towards it, and revolve round it, in regulated periods: the satellites of these planets gravitate towards those which are in the centre of their sphere of action, and describe round them their periodical route. One of these planets, the earth which man inhabits, turns on its own axis; and by the various aspects which its revolution obliges it to present to the sun, experiences those regular variations which are called SEASONS. By a sequence of the sun's action upon different parts of this globe, all its productions undergo vicissitudes: plants, animals, men, are in a sort of morbid drowsiness during *Winter*: in *Spring*, these beings re-animate, to come as it were out of a long lethargy. In short, the mode in which the earth receives the sun's beams, has an influence on all its productions; these rays, when darted obliquely, do not act in the same manner as when they fall perpendicularly; their periodical absence, caused by the revolution of this sphere on itself, produces *night* and *day*. However, in all this, man never witnesses more than necessary effects, flowing from the nature of things, which, whilst that remains the same, can never be opposed with propriety. These effects are owing to gravitation, attraction, centrifugal power, &c.

On the other hand, this *order*, which man admires as a supernatural effect, is sometimes disturbed, or changed into what he calls *confusion*: this confusion is, however, always a necessary consequence of the laws of Nature; in which it is requisite to the support of the whole that some of her parts should be deranged and thrown out of the ordinary course. It is thus, COMETS present themselves so unexpectedly to man's wondering eyes; their eccentric motion disturbs the tranquillity of his planetary system; they excite the terror of the misinstructed to whom every thing unusual is marvellous. The natural philosopher, himself, conjectures that in former ages, these comets have overthrown the surface of this mundane ball, and caused great revolutions on the earth. Independent of this extraordinary *confusion*, he is exposed to others more familiar to him: sometimes, the seasons appear to have usurped each other's place; to have quitted their regular order: sometimes the opposing elements seem to dispute among themselves the dominion of the world; the sea bursts its limits; the solid earth is shaken and rent asunder; mountains are in a state of conflagration; pestilential diseases destroy both men and animals; sterility desolates a country: then affrighted man utters piercing cries, offers up his prayers to recall order; tremblingly raises his hands towards the Being he supposes to be the author of all these calamities; nevertheless, the whole of this afflicting confusion are necessary effects, produced by natural causes; which act according to fixed laws, determined by their own peculiar essence, and the universal essence of Nature: in which every thing must necessarily be changed, moved, and dissolved; where that which is called ORDER, must sometimes be disturbed and altered into a new mode of existence; which to his deluded mind, to his imagination, led astray by ignorance and want of reflection, appears CONFUSION.

There cannot possibly exist what is generally termed *a confusion of Nature*: man finds order in every thing that is conformable to his own mode of being; confusion in every thing by which it is opposed: nevertheless, in Nature, all is in order; because none of her parts are ever able to emancipate themselves from those invariable rules which flow from their respective essences: there *is* not, there *cannot* be confusion in a whole, to the maintenance of which what is *called* confusion is absolutely requisite; of which the general course can never be discomposed, although individuals may be, and necessarily are; where all the effects produced are the consequence of natural causes, that under the circumstances in which they are placed, act only as they infallibly are obliged to act.

It therefore follows, there can be neither monsters nor prodigies; wonders nor miracles in Nature: those which are designated MONSTERS, are certain combinations, with which the eyes of man are not familiarized; but which, therefore, are not less the necessary effects of natural causes.

Those which he terms PRODIGIES, WONDERS, or SUPERNATURAL effects, are phenomena of Nature, with whose mode of action he is unacquainted; of which his ignorance does not permit him to ascertain the principles; whose causes he cannot trace; but which his impatience, his heated imagination, aided by a desire to explain, makes him foolishly attribute to imaginary causes; which, like the idea of order, have no existence but in himself; and which, that he may conceal his own ignorance, that he may obtain more respect with the uninformed, he places beyond Nature, out of which his experience is every instant demonstrably proving that none of these things can have existence.

As for those effects which are called MIRACLES, that is to say, contrary to the unalterable laws of Nature, it must be felt such things are impossible; because, nothing can, for an instant, suspend the necessary course of beings, without the whole of Nature was arrested; without she was disturbed in her tendency. There have neither been wonders nor miracles in Nature; except for those, who have not sufficiently studied the laws, who consequently do not feel, that those laws can never be contradicted, even in the most minute parts, without the whole being destroyed, or at least without changing her essence, her mode of action; that it is the height of folly to recur to supernatural causes to explain the phenomena man beholds, before he becomes fully acquainted with natural causes—with the powers and capabilities which Nature herself contains.

Order and *Confusion*, then, are only relative terms, by which man designates the state in which particular beings find themselves. He says, a being is in order, when all the motion it undergoes conspires to favor its tendency to its own preservation; when it is conducive to the maintenance of its actual existence: that it is in confusion when the causes which move it disturb the harmony of its existence, or have a tendency to destroy the equilibrium necessary to the conservation of its actual state. Nevertheless, confusion, as we have shown, is nothing but the passage of a being into a new order; the more rapid the progress, the greater the confusion for the being that is submitted to it: that which conducts man to what is called death, is, for him, the greatest of all possible confusion. Yet this death is nothing more than a passage into a new mode of existence: it is the eternal, the invariable, the unconquerable law of Nature, to which the individuals of his order, each in his turn, is obliged to submit.

The human body is said to be in order, when its various component parts act in that mode, from which results the conservation of the whole; from which emanates that which is the tendency of his actual existence; in other words, when all the impulse he receives, all the motion he communicates, tends to preserve his health, to render him happy, by promoting the happiness of his fellow men. He is said to be in health when the fluids and solids of his body concur to render him robust, to keep his mind in vigour; when each lends mutual aid towards this end. He is said to be in *confusion*, or in ill health, whenever this tendency is disturbed; when any of the essential parts of his body cease to concur to his preservation, or to fulfil its peculiar functions. This it is that happens in a state of sickness, in which, however, the motion excited in the human machine is as necessary, is regulated by laws as certain, as natural, as invariable, as that which concurs to produce health. Sickness merely produces in him a new order of motion, a new series of action, a new chain of things. Man dies: to him, this appears the greatest confusion he can experience; his body is no longer what it was—its parts no longer concur to the same end—his blood has lost its circulation—he is deprived of feeling—his ideas have vanished—he thinks no more—his desires have fled—death is the epoch, the cessation of his human existence.—His frame becomes an inanimate mass, by the subtraction of those principles by which it was animated; that is, which made it act after a determinate manner: its tendency has received a new direction; its action is changed; the motion excited in its ruins conspires to a new end. To that motion, the harmony of which he calls order, which produced life, sentiment, thought, passions, health, succeeds a series of motion of another species; that, nevertheless, follows laws as necessary as the first; all the parts of the dead man conspire to produce what is called dissolution, fermentation, putrefaction: these new modes of being, of acting, are just as natural to man, reduced to this state, as sensibility, thought, the periodical motion of the blood, &c. were to the living man: his essence having changed, his mode of action can no longer be the same. To that regulated motion, to that necessary action, which conspired to the production of life, succeeds that determinate motion, that series of action which concurs to produce the dissolution of the dead carcass; the dispersion of its parts; the formation of new combinations, from which result new beings; and which, as we have before seen, is the immutable order of active Nature.

How then can it be too often repeated, that relatively to the great whole, all the motion of beings, all their modes of action, can never be but in order, that is to say, are always conformable to Nature; that in all the stages through which beings are obliged to pass, they invariably act after a mode necessarily subordinate to the universal whole? To say more, each individual being always acts in order; all its actions, the whole system of its motion, are the necessary consequence of its peculiar mode of existence; whether that be momentary or durable. Order, in political society, is the effect of a necessary series of ideas, of wills, of actions, in those who compose it; whose movements are regulated in a manner, either calculated to maintain its indivisibility, or to hasten its dissolution. Man constituted, or modified, in the manner we term virtuous, acts necessarily in that mode, from whence results the welfare of his associates: the man we stile wicked, acts necessarily in that mode, from whence springs the misery of his fellows: his Nature, being essentially different, he must necessarily act after a different mode: his individual order is at variance, but his relative order is complete: it is equally the essence of the one, to promote happiness, as it is of the other to induce misery.

Thus, order and confusion in individual beings, is nothing more than the manner of man's considering the natural and necessary effects, which they produce relatively to himself. He fears the wicked man; he says that he will carry confusion into society, because he disturbs its tendency and places obstacles to its happiness. He avoids a falling stone, because it will derange in him the order necessary to his conservation. Nevertheless, order and confusion, are always, as we have shewn, consequences, equally necessary to either the transient or durable state of beings. It is in order that fire burns, because it is of its essence to burn; on the other hand, it is in order, that an intelligent being should remove himself from whatever can disturb his mode of existence. A being, whose organization renders him sensible, must in virtue of his essence, fly from every thing that can injure his organs, or that can place his existence in danger.

Man calls those beings *intelligent*, who are organized after his own manner; in whom he sees faculties proper for their preservation; suitable to maintain their existence in the order that is convenient to them; that can enable them to take the necessary measures towards this end, with a consciousness of the motion they undergo. From hence, it will be perceived, that the faculty called intelligence, consists in a possessing capacity to act comformably to a known end, in the being to which it is attributed. He looks upon these beings as deprived of intelligence, in which he finds no conformity with himself; in whom he discovers neither the same construction, nor the same faculties: of which he knows neither the essence, the end to which they tend, the energies by which they act, nor the order that is necessary to them. The whole cannot have a distinct name, or end, because there is nothing out of itself, to which it can have a tendency. If it be in himself, that he arranges the idea of *order*, it is also in himself, that he draws up that of *intelligence*. He refuses to ascribe it to those beings, who do not act after his own manner: he accords it to all those whom he supposes to act like himself: the latter he calls intelligent agents: the former blind causes; that is to say, intelligent agents who act by *chance*: thus chance is an empty word without sense, but which is always opposed to that of intelligence, without attaching any determinate, or any certain idea.

Man, in fact, attributes to *chance* all those effects, of which the connection they have with their causes is not seen. Thus he uses the word *chance*, to cover his ignorance of those natural causes, which produce visible effects, by means which he cannot form an idea of; or that act by a mode of which he does not perceive the order; or whose system is not followed by actions conformable to his own. As soon as he sees, or believes he sees, the order of action, or the manner of motion, he attributes this order to an *intelligence*; which is nothing more than a quality borrowed from himself—from his own peculiar mode of action—from the manner in which he is himself affected.

Thus an *intelligent being* is one who thinks, who wills, and who acts, to compass an end. If so, he must have organs, an aim conformable to those of man: therefore, to say Nature is governed by an intelligence, is to affirm that she is governed by a being, furnished with organs; seeing that without this organic construction, he can neither have sensations, perceptions, ideas, thought, will, plan, nor action which he understands.

Man always makes himself the center of the universe: it is to himself that he relates all he beholds. As soon as he believes he discovers a mode of action that has a conformity with his own, or some phenomenon that interests his feelings, he attributes it to a cause that resembles himself—that acts after his manner—that has faculties similar to those he possesses—whose interests are like his own—whose projects are in unison with and have the same tendency as those he himself indulges: in short, it is from himself, or the properties which actuate him, that he forms the model of this cause. It is thus that man beholds, out of his own species, nothing but beings who act differently from himself; yet believes that he remarks in Nature an order similar to his own ideas—views conformable to those which he himself possesses. He imagines that Nature is governed by a cause whose intelligence is conformable to his own, to whom he ascribes the honor of the order which he believes he witnesses—of those views that fall in with those that are peculiar to himself—of an aim which quadrates with that which is the great end of all his own actions. It is true that man, feeling his incapability of producing the vast, the multiplied effects of which he witnesses the operation, when contemplating the universe, was under the necessity of making a distinction between himself and the cause which he supposed to be the author of such stupendous effects; he believed he removed every difficulty, by amplifying in this cause all those faculties of which he was himself in possession; adding others of which his own self-love made him desirous, or which he thought would render his being more perfect: thus, he gave JUPITER wings, with the faculty of assuming any form he might deem convenient: it was thus, by degrees, he arrived at forming an idea of that intelligent cause, which he has placed above Nature, to preside over action—to give her that motion of which he has chosen to believe she was in herself incapable. He obstinately persists in regarding this Nature as a heap of dead, inert matter, without form, which has not within itself the power of producing any of those great effects, those regular phenomena, from which emanates what he styles *the order of the Universe*. ANAXAGORAS is said to have been the first who supposed the universe created and governed by an intelligence: ARISTOTLE reproaches him with having made an automaton of this intelligence; or in other words, with ascribing to it the production of things, only when he was at a loss to account for their appearance. From whence it may be deduced, that it is for want of being acquainted with the powers of Nature, or the properties of matter, that man has multiplied beings without necessity—that he has supposed the universe under the government of an intelligent cause, which he is, and perhaps always will be, himself the model: in fine, this cause has been personified under such a variety of shapes, sexes, and names, that a list of the deities he has at various times supposed to guide this Nature, or to whom he has submitted her, makes a large volume that occupies some years of his youthful education to understand. He only rendered this cause more inconceivable, when he extended in it his own faculties too much. He either annihilates, or renders it altogether impossible, when he would attach to it incompatible qualities, which he is obliged to do, to enable him to account for the contradictory and disorderly effects he beholds in the world. In fact, he sees confusion in the world; yet, notwithstanding his confusion contradicts the plan, the power, the wisdom, the bounty of this intelligence, and the miraculous order which he ascribes to it; he says, the extreme beautiful arrangement of the whole, obliges him to suppose it to be the work of a sovereign intelligence: unable, however, to reconcile this seeming confusion with the benevolence he attaches to this cause, he had recourse to another effort of his imagination; he made a new cause, to whom he ascribed all the evil, all the misery, resulting from this confusion: still, his own person served for the model; to which he added those deformities which he had learned to hold in disrespect: in multiplying these counter or destroying causes, he peopled Pandemonium.

It will no doubt be argued, that as Nature contains and produces intelligent beings, either she must be herself intelligent, or else she must be governed by an intelligent cause. We reply, intelligence is a faculty peculiar to organized beings, that is to say, to beings constituted and combined after a determinate manner; from whence results certain modes of action, which are designated under various names; according to the different effects which these beings produce: wine has not the properties called *wit* and *courage*; nevertheless, it is sometimes seen that it communicates those qualities to men, who are supposed to be in themselves entirely devoid of them. It cannot be said Nature is intelligent after the manner of any of the beings she contains; but she can produce intelligent beings by assembling matter suitable to their particular organization, from whose peculiar modes of action will result the faculty called intelligence; who shall be capable of producing certain effects which are the necessary consequence of this property. I therefore repeat, that to have intelligence, designs and views, it is requisite to have ideas; to the production of ideas, organs or senses are necessary: this is what is neither said of Nature nor of the causes he has supposed to preside over her actions. In short experience warrants the assertion, it does more, it proves beyond a doubt, that matter, which is regarded as inert and dead, assumes sensible action, intelligence, and life, when it is combined and organized after particular modes.

From what has been said, it must rationally be concluded that *order* is never more than the necessary or uniform connection of causes with their effects; or that series of action which flows from the peculiar properties of beings, so long as they remain in a given state; that *confusion* is nothing more than the change of this state; that in the universe, all is necessarily in order, because every thing acts and moves according to the various properties of the different beings it contains; that in Nature there cannot be either confusion or real evil, since every thing follows the laws of its natural existence; that there is neither *chance* nor any thing fortuitous in this Nature, where no effect is produced without a sufficient, without a substantial cause; where all causes act necessarily according to fixed and certain laws, which are themselves dependant on the essential properties of these causes or beings, as well as on the combination, which constitutes either their transitory or permanent state; that intelligence is a mode of acting, a method of existence natural to some particular beings; that if this intelligence should be attributed to Nature, it would then be nothing more than the faculty of conserving herself in active existence by necessary means. In refusing to Nature the intelligence he himself enjoys—in rejecting the intelligent cause which is supposed to be the contriver of this Nature, or the principle of that *order* he discovers in her course, nothing is given to *chance*, nothing to a blind cause, nothing to a power which is indistinguishable; but every thing he beholds is attributed to real, to known causes; or to those which by analogy are easy of comprehension. All that exists is acknowledged to be a consequence of the inherent properties of eternal matter, which by contact, by blending, by combination, by change of form, produces order and confusion; with all those varieties which assail his sight, it is himself who is blind, when he imagines blind causes:—man only manifested his ignorance of the powers of motion, of the laws of Nature, when he attributed, any of its effects to *chance*. He did not shew a more enlightened feeling when he ascribed them to an intelligence, the idea of which he borrowed from himself, but which is never in conformity with the effects which he attributes to its intervention—he only imagined words to supply the place of things—he made JUPITER, SATURN, JUNO, and a thousand others, operate that which he found himself inadequate to perform; he distinguished them from Nature, gave them an amplification of his own properties, and believed he understood them by thus obscuring ideas, which he never dared either define or analyze.

CHAP. VI.

Moral and Physical Distinctions of Man.—His Origin.

Let us now apply the general laws we have scrutinized, to those beings of Nature who interest us the most. Let us see in what man differs from the other beings by which he is surrounded. Let us examine if he has not certain points in conformity with them, that oblige him, notwithstanding the different properties they respectively possess, to act in certain respects according to the universal laws to which every thing is submitted. Finally, let us enquire if the ideas he has formed of himself in meditating on his own peculiar mode of existence, be chimerical, or founded in reason.

Man occupies a place amidst that crowd, that multitude of beings, of which Nature is the assemblage. His essence, that is to say, the peculiar manner of existence, by which he is distinguished from other beings, renders him susceptible of various modes of action, of a variety of motion, some of which are simple and visible, others concealed and complicated. His life itself is nothing more than a long series, a succession of necessary and connected motion; which operates perpetual changes in his machine; which has for its principle either causes contained within himself, such as blood, nerves, fibres, flesh, bones; in short, the matter, as well solid as fluid, of which his body is composed—or those exterior causes, which, by acting upon him, modify him diversely; such as the air with which he is encompassed, the aliments by which he is nourished, and all those objects from which he receives any impulse whatever, by the impression they make on his senses.

Man, like all other beings in Nature, tends to his own destruction—he experiences inert force—he gravitates upon himself—he is attracted by objects that are contrary or repugnant to his existence—he seeks after some—he flies, or endeavours to remove himself from others. It is this variety of action, this diversity of modification of which the human being is susceptible, that has been designated under such different names, by such varied nomenclature. It will be necessary, presently, to examine these closely and go more into detail.

However marvellous, however hidden, however secret, however complicated may be the modes of action, which the human frame undergoes, whether interiorly or exteriorly; whatever may be, or appear to be the impulse he either receives or communicates, examined closely, it will be found that all his motion, all his operations, all his changes, all his various states, all his revolutions, are constantly regulated by the same laws, which Nature has prescribed to all the beings she brings forth—which she developes—which she enriches with faculties—of which she increases the bulk—which she conserves for a season—which she ends by decomposing, by destroying: obliging them to change their form.

Man, in his origin, is an imperceptible point, a speck, of which the parts are without form; of which the mobility, the life, escapes his senses; in short, in which he does not perceive any sign of those qualities, called SENTIMENT, FEELING, THOUGHT, INTELLIGENCE, FORCE, REASON, &c. Placed in the womb suitable to his expansion, this point unfolds, extends, increases, by the continual addition of matter he attracts, that is analogous to his being, which consequently assimilates itself with him. Having quitted this womb, so appropriate to conserve his existence, to unfold his qualities, to strengthen his habits; so competent to give, for a season, consistence to the weak rudiments of his frame; he travels through the stage of infancy; he becomes adult: his body has then acquired a considerable extension of bulk, his motion is marked, his action is visible, he is sensible in all his parts; he is a living, an active mass; that is to say, a combination that feels and thinks; that fulfils the functions peculiar to beings of his species. But how has he become sensible? Because he has been by degrees nourished, enlarged, repaired by the continual attraction that takes place within himself, of that kind of matter which is pronounced inert, insensible, inanimate; which is, nevertheless, continually combining itself with his machine; of which it forms an active whole, that is living, that feels, judges, reasons, wills, deliberates, chooses, elects; that has the capability of labouring, more or less efficaciously, to his own individual preservation; that is to say, to the maintenance of the harmony of his existence.

All the motion and changes that man experiences in the course of his life, whether it be from exterior objects or from those substances contained within himself, are either favorable or prejudicial to his existence; either maintain its order, or throw it into confusion; are either in conformity with, or repugnant to, the essential tendency of his peculiar mode of being. He is compelled by Nature to approve of some, to disapprove of others; some of necessity render him happy, others contribute to his misery; some become the objects of his most ardent desire, others of his determined aversion: some elicit his confidence, others make him tremble with fear.

In all the phenomena man presents, from the moment he quits the womb of his mother, to that wherein he becomes the inhabitant of the silent tomb, he perceives nothing but a succession of necessary causes and effects, which are strictly conformable to those laws that are common to all the beings in Nature. All his modes of action—all his sensations—all his ideas—all his passions—every act of his will—every impulse which he either gives or receives, are the necessary consequences of his own peculiar properties, and those which he finds in the various beings by whom he is moved. Every thing he does—every thing that passes within himself—his concealed motion—his visible action, are the effects of inert force—of self-gravitation—the attractive or repulsive powers contained in his machine—of the tendency he has, in common with other beings, to his own individual preservation; in short, of that energy which is the common property of every being he beholds. Nature, in man, does nothing more than shew, in a decided manner, what belongs to the peculiar nature by which he is distinguished from the beings of a different system or order.

The source of those errors into which man has fallen, when he has contemplated himself, has its rise, as will presently be shown, in the opinion he has entertained, that he moved by himself—that he always acts by his own natural energy—that in his actions, in the will that gave him impulse, he was independent of the general laws of Nature; and of those objects which, frequently, without his knowledge, always in spite of him, in obedience to these laws, are continually acting upon him. If he had examined himself attentively, he must have acknowledged, that none of the motion he underwent was spontaneous—he must have discovered, that even his birth depended on causes, wholly out of the reach of his own powers—that, it was without his own consent he entered into the system in which he occupies a place—that, from the moment in which he is born, until that in which he dies, he is continually impelled by causes, which, in spite of himself, influence his frame, modify his existence, dispose of his conduct. Would not the slightest reflection have sufficed to prove to him, that the fluids, the solids, of which his body is composed, as well as that concealed mechanism, which he believes to be independent of exterior causes, are, in fact, perpetually under the influence of these causes; that without them he finds himself in a total incapacity to act? Would he not have seen, that his temperament, his constitution, did in no wise depend on himself—that his passions are the necessary consequence of this temperament—that his will is influenced, his actions determined by these passions; consequently by opinions, which he has not given to himself, of which he is not the master? His blood, more or less heated or abundant; his nerves more or less braced, his fibres more or less relaxed, give him dispositions either transitory or durable—are not these, at every moment decisive of his ideas; of his thoughts: of his desires: of his fears: of his motion, whether visible or concealed? The state in which he finds himself, does it not necessarily depend on the air which surrounds him diversely modified; on the various properties of the aliments which nourish him; on the secret combinations that form themselves in his machine, which either preserve its order, or throw it into confusion? In short, had man fairly studied himself, every thing must have convinced him, that in every moment of his duration, he was nothing more than a passive instrument in the hands of necessity.

Thus it must appear, that where all is connected, where all the causes are linked one to the other, where the whole forms but one immense chain, there cannot be any independent, any isolated energy; any detached power. It follows then, that Nature, always in action, marks out to man each point of the line he is bound to describe; establishes the route, by which he must travel. It is Nature that elaborates, that combines the elements of which he must be composed;—It is Nature that gives him his being, his tendency, his peculiar mode of action. It is Nature that develops him, expands him, strengthens him, increases his bulk—preserves him for a season, during which he is obliged to fulfil the task imposed on him. It is Nature, that in his journey through life, strews on the road those objects, those events; those adventures, that modify him in a variety of ways, that give him impulses which are sometimes agreeable and beneficial, at others prejudicial and disagreeable. It is Nature, that in giving him feeling, in supplying him with sentiment, has endowed him with capacity to choose, the means to elect those objects, to take those methods that are most conducive, most suitable, most natural, to his conservation. It is Nature, who when he has run his race, when he has finished his career, when he has described the circle marked out for him, conducts him in his turn to his destruction; dissolves the union of his elementary particles, and obliges him to undergo the constant, the universal law; from the operation of which nothing is exempted. It is thus, motion places man in the matrix of his mother; brings him forth out of her womb; sustains him for a season; at length destroys him; obliges him to return into the bosom of Nature; who speedily reproduces him, scattered under an infinity of forms; in which each of his particles run over again, in the same manner, the different stages, as necessary as the whole had before run over those of his preceding existence.

The beings of the human species, as well as all other beings, are susceptible of two sorts of motion: the one, that of the mass, by which an entire body, or some of its parts, are visibly transferred from one place to another; the other, internal and concealed, of some of which man is sensible, while some takes place without his knowledge, and is not even to be guessed at, but by the effect it outwardly produces. In a machine so extremely complex as man, formed by the combination of such a multiplicity of matter, so diversified in its properties, so different in its proportions, so varied in its modes of action, the motion necessarily becomes of the most complicated kind; its dullness, as well as its rapidity, frequently escapes the observation of those themselves, in whom it takes place.

Let us not, then, be surprised, if, when man would account to himself for his existence, for his manner of acting, finding so many obstacles to encounter, he invented such strange hypotheses to explain the concealed spring of his machine—if then this motion appeared to him, to be different from that of other bodies, he conceived an idea, that he moved and acted in a manner altogether distinct from the other beings in Nature. He clearly perceived that his body, as well as different parts of it, did act; but, frequently, he was unable to discover what brought them into action: from whence he received the impulse: he then conjectured he contained within himself a moving principle distinguished from his machine, which secretly gave an impulse to the springs which set this machine in motion; that moved him by its own natural energy; that consequently he acted according to laws totally distinct from those which regulated the motion of other beings: he was conscious of certain internal motion, which he could not help feeling; but how could he conceive, that this invisible motion was so frequently competent to produce such striking effects? How could he comprehend, that a fugitive idea, an imperceptible act of thought, was so frequently capacitated to bring his whole being into trouble and confusion? He fell into the belief, that he perceived within himself a substance distinguished from that self, endowed with a secret force; in which he supposed existed qualities distinctly differing from those, of either the visible causes that acted on his organs, or those organs themselves. He did not sufficiently understand, that the primitive cause which makes a stone fall, or his arm move, are perhaps as difficult of comprehension, as arduous to be explained, as those internal impulses, of which his thought or his will are the effects. Thus, for want of meditating Nature—of considering her under her true point of view—of remarking the conformity—of noticing the simultaneity, the unity of the motion of this fancied motive-power with that of his body—of his material organs—he conjectured he was not only a distinct being, but that he was set apart, with different energies, from all the other beings in Nature; that he was of a more simple essence having nothing in common with any thing by which he was surrounded; nothing that connected him with all that he beheld.

It is from thence has successively sprung his notions of SPIRITUALITY, IMMATERIALITY, IMMORTALITY; in short, all those vague unmeaning words he has invented by degrees, in order to subtilize and designate the attributes of the unknown power, which he believes he contains within himself; which he conjectures to be the concealed principle of all his visible actions when man once imbibes an idea that he cannot comprehend, he meditates upon it until he has given it a complete personification: Thus he saw, or fancied he saw, the igneous matter pervade every thing; he conjectured that it was the only principle of life and activity; he proceeded to embody it; he gave it his own form; called it JUPITER, and ended by worshipping this image of his own creation, as the power from whom he derived every good he experienced, every evil he sustained. To crown the bold conjectures he ventured to make on this internal motive-power, he supposed, that different from all other beings, even from the body that served to envelope it, it was not bound to undergo dissolution; that such was its perfect simplicity, that it could not be decomposed, nor even change its form; in short, that it was by its essence exempted from those revolutions to which he saw the body subjected, as well as all the compound beings with which Nature is filled.

Thus man, in his own ideas, became double; he looked upon himself as a whole, composed by the inconceivable assemblage of two different, two distinct natures, which have no point of analogy between themselves: he distinguished two substances in himself; one evidently submitted to the influence of gross beings, composed of coarse inert matter: this he called BODY;—the other, which he supposed to be simple, of a purer essence, was contemplated as acting from itself: giving motion to the body, with which it found itself so miraculously united: this he called SOUL, or SPIRIT; the functions of the one, he denominated *physical, corporeal, material*; the functions of the other he styled *spiritual, intellectual.* Man, considered relatively to the first, was termed the PHYSICAL MAN; viewed with relation to the last, he was designated the MORAL MAN. These distinctions, although adopted by the greater number of the philosophers of the present day, are, nevertheless, only founded on gratuitous suppositions. Man has always believed he remedied his ignorance of things, by inventing words to which he could never attach any true sense or meaning. He imagined he understood matter, its properties, its faculties, its resources, its different combinations, because he had a superficial glimpse of some of its qualities: he has, however, in reality, done nothing more than obscure the faint ideas he has been capacitated to form of this matter, by associating it with a substance much less intelligible than itself. It is thus, speculative man, in forming words, in multiplying beings, has only plunged himself into greater difficulties than those he endeavoured to avoid; and thereby placed obstacles to the progress of his knowledge: whenever he has been deficient of facts, he has had recourse to conjecture, which he quickly changed into fancied realities. Thus, his imagination, no longer guided by experience, hurried on by his new ideas, was lost, without hope of return, in the labyrinth of an ideal, of an intellectual world, to which he had himself given birth; it was next to impossible to withdraw him from this delusion, to place him in the right road, of which nothing but experience can furnish him the clue. Nature points out to man, that in himself, as well as in all those objects which act upon him, there is never more than matter endowed with various properties, diversely modified, that acts by reason of these properties: that man is an organized whole, composed of a variety of matter; that like all the other productions of Nature, he follows general and known laws, as well as those laws or modes of action which are peculiar to himself and unknown.

Thus, when it shall be inquired, what is man?

We say, he is a material being, organized after a peculiar manner; conformed to a certain mode of thinking—of feeling; capable of modification in certain modes peculiar to himself—to his organization—to that particular combination of matter which is found assembled in him.

If, again, it be asked, what origin we give to beings of the human species?

We reply, that, like all other beings, man is a production of Nature, who resembles them in some respects, and finds himself submitted to the same laws; who differs from them in other respects, and follows particular laws, determined by the diversity of his conformation.

If, then, it be demanded, whence came man?

We answer, our experience on this head does not capacitate us to resolve the question: but that it cannot interest us, as it suffices for us to know that man exists; that he is so constituted, as to be competent to the effects we witness.

But it will be urged, has man always existed? Has the human species existed from all eternity; or is it only an instantaneous production of Nature? Have there been always men like ourselves? Will there always be such? Have there been, in all times, males and females? Was there a first man, from whom all others are descended? Was the animal anterior to the egg, or did the egg precede the animal? Is this species without beginning? Will it also be without end? The species itself, is it indestructible, or does it pass away like its individuals? Has man always been what he now is; or has he, before he arrived at the state in which we see him, been obliged to pass under an infinity of successive developements? Can man at last flatter himself with having arrived at a fixed being, or must the human species again change? If man is the production of Nature, it will perhaps be asked, Is this Nature competent to the production of new beings, to make the old species disappear? Adopting this supposition, it may be inquired, why Nature does not produce under our own eyes new beings—new species?

It would appear on reviewing these questions, to be perfectly indifferent, as to the stability of the argument we have used, which side was taken; that, for want of experience, hypothesis must settle a curiosity that always endeavours to spring forward beyond the boundaries prescribed to our mind. This granted, the contemplator of Nature will say, that he sees no contradiction, in supposing the human species, such as it is at the present day, was either produced in the course of time, or from all eternity: he will not perceive any advantage that can arise from supposing that it has arrived by different stages, or successive developements, to that state in which it is actually found. Matter is eternal, it is necessary, but its forms are evanescent and contingent. It may be asked of man, is he any thing more than matter combined, of which the former varies every instant?

Notwithstanding, some reflections seem to favor the supposition, to render more probable the hypothesis, that man is a production formed in the course of time; who is peculiar to the globe he inhabits, who is the result of the peculiar laws by which it is directed; who, consequently, can only date his formation as coeval with that of his planet. Existence is essential to the universe, or the total assemblage of matter essentially varied that presents itself to our contemplation; the combinations, the forms, however, are not essential. This granted, although the matter of which the earth is composed has always existed, this earth may not always have had its present form—its actual properties; perhaps it may be a mass detached in the course of time from some other celestial body;—perhaps it is the result of the spots, or those encrustations which astronomers discover in the sun's disk, which have had the faculty to diffuse themselves over our planetary system;—perhaps the sphere we inhabit may be an extinguished or a displaced comet, which heretofore occupied some other place in the regions of space;—which, consequently, was then competent to produce beings very different from those we now behold spread over its surface; seeing that its then position, its nature, must have rendered its productions different from those which at this day it offers to our view.

Whatever may be the supposition adopted, plants, animals, men, can only be regarded as productions inherent in and natural to our globe, in the position and in the circumstances in which it is actually found: these productions it would be reasonable to infer would be changed, if this globe by any revolution should happen to shift its situation. What appears to strengthen this hypothesis, is, that on our ball itself, all the productions vary, by reason of its different climates: men, animals, vegetables, minerals, are not the same on every part of it: they vary sometimes in a very sensible manner, at very inconsiderable distances. The elephant is indigenous to, or native of the torrid zone: the rein deer is peculiar to the frozen climates of the North; Indostan is the womb that matures the diamond; we do not find it produced in our own country: the pine-apple grows in the common atmosphere of America; in our climate it is never produced in the open ground, never until art has furnished a sun analogous to that which it requires—the European in his own climate finds not this delicious fruit. Man in different climates varies in his colour, in his size, in his conformation, in his powers, in his industry, in his courage, and in the faculties of his mind. But, what is it that constitutes climate? It is the different position of parts of the same globe, relatively to the sun; positions that suffice to make a sensible variety in its productions.

There is, then, sufficient foundation to conjecture that if by any accident our globe should become displaced, all its productions would of necessity be changed; seeing that causes being no longer the same, or no longer acting after the same manner, the effects would necessarily no longer be what they now are, all productions, that they may be able to conserve themselves, or maintain their actual existence, have occasion to co-order themselves with the whole from which they have emanated. Without this they would no longer be in a capacity to subsist: it is this faculty of co-ordering themselves,—this relative adaption, which is called the ORDER OF THE UNIVERSE: the want of it is called CONFUSION. Those productions which are treated as MONSTROUS, are such as are unable to co-order themselves with the general or particular laws of the beings who surround them, or with the whole in which they find themselves placed: they have had the faculty in their formation to accommodate themselves to these laws; but these very laws are opposed to their perfection: for this reason they are unable to subsist. It is thus that by a certain analogy of conformation, which exists between animals of different species, mules are easily produced; but these mules, unable to co-order themselves with the beings that surround them, are not able to reach perfection, consequently cannot propagate their species. Man can live only in air, fish only in water: put the man into the water, the fish into the air, not being able to co-order themselves with the fluids which surround them, these animals will quickly be destroyed. Transport by imagination, a man from our planet into SATURN, his lungs will presently be rent by an atmosphere too rarified for his mode of being, his members will be frozen with the intensity of the cold; he will perish for want of finding elements analogous to his actual existence: transport another into MERCURY, the excess of heat, beyond what his mode of existence can bear, will quickly destroy him.

Thus, every thing seems to authorise the conjecture, that the human species is a production peculiar to our sphere, in the position in which it is found: that when this position may happen to change, the human species will, of consequence, either be changed or will be obliged to disappear; seeing that there would not then be that with which man could co-order himself with the whole, or connect himself with that which can enable him to subsist. It is this aptitude in man to co-order himself with the whole, that not only furnishes him with the idea of order, but also makes him exclaim "*whatever is, is right*;" whilst every thing is only that which it can be, as long as the whole is necessarily what it is; whilst it is positively neither good nor bad, as we understand those terms: it is only requisite to displace a man, to make him accuse the universe of confusion.

These reflections would appear to contradict the ideas of those, who are willing to conjecture that the other planets, like our own, are inhabited by beings resembling ourselves. But if the LAPLANDER differs in so marked a manner from the HOTTENTOT, what difference ought we not rationally to suppose between an inhabitant of our planet and one of SATURN or of VENUS?

However it may be, if we are obliged to recur by imagination to the origin of things, to the infancy of the human species, we may say that it is probable that man was a necessary consequence of the disentangling of our globe; or one of the results of the qualities, of the properties, of the energies, of which it is susceptible in its present position—that he was born male and female—that his existence is co-ordinate with that of the globe, under its present position—that as long as this co-ordination shall subsist, the human specie will conserve himself, will propagate himself, according to the impulse, after the primitive laws, which he has originally received—that if this co-ordination should happen to cease; if the earth, displaced, should cease to receive the same impulse, the same influence, on the part of those causes which actually act upon it, or which give it energy; that then the human species would change, to make place for new beings, suitable to co-order themselves with the state that should succeed to that which we now see subsist.

In thus supposing the changes in the position of our globe, the primitive man did, perhaps, differ more from the actual man, than the quadruped differs from the insect. Thus man, the same as every thing else that exists on our planet, as well as in all the others, may be regarded as in a state of continual vicissitude: thus the last term of the existence of man is to us as unknown and as indistinct as the first: there is, therefore, no contradiction in the belief that the species vary incessantly—that to us it is as impossible to know what he will become, as to know what he has been.

With respect to those who may ask why Nature does not produce new beings? we may enquire of them in turn, upon what foundation they suppose this fact? What it is that authorizes them to believe this sterility in Nature? Know they if, in the various combinations which she is every instant forming, Nature be not occupied in producing new beings, without the cognizance of these observers? Who has informed them that this Nature is not actually assembling, in her immense elaboratory, the elements suitable to bring to light, generations entirely new, that will have nothing in common with those of the species at present existing? What absurdity then, or what want of just inference would there be, to imagine that the man, the horse, the fish, the bird, will be no more? Are these animals so indispensably requisite to Nature, that without them she cannot continue her eternal course? Does not all change around us? Do we not ourselves change? Is it not evident that the whole universe has not been, in its anterior eternal duration, rigorously the same that it now is? that it is impossible, in its posterior eternal duration, it can be rigidly in the same state that it now is for a single instant? How, then, pretend to divine that, to which the infinite succession of destruction, of reproduction, of combination, of dissolution, of metamorphosis, of change, of transposition, may be able eventually to conduct it by their consequence? Suns encrust themselves, and are extinguished; planets perish and disperse themselves in the vast plains of air; other suns are kindled, and illumine their systems; new planets form themselves, either to make revolutions round these suns, or to describe new routes; and man, an infinitely small portion of the globe, which is itself but an imperceptible point in the immensity of space, vainly believes it is for himself this universe is made; foolishly imagines he ought to be the confident of Nature; confidently flatters himself he is eternal: and calls himself KING OF THE UNIVERSE!!!

O man! wilt thou never conceive, that thou art but an ephemeron? All changes in the great macrocosm: nothing remains the same an instant, in the planet thou inhabitest: Nature contains no one constant form, yet thou pretendest thy species can never disappear; that thou shalt be exempted from the universal law, that wills all shall experience change! Alas! In thy actual being, art not thou submitted to continual alterations? Thou, who in thy folly, arrogantly assumest to thyself the title of KING OF NATURE! Thou, who measurest the earth and the heavens! Thou, who in thy vanity imaginest, that the whole was made, because thou art intelligent! There requires but a very slight accident, a single atom to be displaced, to make thee perish; to degrade thee; to ravish from thee this intelligence of which thou appearest so proud.

If all the preceding conjectures be refused by those opposed to us; if it be pretended that Nature acts by a certain quantum of immutable and general laws; if it be believed that men, quadrupeds, fish, insects, plants, are from all eternity, and will remain eternally, what they now are: if I say it be contended, that from all eternity the stars have shone, in the immense regions of space, have illuminated the firmament; if it be insisted, we must no more demand why man is such as he appears, then ask why Nature is such as we behold her, or why the world exists? We are no longer opposed to such arguments. Whatever may be the system adopted, it will perhaps reply equally well to the difficulties with which our opponents endeavour to embarrass the way: examined closely, it will be perceived they make nothing against those truths, which we have gathered from experience. It is not given to man to know every thing—it is not given him to know his origin—it is not given him to penetrate into the essence of things, nor to recur to first principles—but it is given him, to have reason, to have honesty, to ingenuously allow he is ignorant of that which he cannot know, and not to substitute unintelligible words, absurd suppositions, for his uncertainty. Thus, we say to those, who to solve difficulties far above their reach, pretend that the human species descended from a first man and a first woman, created diversely according to different creeds;—that we have some ideas of Nature, but that we have none of creation;—that the human mind is incapable of comprehending the period when all was nothing;—that to use words we cannot understand, is only in other terms to acknowledge our ignorance of the powers of Nature;—that we are unable to fathom the means by which she has been capacitated to produce the phenomena we behold.

Let us then conclude, that man has no just, no solid reason to believe himself a privileged being in Nature; because he is subject to the same vicissitudes, as all her other productions. His pretended prerogatives have their foundation in error, arising from mistaken opinions concerning his existence. Let him but elevate himself by his thoughts above the globe he inhabits, he will look upon his own species with the same eyes he does all other beings in Nature: He will then clearly perceive that in the same manner that each tree produces its fruit, by reason of its energies, in consequence of its species: so each man acts by reason of his particular energy; that he produces fruit, actions, works, equally necessary: he will feel that the illusion which he anticipates in favour of himself, arises from his being, at one and the same time, a spectator and a part of the universe. He will acknowledge, that the idea of excellence which he attaches to his being, has no other foundation than his own peculiar interest; than the predilection he has in favour of himself—that the doctrine he has broached with such seeming confidence, bottoms itself on a very suspicious foundation, namely IGNORANCE and SELF-LOVE.

CHAP. VII.

The Soul and the Spiritual System.

Man, after having gratuitously supposed himself composed of two distinct independent substances, that have no common properties, relatively with each other; has pretended, as we have seen, that that which actuated him interiorly, that motion which is invisible, that impulse which is placed within himself, is essentially different from those which act exteriorly. The first he designated, as we have already said, by the name of a SPIRIT or a SOUL. If however it be asked, what is a spirit? The moderns will reply, that the whole fruit of their metaphysical researches is limited to learning that this motive-power, which they state to be the spring of man's action, is a substance of an unknown nature; so simple, so indivisible, so deprived of extent, so invisible, so impossible to be discovered by the senses, that its parts cannot be separated, even by abstraction or thought. The question then arises, how can we conceive such a substance, which is only the negation of every thing of which we have a knowledge? How form to ourselves an idea of a substance, void of extent, yet acting on our senses; that is to say, on those organs which are material, which have extent? How can a being without extent be moveable; how put matter in action? How can a substance devoid of parts, correspond successively with different parts of space? But a very cogent question presents itself on this occasion: if this distinct substance that is said to form one of the component parts of man, be really what it is reported, and if it be not, it is not what it is described; if it be unknown, if it be not pervious to the senses; if it be invisible, by what means did the metaphysicians themselves become acquainted with it? How did they form ideas of a substance, that taking their own account of it, is not, under any of its circumstances, either directly or by analogy, cognizable to the mind of man? If they could positively achieve this, there would no longer be any mystery in Nature: it would be as easy to conceive the time when all was nothing, when all shall have passed away, to account for the production of every thing we behold, as to dig in a garden or read a lecture.—Doubt would vanish from the human species; there could no longer be any difference of opinion, since all must necessarily be of one mind on a subject so accessible to every enquirer.

But it will be replied, the materialist himself admits, the natural philosophers of all ages have admitted, elements and atoms, beings simple and indivisible, of which bodies are composed:—granted; they have no more: they have also admitted that many of these atoms, many of these elements, if not all, are unknown to them: nevertheless, these simple beings, these atoms of the materialist, are not the same thing with the spirit, or the soul of the metaphysician. When the natural philosopher talks of atoms—when he describes them as simple beings, he indicates nothing more than that they are homogeneous, pure, without mixture: but then he allows that they have extent, consequently parts, are separable by thought, although no other natural agent with which he is acquainted is capable of dividing them: that the simple beings of this genus are susceptible of motion—can impart action—receive impulse—are material—are placed in Nature—are indestructible;—that consequently, if he cannot know them from themselves, he can form some idea of them by analogy: thus he has done that intelligibly, which the metaphysician would do unintelligibly: the latter, with a view to render man immortal, finding difficulties to his wish, from seeing that the body decayed—that it has submitted to the great, the universal law—has, to solve the difficulty, to remove the impediment, given him a soul, distinct from the body, which he says is exempted from the action of the general law: to account for this, he has called it a spiritual being, whose properties are the negation of all known properties, consequently inconceivable: had he, however, had recourse to the atoms of the former—had he made this substance the last possible term of the division of matter—it would at least have been intelligible; it would also have been immortal, since, according to the reasonings of all men, whether metaphysicians, theologians, or natural philosophers, an atom is an indestructible element, that must exist to all eternity.

All men are agreed in this position, that motion is the successive change of the relations of one body with other bodies, or with the different parts of space. If that which is called *spirit* be susceptible of communicating or receiving motion—if it acts—if it gives play to the organs of body—to produce these effects, it necessarily follows that this being changes successively its relation, its tendency, its correspondence, the position of its parts, either relatively to the different points of space, or to the different organs of the body which it puts in action: but to change its relation with space, with the organs to which it gives impulse, it follows of necessity that this spirit most have extent, solidity, consequently distinct parts: whenever a substance possesses these qualities, it is what we call MATTER, it can no longer be regarded as a simple pure being, in the sense attached to it by the moderns, or by theologians.

Thus it will be seen, that those who, to conquer insurmountable difficulties, have supposed in man an immaterial substance, distinguished from his body, have not thoroughly understood themselves; indeed they have done nothing more than imagined a negative quality, of which they cannot have any correct idea: matter alone is capable of acting on our senses; without this action nothing would be capable of making itself known to us. They have not seen that a being without extent is neither in a capacity to move itself, nor has the capability of communicating motion to the body; since such a being, having no parts, has not the faculty of changing its relation, or its distance, relatively to other bodies, nor of exciting motion in the human body, which is itself material. That which is called our soul moves itself with us; now motion is a property of matter—this soul gives impulse to the arm; the arm, moved by it, makes an impression, a blow, that follows the general law of motion: in this case, the force remaining the same, if the mass was two-fold, the blow should be double. This soul again evinces its materiality in the invincible obstacles it encounters on the part of the body. If the arm be moved by its impulse when nothing opposes it, yet this arm can no longer move, when it is charged with a weight beyond its strength. Here then is a mass of matter that annihilates the impulse given by a spiritual cause, which spiritual cause having no analogy with matter, ought not to find more difficulty in moving the whole world, than in moving a single atom, nor an atom, than the universe. From this, it is fair to conclude, such a substance is a chimera—a being of the imagination. That it required a being differently endowed, differently constituted, to set matter in motion—to create all the phenomena we behold: nevertheless, it is a being the metaphysicians have made the contriver, the Author of Nature. As man, in all his speculations, takes himself for the model, he no sooner imagined a spirit within himself, than giving it extent, he made it universal; then ascribed to it all those causes with which his ignorance prevents him from becoming acquainted, thus he identified himself with the Author of Nature—then availed himself of the supposition to explain the connection of the soul with the body: his self-complacency prevented his perceiving that he was only enlarging the circle of his errors, by pretending to understand that which it is more than possible he will never be permitted to know; his self-love prevented him from feeling, that whenever he punished another for not thinking as he did, that he committed the greatest injustice, unless he was satisfactorily able to prove that other wrong, and himself right: that if he himself was obliged to have recourse to hypothesis—to gratuitous suppositions, whereon to found his doctrine, that from the very fallibility of his nature, these might be erroneous: thus GALLILEO was persecuted, because the metaphysicians, the theologians of his day, chose to make others believe what it was evident they did not themselves understand.

As soon as I feel an impulse, or experience motion, I am under the necessity to acknowledge extent, solidity, density, impenetrability in the substance I see move, or from which I receive impulse: thus, when action is attributed to any cause whatever, I am obliged to consider it MATERIAL. I may be ignorant of its individual nature, of its mode of action, or of its generic properties; but I cannot deceive myself in general properties, which are common to all matter: this ignorance will only be increased, when I shall take that for granted of a being, of which from that moment I am precluded by what I admit from forming any idea, which moreover deprives it completely either of the faculty of moving itself, giving an impulse, or acting. Thus, according to the received idea of the term, a spiritual substance that moves itself, that gives motion to matter, and that acts, implies a contradiction, that necessarily infers a total impossibility.

The partizans of spirituality believe they answer the difficulties they have accumulated, by asserting that "*the soul is entire—is whole under each point of its extent.*" If an absurd answer will solve difficulties, they certainly have done it. But let us examine this reply:—it will be found that this indivisible part which is called soul, however insensible or however minute, must yet remain something: then an infinity of unextended substances, or the same substance having no dimensions, repeated an infinity of times, would constitute a substance that has extent: this cannot be what they mean, because according to this principle, the human soul would then be as infinite as the Author of Nature; seeing that they have stated this to be a being without extent, who is an infinity of times whole in each part of the universe. But when there shall appear as much solidity in the answer as there is a want of it, it must be acknowledged that in whatever manner the spirit or the soul finds itself in its extent, when the body moves forward the soul does not remain behind; if so, it has a quality in common with the body, peculiar to matter; since it is conveyed from place to place jointly with the body. Thus, when even the soul should be admitted to be immaterial, what conclusion must be drawn? Entirely submitted to the motion of the body, without this body it would remain dead and inert. This soul would only be part of a two-fold machine, necessarily impelled forward by a concatenation, or connection with the whole. It would resemble a bird, which a child conducts at its pleasure, by the string with which it is bound.

Thus, it is for want of consulting experience, by not attending to reason, that man has darkened his ideas upon the concealed principle of his motion. If, disentangled from prejudice—if, destitute of gratuitous suppositions—if, throwing aside error, he would contemplate his soul, or the moving principle that acts within him, he would be convinced that it forms a part of its body, that it cannot be distinguished from it, but by abstraction; that it is only the body itself, considered relatively with some of its functions, or with those faculties of which its nature, or its peculiar organization, renders it susceptible:—he will perceive that this soul is obliged to undergo the same changes as the body; that it is born with it;

that it expands itself with it; that like the body, it passes through a state of infancy, a period of weakness, a season of inexperience; that it enlarges itself, that it strengthens itself, in the same progression; that like the body, it arrives at an adult age or reaches maturity; that it is then, and not till then, it obtains the faculty of fulfilling certain functions; that it is in this stage, and in no other, that it enjoys reason; that it displays more or less wit, judgment, and manly activity; that like the body, it is subject to those vicissitudes which exterior causes obliges it to undergo by their influence; that, conjointly with the body, it suffers, enjoys, partakes of its pleasures, shares its pains, is sound when the body is healthy, and diseased when the body is oppressed with sickness; that like the body, it is continually modified by the different degrees of density in the atmosphere; by the variety of the seasons, and by the various properties of the aliments received into the stomach: in short, he would be obliged to acknowledge that at some periods it manifests visible signs of torpor, stupefaction, decrepitude, and death.

In despite of this analogy, or rather this continual identity, of the soul with the body, man has been desirous of distinguishing their essence; he has therefore made the soul an inconceivable being: but in order that he might form to himself some idea of it, he was, notwithstanding, obliged to have recourse to material beings, and to their manner of acting. The word *spirit*, therefore, presents to the mind no other ideas than those of breathing, of respiration, of wind. Thus, when it is said the *soul is a spirit*, it really means nothing more than that its mode of action is like that of breathing: which though invisible in itself, or acting without being seen, nevertheless produces very visible effects. But breath, it is acknowledged, is a material cause; it is allowed to be air modified; it is not, therefore, a simple or pure substance, such as the moderns designate under the name of SPIRIT.

It is rather singular that in the Hebrew, the Greek, and the Latin, the synonymy, or corresponding term for spirit should signify *breath*. The metaphysicians themselves can best say why they have adopted such a word, to designate the substance they have distinguished from matter: some of them, fearful they should not have distinct beings enough, have gone farther, and compounded man of three substances, BODY, SOUL, and INTELLECT.

Although the word *spirit* is so very ancient among men, the sense attached to it by the moderns is quite new: the idea of spirituality, as admitted at this day, is a recent production of the imagination. Neither PYTHAGORAS nor PLATO, however heated their brain, however decided their taste for the marvellous, appear to have understood by spirit an immaterial substance, or one without extent, devoid of parts; such as that of which the moderns have formed the human soul, the concealed author of motion. The ancients, by the word spirit, were desirous to define matter of an extreme subtilty, of a purer quality than that which acted grossly on our senses. In consequence, some have regarded the soul as an ethereal substance; others as igneous matter; others again have compared it to light. DEMOCRITUS made it consist in motion, consequently gave it a manner of existence. ARISTOXENES, who was himself a musician, made it harmony. ARISTOTLE regarded the soul as the moving faculty, upon which depended the motion of living bodies.

The earliest doctors of Christianity had no other idea of the soul, than that it was material. TERTULLIAN, ARNOBIUS, CLEMENT of ALEXANDRIA, ORIGEN, SAINT JUSTIN, IRENAEUS, have all of them discoursed upon it; but have never spoken of it other than as a corporeal substance—as matter. It was reserved for their successors at a great distance of time, to make the human soul and the soul of the world *pure spirits*; that is to say, immaterial substances, of which it is impossible they could form any accurate idea: by degrees this incomprehensible doctrine of spirituality, conformable without doubt to the views of those who make it a principle to annihilate reason, prevailed over the others: But it might be fairly asked, if the pretended proofs of this doctrine owe themselves to a man, who on a much more comprehensible point has been proved in error; if, on that which time has shewn was accessible to man's reason, the great champion in support of this dogma was deceived; are we not bound to examine, with the most rigorous investigation, the reasonings, the evidence, of one who was the decided, the proven child of enthusiasm and error? Yet DESCARTES, to whose sublime errors the world is indebted for the Newtonian system, although before him the soul had been considered spiritual, was the first who established that, "*that which thinks ought to be distinguished from matter*," from whence he concludes rather hastily, that the soul, or that which thinks in man, is a spirit; or a simple indivisible substance. Perhaps it would have been more logical, more consistent with reason, to have said, since man, who is matter, who has no idea but of matter, enjoys the faculty of thought, matter can think; that is, it is susceptible of that particular modification called thought.

However this may be, this doctrine was believed divine, supernatural, because it was inconceivable to man. Those who dared believe even that which was believed before; namely, *that the soul was material*, were held as rash inconsiderate madmen, or else treated as enemies to the welfare and happiness of the human race. When man had once renounced experience; when he had abjured his reason; when he had joined the banner of this enthusiastic novelty; he did nothing more, day after day, than subtilize the delirium, the ravings of his imagination: he pleased himself by continually sinking deeper into the most unfathomable depths of error: he felicitated himself on his discoveries; on his pretended knowledge; in an exact ratio as his understanding became enveloped in the mists of darkness, environed with the clouds of ignorance. Thus, in consequence of man's reasoning upon false principles; of having relinquished the evidence of his senses; the moving principle within him, the concealed author of motion, has been made a mere chimera, a mere being of the imagination, because he has divested it of all known properties; because he has attached to it nothing but properties which, from the very nature of his existence, he is incapacitated to comprehend.

The doctrine of spirituality, such as it now exists, offers nothing but vague ideas; or rather is the absense of all ideas. What does it present to the mind, but a substance which possesses nothing of which our senses enable us to have a knowledge? Can it be truth that a man is able to figure to himself a being not material, having neither extent nor parts, which, nevertheless, acts upon matter without having any point of contact, any kind of analogy with it; and which itself receives the impulse of matter by means of material organs, which announce to it the presence of other beings? Is it possible to conceive the union of the soul with the body; to comprehend how this material body can bind, enclose, constrain, determine a fugitive being which escapes all our senses? Is it honest, is it plain dealing, to solve these difficulties, by saying there is a mystery in them; that they are the effects of a power, more inconceivable than the human soul; than its mode of acting, however concealed from our view? When to resolve these problems, man is obliged to have recourse to miracles or to make the Divinity interfere, does he not avow his own ignorance? When, notwithstanding the ignorance he is thus obliged to avow by availing himself of the divine agency, he tells us, this immaterial substance, this soul, shall experience the action of the element of fire, which he allows to be material; when he confidently says this soul shall be burnt; shall suffer in purgatory; have we not a right to believe, that either he has a design to deceive us, or else that he does not himself understand that which he is so anxious we should take upon his word?

Let us not then be surprised at those subtile hypotheses, as ingenious as they are unsatisfactory, to which theological prejudice has obliged the most profound modern speculators to recur; when they have undertaken to reconcile the spirituality of the soul, with the physical action of material beings, on this incorporeal substance; its re-action upon these beings; its union with the body. When the human mind permits itself to be guided by authority without proof, to be led forward by enthusiasm; when it renounces the evidence of its senses; what can it do more than sink into error? Let those who doubt this, read the metaphysical romances of LEIBNITZ, DESCARTES, MALEBRANCHE, CUDWORTH, and many others: let them coolly examine the ingenious, but fanciful systems entitled *the pre-established harmony of occasional causes; physical pre-motion, &c.*

If man wishes to form to himself clear, perspicuous ideas of his soul, let him throw himself back on his experience—let him renounce his prejudices—let him avoid theological conjecture—let him tear the bandages which he has been taught to think necessary, but with which he has been blind-folded, only to confound his reason. If it be wished to draw man to virtue, let the natural philosopher, let the anatomist, let the physician, unite their experience; let them compare their observations, in order to show what ought to be thought of a substance, so disguised, so hidden by absurdities, as not easily to be known. Their discoveries may perhaps teach moralists the true motive-power that ought to influence the actions of man—legislators, the true motives that should actuate him, that should excite him to labour to the welfare of society—sovereigns, the means of rendering their subjects truly happy; of giving solidity to the power of the nations committed to their charge. Physical souls have physical wants, and demand physical happiness. These are real, are preferable objects, to that variety of fanciful chimeras, each in its turn giving place to the other, with which the mind of man has been fed during so many ages. Let us, then, labour to perfect the morality of man; let us make it agreeable to him; let us excite in him an ardent thirst for its purity: we shall presently see his morals become better, himself become happier; his soul become calm and serene; his will determined to virtue, by the natural, by the palpable motives held out to him. By the diligence, by the care which legislators shall bestow on natural philosophy, they will form citizens of sound understandings; robust and well constituted; who, finding themselves happy, will be themselves accessary to that useful impulse so necessary for their soul. When the body is suffering, when nations are unhappy, the soul cannot be in a proper state. *Mens sana in corpore sano*, a sound mind in a sound body, will be always able to make a good citizen.

The more man reflects, the more he will be convinced that the soul, very far from being distinguished from the body, is only the body itself, considered relatively to some of its functions, or to some of the modes of existing or acting, of which it is susceptible whilst it enjoys life. Thus, the soul is man, considered relatively to the faculty he has of feeling, of thinking, of acting in a mode resulting from his peculiar nature; that is to say, from his properties, from his particular organization: from the modifications, whether durable or transitory, which the beings who act upon him cause his machine to undergo.

Those who have distinguished the soul from the body, appear only to have distinguished their brain from themselves. Indeed, the brain is the common center, where all the nerves, distributed through every part of the body, meet and blend themselves: it is by the aid of this interior organ that all those operations are performed which are attributed to the soul: it is the impulse, or the motion, communicated to the nerve, which modifies the brain: in consequence, it re-acts, or gives play to the bodily organs; or rather it acts upon itself, and becomes capable of producing within itself a great variety of motion, which has been designated *intellectual faculties.*

From this it may be seen that some philosophers have been desirous to make a spiritual substance of the brain. It is evidently nothing but ignorance that has given birth to and accredited this system, which embraces so little, either of the natural or the rational. It is from not having studied himself, that man has supposed he was compounded with an agent, essentially different from his body: in examining this body, he will find that it is quite useless to recur to hypothesis for the explanation of the various phenomena it presents to his contemplation; that hypothesis can do nothing more than lead him out of the right road to the information after which he seeks. What obscures this question, arises from this, that man cannot see himself: indeed, for this purpose, that would be requisite which is impossible; namely, that he could he at one and the same moment both within and without himself: he may be compared to an Eolian harp, that issues sounds of itself, and should demand what it is that causes it to give them forth? It does not perceive that the sensitive quality of its chords causes the air to brace them; that being so braced, it is rendered sonorous by every gust of wind with which it happens to come in contact.

When a theologian, obstinately bent on admitting into man two substances essentially different, is asked why he multiplies beings without necessity? he will reply, because *"thought cannot be a property of matter."* If, then, it be enquired of him, *cannot God give to matter the faculty of thought?* he will answer, *"no! seeing that God cannot do impossible things!"* According to his principles, it is as impossible that spirit or thought can produce matter, as it is impossible that matter can produce spirit or thought: it might, therefore, be concluded against him, that the world was not made by a spirit, any more than a spirit was made by the world. But in this case, does not the theologian, according to his own assertion, acknowledge himself to be the true atheist? Does he not, in fact, circumscribe the attributes of the Deity, and deny his power, to suit his own purpose? Yet these men demand implicit belief in doctrines, which they are obliged to maintain by the most contradictory assertions.

The more experience we collect, the more we shall be convinced that the word *spirit*, in its present received usage, conveys no one sense that is tangible, either to ourselves or to those that invented it; consequently cannot be of the least use, either in physics or morals. What modern metaphysicians believe and understand by the word, is nothing more than an *occult* power, imagined to explain *occult* qualities and actions, but which, in fact, explains nothing. Savage nations admit of spirits, to account to themselves for those effects, which to them appear marvellous, as long as their ignorance knows not the cause to which they ought to be attributed. In attributing to spirits the phenomena of Nature, as well as those of the human body, do we, in fact, do any thing more than reason like savages? Man has filled Nature with spirits, because he has almost always been ignorant of the true causes of those effects by which he was astonished. Not being acquainted with the powers of Nature, he has supposed her to be animated by a *great spirit*: not understanding the energy of the human frame, he has in like manner conjectured it to be animated by a *minor spirit*: from this it would appear, that whenever he wished to indicate the unknown cause of a phenomena, he knew not how to explain in a natural manner, he had recourse to the word *spirit*. In short, *spirit* was a term by which he solved all his doubts, and cleared up his ignorance to himself. It was according to these principles that when the AMERICANS first beheld the terrible effects of gunpowder, they ascribed the cause to wrathful spirits, to their enraged divinities: it was by adopting these principles, that our ancestors believed in a plurality of gods, in ghosts, in genii, &c. Pursuing the same track, we ought to attribute to spirits gravitation, electricity, magnetism, &c. &c. It is somewhat singular, that priests have in all ages so strenuously upheld those systems which time has exploded; that they have appeared to be either the most crafty or the most ignorant of men. Where are now the priests of Apollo, of Juno, of the Sun, and a thousand others? Yet these are the men, who in all times have persecuted those who have been the first to give natural explanations of the phenomena of Nature, as witness ANAXAGORAS, ARISTOTLE, GALLILEO, DESCARTES, &c. &c.

CHAP. VIII.

The Intellectual Faculties derived from the Faculty of Feeling.

To convince ourselves that the faculties called *intellectual*, are only certain modes of existence, or determinate manners of acting, which result from the peculiar organization of the body, we have only to analyze them; we shall then see that all the operations which are attributed to the soul, are nothing more than certain modifications of the body; of which a substance that is without extent, that has no parts, that is immaterial, is not susceptible.

The first faculty we behold in the living man, and that from which all his others flow, is *feeling*: however inexplicable this faculty may appear, on a first view, if it be examined closely, it will be found to be a consequence of the essence, or a result of the properties of organized beings; the same as *gravity, magnetism, elasticity, electricity*, &c. result from the essence or nature of some others. We shall also find these last phenomena are not less inexplicable than that of feeling. Nevertheless, if we wish to define to ourselves a clear and precise idea of it, we shall find that feeling is a particular manner of being moved—a mode of receiving an impulse peculiar to certain organs of animated bodies, which is occasioned by the presence of a material object that acts upon these organs, and transmit the impulse or shock to the brain.

Man only feels by the aid of nerves dispersed through his body; which is itself, to speak correctly, nothing more than a great nerve; or may be said to resemble a large tree, of which the branches experience the action of the root, communicated through the trunk. In man the nerves unite and lose themselves in the brain; that intestine is the true seat of feeling: like the spider in the centre of his web, it is quickly warned of all the changes that happen to the body, even at the extremities to which it sends its filaments and branches. Experience enables us to ascertain, that man ceases to feel in those parts of his body of which the communication with the brain is intercepted; he feels very little, or not at all, whenever this organ is itself deranged or affected in too lively a manner. A proof of this is afforded in the transactions of the Royal Academy of Sciences at Paris: they inform us of a man who had his scull taken off, in the room of which his brain was recovered with skin; in proportion as a pressure was made by the hand on his brain, the man fell into a kind of insensibility, which deprived him of all feeling. BARTOLIN says, the brain of a man is twice as big as that of an ox. This observation had been already made by ARISTOTLE. In the dead body of an idiot dissected by WILLIS, the brain was found smaller than ordinary: he says the greatest difference he found between the parts of the body of this idiot, and those of wiser men, was, that the plexus of the intercostal nerves, which is the mediator between the brain and the heart, was extremely small, accompanied by a less number of nerves than usual. According to WILLIS, the ape is, of all animals, that which has the largest brain, relatively to his size: he is also, after man, that which has the most intelligence: this is further confirmed, by the name he bears in the soil, to which he is indigenous, which is *ourang outang*, or the man beast. There is, therefore, every reason to believe that it is entirely in the brain, that consists the difference, that is found not only between man and beasts, but also between the man of wit, and the fool: between the thinking man, and he who is ignorant; between the man of sound understanding, and the madman: a multitude of experience, serves to prove, that those persons who are most accustomed to use their intellectual faculties, have their brain more extended than others: the same has been remarked of watermen, that they have arms much longer than other men.

However this may be, the sensibility of the brain, and all its parts, is a fact: if it be asked, whence comes this property? We shall reply, it is the result of an arrangement, of a combination, peculiar to the animal: it is thus that milk, bread, wine, change themselves in the substance of man, who is a sensible being: this insensible matter becomes sensible, in combining itself with a sensible whole. Some philosophers think that sensibility is a universal quality of matter: in this case, it would be useless to seek from whence this property is derived, as we know it by its effects. If this hypothesis be admitted, in like manner as two kinds of motion are distinguished in Nature, the one called *live* force, the other *dead*, or *inert* force, two sorts of sensibility will be distinguished, the one active or alive, the other inert or dead. Then to animalize a substance, is only to destroy the obstacles that prevent its being active or sensible. In fact, sensibility is either a quality which communicates itself like motion, and which is acquired by combination; or this sensibility is a property inherent in all matter: in both, or either case, an unextended being, without parts, such as the human soul is said to be, can neither be the cause of it nor submitted to its operation; but we may fairly conclude, that all the parts of Nature enjoy the capability to arrive at animation; the obstacle is only in the state, not in the quality. Life is the perfection of Nature: she has no parts which do not tend to it— which do not attain it by the same means. Life in an insect, a dog, a man, has no other difference, than that this act is more perfect, relatively to ourselves in proportion to the structure of the organs: if, therefore, it be asked, what is requisite to animate a body? we reply, it needs no foreign aid; it is sufficient that the power of Nature be joined to its organization.

The conformation, the arrangement, the texture, the delicacy of the organs, as well exterior as interior, which compose men and animals, render their parts extremely mobile, or make their machine susceptible of being moved with great facility. In a body, which is only a heap of fibres, a mass of nerves, contiguous one to the other, united in a common center, always ready to act; in a whole, composed of fluids and solids, of which the parts are in equilibrium, the smallest touching each other, are active in their motion, communicating reciprocally, alternately and in succession, the impression, oscillations, and shocks they receive; in such a composition, it is not surprising that the slightest impulse propagates itself with celerity; that the shocks excited in its remotest parts, make themselves quickly felt in the brain, whose delicate texture renders it susceptible of being itself very easily modified. Air, fire, water, agents the most inconstant, possessing the most rapid motion, circulate continually in the fibres, incessantly penetrate the nerves: without doubt these contribute to that incredible celerity with which the brain is acquainted with what passes at the extremities of the body.

Notwithstanding the great mobility with which man's organization renders him susceptible, although exterior as well as interior causes are continually acting upon him, he does not always feel in a distinct, in a decided manner, the impulse given to his senses: indeed, he does not feel it, until it has produced some change, or given some shock to his brain. Thus, although completely environed by air, he does not feel its action, until it is so modified, as to strike with a sufficient degree of force on his organs; to penetrate his skin, through which his brain is warned of its presence. Thus, during a profound and tranquil sleep, undisturbed by any dream, man ceases to feel. In short, notwithstanding the continued motion that agitates his frame, man does not appear to feel, when this motion acts in a convenient order; he does not perceive a state of health, but he discovers a state of grief or sickness; because, in the first, his brain does not receive too lively an impulse, whilst in the others, his nerves are contracted, shocked, and agitated, with violent, with disorderly motion: these communicating with his brain, give notice that some cause acts strongly upon them— impels them in a manner that bears no analogy with their natural habit: this constitutes, in him, that peculiar mode of existing which he calls *grief.*

On the other hand, it sometimes happens that exterior objects produce very considerable changes on his body, without his perceiving them at the moment. Often, in the heat of battle, the soldier perceives not that he is dangerously wounded, because, at the time, the rapidity, the multiplicity of impetuous motion that assails his brain, does not permit him to distinguish the particular change a part of his body has undergone by the wound. In short, when a great number of causes are simultaneously acting on him with too much vivacity, he sinks under their accumulated pressure,—he swoons—he loses his senses—he is deprived of feeling.

In general, feeling only obtains, when the brain can distinguish distinctly, the impressions made on the organs with which it has communication; it is the distinct shock, the decided modification man undergoes, that constitutes *conscience*. Doctor Clarke, says to this effect: "Conscience is the act of reflecting, by means of which I know that I think, and that my thoughts, or my actions belong to me, and not to another." From this it will appear, that *feeling* is a mode of being, a marked change, produced on our brain, occasioned by the impulse communicated to our organs, whether by interior or exterior agents, by which it is modified either in a durable or transient manner: it is not always requisite that man's organs should be moved by an exterior object, to enable him to feel that he should be conscious of the changes effected in him: he can feel them within himself by means of an interior impulse; his brain is then modified, or rather he renews within himself the anterior modifications. We are not to be astonished that the brain should be necessarily warned of the shocks, of the impediments, of the changes that may happen to so complicated a machine as the human body, in which, notwithstanding all the parts are contiguous to the brain, and concentrate themselves in this brain, and are by their essence in a continual state of action and re-action.

When a man experiences the pains of the gout, he is conscious of them; in other words, he feels interiorly, that it has produced very marked, very distinct changes in him, without his perceiving, that he has received an impulse from any exterior cause; nevertheless, if he will recur to the true source of these changes, he will find that they have been wholly produced by exterior agents: they have been the consequence, either of his temperament; of the organization received from his parents; of the aliments with which his frame has been nourished; besides a thousand trivial, inappreciable causes, which congregating themselves by degrees produce in him the gouty humour; the effect of which is to make him feel in an acute and very lively manner. The pain of the gout engenders in his brain an idea, so modifies it that it acquires the faculty of representing to itself, of reiterating as it were, this pain when even he shall be no longer tormented with the gout: his brain, by a series of motion interiorly excited, is again placed in a state analogous to that in which it was when he really experienced this pain: but if he had never felt it, he would never have been in a capacity to form to himself any just idea of its excruciating torments.

The visible organs of man's body, by the intervention of which his brain is modified, take the name of *senses*. The various modifications which his brain receives by the aid of these senses, assumes a variety of names. *Sensation, perception,* and *idea,* are terms that designate nothing more than the changes produced in this interior organ, in consequence of impressions made on the exterior organs by bodies acting on them: these changes considered by themselves, are called *sensations*; they adopt the term *perception* when the brain is warned of their presence; *ideas* is that state of them in which the brain is able to ascribe them to the objects by which they have been produced.

Every *sensation*, then, is nothing more than the shock given to the organs, every *perception* is this shock propagated to the brain; every *idea* is the image of the object to which the sensation and the perception is to be ascribed. From whence it will be seen, that if the senses be not moved, there can neither be sensations, perceptions, nor ideas: this will be proved to those, who can yet permit themselves to doubt so demonstrable and striking a truth.

It is the extreme mobility of which man is capable, owing to his peculiar organization, that distinguishes him from other beings that are called insensible or inanimate; the different degrees of this mobility, of which the individuals of his species are susceptible, discriminate them from each other; make that incredible variety, that infinity of difference which is to be found, as well in their corporeal faculties, as in those which are mental or intellectual. From this mobility, more or less remarkable in each human being, results wit, sensibility, imagination, taste, &c.: for the present, however, let us follow the operation of the senses; let us examine in what manner they are acted upon, and are modified by exterior objects:—we will afterwards scrutinize the re-action of the interior organ or brain.

The eyes are very delicate, very movable organs, by means of which the sensation of light or colour is experienced: these give to the brain a distinct perception, in consequence of which, man forms an idea, generated by the action of luminous or coloured bodies: as soon as the eyelids are opened, the retina is affected in a peculiar manner; the fluid, the fibres, the nerves, of which they are composed, are excited by shocks which they communicate to the brain; to which they delineate the images of the bodies from which they have received the impulse; by this means, an idea is acquired of the colour, the size, the form, the distance of these bodies: it is thus that may be explained the mechanism of *sight*.

The mobility and the elasticity of which the skin is rendered susceptible, by the fibres and nerves which form its texture, accounts for the rapidity with which this envelope to the human body is affected when applied to any other body; by their agency, the brain has notice of its presence, of its extent, of its roughness, of its smoothness, of its surface, of its pressure of its ponderosity, &c. Qualities from which the brain derives distinct perceptions, which breed in it a diversity of ideas; it is this that constitutes the *touch* or *feeling*.

The delicacy of the membrane by which the interior of the nostrils is covered, renders them easily susceptible of irritation, even by the invisible and impalpable corpuscles that emanate from odorous bodies: by these means sensations are excited, the brain has perceptions, and generates ideas: it is this that forms the sense of *smelling*.

The mouth, filled with nervous, sensible, movable, irritable glands, saturated with juices suitable to the dissolution of saline substances, is affected in a very lively manner by the aliments which pass through it for the nourishment of the body; these glands transmit to the brain the impressions received: perceptions are of consequence; ideas follow: it is from this mechanism that results *taste*.

The ear, whose conformation fits it to receive the various impulses of air, diversely modified, communicates to the brain the shocks or sensations; these breed the perception of sound, and generate the idea of sonorous bodies: it is this that constitutes *hearing*.

Such are the only means by which man receives sensations, perceptions, and ideas. These successive modifications of his brain are effects produced by objects that give impulse to his senses; they become themselves causes, producing in his soul new modifications, which are denominated *thought, reflection, memory, imagination, judgment, will, action*; the basis, however, of all these is *sensation*.

To form a precise notion of *thought*, it will be requisite to examine, step by step, what passes in man during the presence of any object whatever. Suppose for a moment this object to be a peach: this fruit makes, at the first view, two different impressions on his eyes; that is to say, it produces two modifications, which are transmitted to the brain, which on this occasion experiences two new perceptions, or has two new ideas or modes of existence, designated by the terms *colour* and *rotundity*; in consequence, he has an idea of a body possessing roundness and colour: if he places his hand on this fruit, the organ of feeling having been set in action, his hand experiences three new impressions, which are called *softness, coolness, weight*, from whence result three new perceptions in the brain, he has consequently three new ideas: if he approximates this peach to his nose, the organ of *smelling* receives an impulse, which, communicated to the brain, a new perception arises, by which he acquires a new idea, called *odour*: if he carries this fruit to his mouth, the organ of taste becomes affected in a very lively manner: this impulse communicated to the brain, is followed by a perception that generates in him the idea of *flavour*. In re-uniting all these impressions, or these various modifications of his organs, which it have been consequently transmitted to his brain; that is to say, in combining the different sensations, perceptions, and ideas, that result from the impulse he has received, he has an idea of a whole, which he designates by the name of a peach, with which he can then occupy his thoughts.

From this it is sufficiently proved that thought has a commencement, a duration, an end; or rather a generation, a succession, a dissolution, like all the other modifications of matter; like them, thought is excited, is determined, is increased, is divided, is compounded, is simplified, &c. If, therefore, the soul, or the principle that thinks, be indivisible; how does it happen, that this soul has the faculty of memory, or of forgetfulness; is capacitated to think successively, to divide, to abstract, to combine, to extend its ideas, to retain them, or to lose them? How can it cease to think? If forms appear divisible in matter, it is only in considering them by abstraction, after the method, of geometricians; but this divisibility of form exists not in Nature, in which there is neither a point, an atom, nor form perfectly regular; it must therefore be concluded, that the forms of matter are not less indivisible than thought.

What has been said is sufficient to show the generation of sensations, of perceptions, of ideas, with their association, or connection in the brain: it will be seen that these various modifications are nothing more than the consequence of successive impulses, which the exterior organs transmit to the interior organ, which enjoys the faculty of thought, that is to say, to feel in itself the different modifications it has received, or to perceive the various ideas which it has generated; to combine them, to separate them, to extend them, to abridge them, to compare them, to renew them, &c. From whence it will be seen, that thought is nothing more than the perception of certain modifications, which the brain either gives to itself, or has received from exterior objects.

Indeed, not only the interior organ perceives the modifications it receives from without, but again it has the faculty of modifying itself; of considering the changes which take place in it, the motion by which it is agitated in its peculiar operations, from which it imbibes new perceptions and new ideas. It is the exercise of this power to fall back upon itself, that is called *reflection*.

From this it will appear, that for man to think and to reflect, is to feel, or perceive within himself the impressions, the sensations, the ideas, which have been furnished to his brain by those objects which give impulse to his senses, with the various changes which his brain produced on itself in consequence.

Memory is the faculty which the brain has of renewing in itself the modifications it has received, or rather, to restore itself to a state similar to that in which it has been placed by the sensations, the perceptions, the ideas, produced by exterior objects, in the exact order it received them, without any new action on the part of these objects, or even when these objects are absent; the brain perceives that these modifications assimilate with those it formerly experienced in the presence of the objects to which it relates, or attributes them. Memory is faithful, when these modifications are precisely the same; it is treacherous, when they differ from those which the organs have exteriorly experienced.

Imagination in man is only the faculty which the brain has of modifying itself, or of forming to itself new perceptions, upon the model of those which it has anteriorly received through the action of exterior objects on the senses. The brain, then, does nothing more than combine ideas which it has already formed, which it recalls to itself, from which it forms a whole, or a collection of modifications, which it has not received, which exists nowhere but in itself, although the individual ideas, or the parts of which this ideal whole is composed, have been previously communicated to it, in consequence of the impulse given to the senses by exterior objects: it is thus man forms to himself the idea of *centaurs*, or a being composed of a man and a horse, of *hyppogriffs*, or a being composed of a horse with wings and a griffin, besides a thousand other objects, equally ridiculous. By memory, the brain renews in itself the sensations, the perceptions, and the ideas which it has received or generated; represents to itself the objects which have actually moved its organs. By imagination it combines them variously: forms objects in their place which have not moved its organs, although it is perfectly acquainted with the elements or ideas of which it composes them. It is thus that man, by combining a great number of ideas borrowed from himself, such as justice, wisdom, goodness, intelligence, &c. by the aid of imagination, has formed various ideal beings, or imaginary wholes, which he has called JUPITER, JUNO, BRAMAH, SATURN, &c.

Judgment is the faculty which the brain possesses of comparing with each other the modifications it receives, the ideas it engenders, or which it has the power of awakening within itself, to the end that it may discover their relations, or their effects.

Will is a modification of the brain, by which it is disposed to action, that is to say, to give such an impulse to the organs of the body, as can induce to act in a manner, that will procure for itself what is requisite to modify it in a mode analogous to its own existence, or to enable it to avoid that by which it can be injured. To *will* is to be disposed to *action*. The exterior objects, or the interior ideas, which give birth to this disposition are called *motives*, because they are the springs or movements which determine it to act, that is to say, which give play to the organs of the body. Thus, *voluntary actions* are the motion of the body, determined by the modification of the brain. Fruit hanging on a tree, through the agency of the visual organs, modifies the brain in such a manner as to dispose the arm to stretch itself forth to cull it; again, it modifies it in another manner, by which it excites the hand to carry it to the mouth.

All the modifications which the interior organ or the brain receives, all the sensations, all the perceptions, all the ideas that are generated by the objects which give impulse to the senses, or which it renews within itself by its own peculiar faculties, are either favourable or prejudicial to man's mode of existence, whether that be transitory or habitual: they dispose the interior organ to action, which it exercises by reason of its own peculiar energy: this action is not, however, the same in all the individuals of the human species, depending much on their respective temperaments. From hence the PASSIONS have their birth: these are more or less violent; they are, however, nothing more than the motion of the will, determined by the objects which give it activity; consequently composed of the analogy or of the discordance which is found between these objects, man's peculiar mode of existence, and the force of his temperament. From this it results, that the passions are modes of existence or modifications of the brain; which either attract or repel those objects by which man is surrounded; that consequently they are submitted in their action to the physical laws of attraction and repulsion.

The faculty of perceiving or of being modified, as well by itself as exterior objects which the brain enjoys is sometimes designated by the term *understanding*. To the assemblage of the various faculties of which this interior organ is susceptible, is applied the name of *intelligence*. To a determined mode in which the brain exercises the faculties peculiar to itself, is given the appellation of *reason*. The dispositions or the modifications of the brain, some of them constant, others transitory, which give impulse to the beings of the human species, causing them to act, are styled *wit, wisdom, goodness, prudence, virtue, &c.*

In short, as there will be an opportunity presently to prove, all the intellectual faculties—that is to say, all the modes of action attributed to the soul, may be reduced to the modifications, to the qualities, to the modes of existence, to the changes produced by the motion of the brain; which is visibly in man the seat of feeling, the principle of all his actions. These modifications are to be attributed to the objects that strike on his senses; of which the impression is transmitted to the brain, or rather to the ideas, which the perceptions caused by the action of these objects on his senses have there generated, and which it has the faculty to re-produce. This brain moves itself in its turn, re-acts upon itself, gives play to the organs, which concentrate themselves in it, or which are rather nothing more than an extension of its own peculiar substance. It is thus the concealed motion of the interior organ, renders itself sensible by outward and visible signs. The brain, affected by a modification which is called FEAR, diffuses a paleness over the countenance, excites a tremulous motion in the limbs called trembling. The brain, affected by a sensation of GRIEF, causes tears to flow from the eyes, even without being moved by any exterior object; an idea which it retraces with great strength, suffices to give it very little modifications, which visibly have an influence on the whole frame.

In all this, nothing more is to be perceived than the same substance which acts diversely on the various parts of the body. If it be objected that this mechanism does not sufficiently explain the principles of the motion or the faculties of the soul; we reply, that it is in the same situation as all the other bodies of Nature, in which the most simple motion, the most ordinary phenomena, the most common modes of action are inexplicable mysteries, of which we shall never be able to fathom the first principles. Indeed, how can we flatter ourselves we shall ever be enabled to compass the true principle of that gravity by which a stone falls? Are we acquainted with the mechanism which produces attraction in some substances, repulsion in others? Are we in a condition to explain the communication of motion from one body to another? But it may be fairly asked,—Are the difficulties that occur, when attempting to explain the manner in which the soul acts, removed by making it a *spiritual being*, a substance of which we have not, nor cannot form one idea, which consequently must bewilder all the notions we are capable of forming to ourselves of this being? Let us then be contented to know that the soul moves itself, modifies itself, in consequence of material causes, which act upon it which give it activity: from whence the conclusion may be said to flow consecutively, that all its operations, all its faculties, prove that it is itself *material*.

CHAP. IX.

The Diversity of the Intellectual Faculties: they depend on Physical Causes, as do their Moral Qualities.—The Natural Principles of Society.—Morals.—Politics.

Nature is under the necessity of diversifying all her works. Elementary matter, different in its essence, must necessarily form different beings, various in their combinations, in their properties, in their modes of action, in their manner of existence. There is not, neither can there be, two beings, two combinations, which are mathematically and rigorously the same; because the place, the circumstances, the relations; the proportions, the modifications, never being exactly alike, the beings that result can never bear a perfect resemblance to each other: their modes of action must of necessity vary in something, even when we believe we find between them the greatest conformity.

In consequence of this principle, which every thing we see conspires to prove to be a truth, there are not two individuals of the human species who have precisely the same traits—who think exactly in the same manner—who view things under the same identical point of sight—who have decidedly the same ideas; consequently no two of them have uniformly the same system of conduct. The visible organs of man, as well as his concealed organs, have indeed some analogy, some common points of resemblance, some general conformity; which makes them appear, when viewed in the gross, to be affected in the same manner by certain causes: but the difference is infinite in the detail. The human soul may be compared to those instruments, of which the chords, already diversified in themselves, by the manner in which they have been spun, are also strung upon different notes: struck by the same impulse, each chord gives forth the sound that is peculiar to itself; that is to say, that which depends on its texture, its tension, its volume, on the momentary state in which it is placed by the circumambient air. It is this that produces the diversified spectacle, the varied scene, which the moral world offers to our view: it is from this that results the striking contrariety that is to be found in the minds, in the faculties, in the passions, in the energies, in the taste, in the imagination, in the ideas, in the opinions of man. This diversity is as great as that of his physical powers: like them it depends on his temperament, which is as much varied as his physiognomy. This variety gives birth to that continual series of action and reaction, which constitutes the life of the moral world: from this discordance results the harmony which at once maintains and preserves the human race.

The diversity found among the individuals of the human species, causes inequalities between man and man: this inequality constitutes the support of society. If all men were equal in their bodily powers, in their mental talents, they would not have any occasion for each other: it is the variation of his faculties, the inequality which this places him in, with regard to his fellows, that renders morals necessary to man: without these, he would live by himself, he would remain an isolated being. From whence it may be perceived, that this inequality of which man so often complains without cause—this impossibility which each man finds when in an isolated state, when left to himself, when unassociated with his fellow men, to labour efficaciously to his own welfare, to make his own security, to ensure his own conservation; places him in the happy situation of associating with his like, of depending on his fellow associates, of meriting their succour, of propitiating them to his views, of attracting their regard, of calling in their aid to chase away, by common and united efforts, that which would have the power to trouble or derange the order of his existence. In consequence of man's diversity, of the inequality that results, the weaker is obliged to seek the protection of the stronger; this, in his turn, recurs to the understanding, to the talents, to the industry of the weaker, whenever his judgment points out he can be useful to him: this natural inequality furnishes the reason why nations distinguish those citizens who have rendered their country eminent services. It is in consequence of his exigencies that man honors and recompenses those whose understanding, good deeds, assistance, or virtues, have procured for him real or supposed advantages, pleasures, or agreeable sensations of any sort: it is by this means that genius gains an ascendancy over the mind of man, and obliges a whole people to acknowledge its powers. Thus, the diversity and inequality of the faculties, as well corporeal as mental or intellectual, renders man necessary to his fellow man, makes him a social being, and incontestibly proves to him the necessity of morals.

According to this diversity of faculties, the individuals of the human species are divided into different classes, each in proportion to the effects produced, or the different qualities that may be remarked: all these varieties in man flow from the individual properties of his soul, or from the particular modification of his brain. It is thus, that wit, imagination, sensibility, talents, &c. diversify to infinity the differences that are to be found in man. It is thus, that some are called good, others wicked; some are denominated virtuous, others vicious; some are ranked as learned, others as ignorant; some are considered reasonable, others unreasonable, &c.

If all the various faculties attributed to the soul are examined, it will be found that like those of the body they are to be ascribed to physical causes, to which it will be very easy to recur. It will be found that the powers of the soul are the same as those of the body; that they always depend on the organization of this body, on its peculiar properties, on the permanent or transitory modifications that it undergoes; in a word, on its temperament.

Temperament is, in each individual, the habitual state in which he finds the fluids and the solids of which his body is composed. This temperament varies, by reason of the elements or matter that predominate in him, in consequence of the different combinations, of the various modifications, which this matter, diversified in itself, undergoes in his machine. Thus, in one, the blood is superabundant; in another, the bile; in a third, phlegm, &c.

It is from Nature—from his parents—from causes, which from the first moment of his existence have unceasingly modified him, that man derives his temperament. It is in his mother's womb that he has attracted the matter which, during his whole life, shall have an influence on his intellectual faculties—on his energies—on his passions—on his conduct. The very nourishment he takes, the quality of the air he respires, the climate he inhabits, the education he receives, the ideas that are presented to him, the opinions he imbibes, modify this temperament. As these circumstances can never be rigorously the same in every point for any two men, it is by no means surprising that such an amazing variety, so great a contrariety, should be found in man; or that there should exist as many different temperaments, as there are individuals in the human species.

Thus, although man may bear a general resemblance, he differs essentially, as well by the texture of his fibres and the disposition of his nerves, as by the nature, the quality, the quantity of matter that gives them play, that sets his organs in motion. Man, already different from his fellow, by the elasticity of his fibres, the tension of his nerves, becomes still more distinguished by a variety of other circumstances: he is more active, more robust, when he receives nourishing aliments, when he drinks wine, when he takes exercise: whilst another, who drinks nothing but water, who takes less juicy nourishment, who languishes in idleness, shall be sluggish and feeble.

All these causes have necessarily an influence on the mind, on the passions, on the will; in a word, on what are called the intellectual faculties. Thus, it may be observed, that a man of a sanguine constitution, is commonly lively, ingenious, full of imagination, passionate, voluptuous, enterprising; whilst the phlegmatic man is dull, of a heavy understanding, slow of conception, inactive, difficult to be moved, pusillanimous, without imagination, or possessing it in a less lively degree, incapable of taking any strong measures, or of willing resolutely.

If experience was consulted, in the room of prejudice, the physician would collect from morals, the key to the human heart: in curing the body, he would sometimes be assured of curing the mind. Man, in making a spiritual substance of his soul, has contented himself with administering to it spiritual remedies, which either have no influence over his temperament, or do it an injury. The doctrine of the spirituality of the soul has rendered morals a conjectural science, that does not furnish a knowledge of the true motives which ought to be put in activity, in order to influence man to his welfare. If, calling experience to his assistance, man sought out the elements which form the basis of his temperament, or of the greater number of the individuals composing a nation, he would then discover what would be most proper for him,—that which could be most convenient to his mode of existence—which could most conduce to his true interest—what laws would be necessary to his happiness—what institutions would be most useful for him—what regulations would be most beneficial. In short, morals and politics would be equally enabled to draw from *materialism*, advantages which the dogma of spirituality can never supply, of which it even precludes the idea. Man will ever remain a mystery, to those who shall obstinately persist in viewing him with eyes prepossessed by metaphysics; he will always be an enigma to those who shall pertinaciously attribute his actions to a principle, of which it is impossible to form to themselves any distinct idea. When man shall be seriously inclined to understand himself, let him sedulously endeavour to discover the matter that enters into his combination, which constitutes his temperament; these discoveries will furnish him with the clue to the nature of his desires, to the quality of his passions, to the bent of his inclinations—will enable him to foresee his conduct on given occasions—will indicate the remedies that may be successfully employed to correct the defects of a vicious organization, of a temperament, as injurious to himself as to the society of which he is a member.

Indeed, it is not to be doubted that man's temperament is capable of being corrected, of being modified, of being changed, by causes as physical as the matter of which it is constituted. We are all in some measure capable of forming our own temperament: a man of a sanguine constitution, by taking less juicy nourishment, by abating its quantity, by abstaining from strong liquor, &c. may achieve the correction of the nature, the quality, the quantity, the tendency, the motion of the fluids, which predominate in his machine. A bilious man, or one who is melancholy, may, by the aid of certain remedies, diminish the mass of this bilious fluid; he may correct the blemish of his humours, by the assistance of exercise; he may dissipate his gloom, by the gaiety which results from increased motion. An European transplanted into Hindostan, will, by degrees, become quite a different man in his humours, in his ideas, in his temperament, in his character.

Although but few experiments have been made with a view to learn what constitutes the temperament of man, there are still enough if he would but deign to make use of them—if he would vouchsafe to apply to useful purposes the little experience he has gleaned. It would appear, speaking generally, that the igneous principle which chemists designate under the name of *phlogiston*, or inflammable matter, is that which in man yields him the most active life, furnishes him with the greatest energy, affords the greatest mobility to his frame, supplies the greatest spring to his organs, gives the greatest elasticity to his fibres, the greatest tension to his nerves, the greatest rapidity to his fluids. From these causes, which are entirely material, commonly result the dispositions or faculties called sensibility, wit, imagination, genius, vivacity, &c. which give the tone to the passions, to the will, to the moral actions of man. In this sense, it is with great justice we apply the expressions, 'warmth of soul,' 'ardency of imagination,' 'fire of genius,' &c.

It is this fiery element, diffused unequally, distributed in various proportions through the beings of the human species, that sets man in motion, gives him activity, supplies him with animal heat, and which, if we may be allowed the expression, renders him more or less alive. This igneous matter, so active, so subtle, dissipates itself with great facility, then requires to be reinstated in his system by means of aliments that contain it, which thereby become proper to restore his machine, to lend new warmth to the brain, to furnish it with the elasticity requisite to the performance of those functions which are called intellectual. It is this ardent matter contained in wine, in strong liquor, that gives to the most torpid, to the dullest, to the most sluggish man, a vivacity of which, without it, he would be incapable—which urges even the coward on to battle. When this fiery element is too abundant in man, whilst he is labouring under certain diseases, it plunges him into delirium; when it is in too weak or in too small a quantity, he swoons, he sinks to the earth. This igneous matter diminishes in his old age—it totally dissipates at his death. It would not be unreasonable to suppose, that what physicians call the nervous fluid, which so promptly gives notice to the brain of all that happens to the body, is nothing more than electric matter; that the various proportions of this matter diffused through his system, is the cause of that great diversity to be discovered in the human being, and in the faculties he possesses.

If the intellectual faculties of man, or his moral qualities, be examined according to the principles here laid down, the conviction must be complete that they are to be attributed to material causes, which have an influence more or less marked, either transitory or durable, over his peculiar organization. But where does he derive this organization, except it be from the parents from whom he receives the elements of a machine necessarily analogous to their own? From whence does he derive the greater or less quantity of igneous matter, or vivifying heat, that decides upon, that gives the tone to his mental qualities? It is from the mother who bore him in her womb, who has communicated to him a portion of that fire with which she was herself animated, which circulated through her veins with her blood;—it is from the aliments that have nourished him,—it is from the climate he inhabits,—it is from the atmosphere that surrounds: all these causes have an influence over his fluids, over his solids, and decide on his natural dispositions. In examining these dispositions, from whence his faculties depend, it will ever be found, that they are *corporeal*, that they are *material*.

The most prominent of these dispositions in man, is that physical sensibility from which flows all his intellectual or moral qualities. To feel, according to what has been said, is to receive an impulse, to be moved, to have a consciousness of the changes operated on his system. To have sensibility is nothing more than to be so constituted as to feel promptly, and in a very lively manner, the impressions of those objects which act upon him. A sensible soul is only man's brain, disposed in a mode to receive the motion communicated to it with facility, to re-act with promptness, by giving an instantaneous impulse to the organs. Thus the man is called sensible, whom the sight of the distressed, the contemplation of the unhappy, the recital of a melancholy tale, the witnessing of an afflicting catastrophe, or the idea of a dreadful spectacle, touches in so lively a manner as to enable the brain to give play to his lachrymal organs, which cause him to shed tears; a sign by which we recognize the effect of great grief, of extreme anguish in the human being. The man in whom musical sounds excite a degree of pleasure, or produce very remarkable effects, is said to have a *sensible* or a fine ear. In short, when it is perceived that eloquence—the beauty of the arts—the various objects that strike his senses, excite in him very lively emotions, he is said to possess a soul full of sensibility.

Wit, is a consequence of this physical sensibility; indeed, wit is nothing more than the facility which some beings, of the human species possess, of seizing with promptitude, of developing with quickness, a whole, with its different relations to other objects. *Genius*, is the facility with which some men comprehend this whole, and its various relations when they are difficult to be known, but useful to forward great and mighty projects. Wit may be compared to a piercing eye which perceives things quickly. Genius is an eye that comprehends at one view, all the points of an extended horizon: or what the French term *coup d'oeil*. True wit is that which perceives objects with their relations such as they really are. False wit is that which catches at relations, which do not apply to the object, or which arises from some blemish in the organization. True wit resembles the direction on a hand-post.

Imagination is the faculty of combining with promptitude ideas or images; it consists in the power man possesses of re-producing with ease the modifications of his brain: of connecting them, of attaching them to the objects to which they are suitable. When imagination does this, it gives pleasure; its fictions are approved, it embellishes Nature, it is a proof of the soundness of the mind, it aids truth: when on the contrary, it combines ideas, not formed to associate themselves with each other—when it paints nothing but disagreeable phantoms, it disgusts, its fictions are censured, it distorts Nature, it advocates falsehood, it is the proof of a disordered, of a deranged mind: thus poetry, calculated to render Nature more pathetic, more touching, pleases when it creates ideal beings, but which move us agreeably: we, therefore, forgive the illusions it has held forth, on account of the pleasure we have reaped from them. The hideous chimeras of superstition displease, because they are nothing more than the productions of a distempered imagination, that can only awaken the most afflicting sensations, fills us with the most disagreeable ideas.

Imagination, when it wanders, produces fanaticism, superstitious terrors, inconsiderate zeal, phrenzy, and the most enormous crimes: when it is well regulated, it gives birth to a strong predilection for useful objects, an energetic passion for virtue, an enthusiastic love of our country, and the most ardent friendship: the man who is divested of imagination, is commonly one in whose torpid constitution phlegm predominates over the igneous fluid, over that sacred fire, which is the great principle of his mobility, of that warmth of sentiment, which vivifies all his intellectual faculties. There must be enthusiasm for transcendent virtues as well as for atrocious crimes; enthusiasm places the soul in a state similar to that of drunkenness; both the one and the other excite in man that rapidity of motion which is approved, when good results, when its effects are beneficial; but which is censured, is called folly, delirium, crime, fury; when it produces nothing but disorder and confusion.

The mind is out of order, it is incapable of judging sanely—the imagination is badly regulated, whenever man's organization is not so modified, as to perform its functions with precision. At each moment of his existence, man gathers experience; every sensation he has, furnishes a fact that deposits in his brain an idea which his memory recalls with more or less fidelity: these facts connect themselves, these ideas are associated; their chain constitutes *experience*; this lays the foundation of *science*. Knowledge is that consciousness which arises from reiterated experience—from experiments made with precision of the sensations, of the ideas, of the effects which an object is capable of producing, either in ourselves or in others. All science, to be just, must be founded on truth. Truth itself rests on the constant, the faithful relation of our senses. Thus, *truth* is that conformity, that perpetual affinity, which man's senses, when well constituted, when aided by experience, discover to him, between the objects of which he has a knowledge, and the qualities with which he clothes them. In short, truth is nothing more than the just, the precise association of his ideas. But how can he, without experience, assure himself of the accuracy, of the justness of this association? How, if he does not reiterate this experience, can he compare it? how prove its truth? If his senses are vitiated, how is it possible they can convey to him with precision, the sensations, the facts, with which they store his brain? It is only by multiplied, by diversified, by repeated experience, that he is enabled to rectify the errors of his first conceptions.

Man is in error every time his organs, either originally defective in their nature, or vitiated by the durable or transitory modifications which they undergo, render him incapable of judging soundly of objects. Error consists in the false association of ideas, by which qualities are attributed to objects which they do not possess. Man is in error, when he supposes those beings really to have existence, which have no local habitation but in his own imagination: he is in error, when he associates the idea of happiness with objects capable of injuring him, whether immediately or by remote consequences which he cannot foresee.

But how can he foresee effects of which he has not yet any knowledge? It is by the aid of experience: by the assistance which this experience affords, it is known that analogous, that like causes, produce analogous, produce like effects. Memory, by recalling these effects, enables him to form a judgment of those he may expect, whether it be from the same causes, or from causes that bear a relation to those of which he has already experienced the action. From this it will appear, that *prudence, foresight,* are faculties that are ascribable to, that grow out of experience. If he has felt that fire excited in his organs painful sensation, this experience suffices him to know, to foresee, that fire so applied, will consequently excite the same sensations. If he has discovered that certain actions, on his part, stirred up the hatred, elicited the contempt of others, this experience sufficiently enables him to foresee, that every time he shall act in a similar manner, he will be either hated or despised.

The faculty man has of gathering experience, of recalling it to himself, of foreseeing effects by which he is enabled to avoid whatever may have the power to injure him, to procure that which may be useful to the conservation of his existence, which may contribute to that which is the sole end of all his actions, whether corporeal or mental,—his felicity— constitutes that, which, in one word, is designated under the name of

Reason. Sentiment, imagination, temperament, may be capable of leading him astray—may have the power to deceive him; but experience and reflection will rectify his errors, point out his mistakes, place him in the right road, teach him what can really conduce to, what can truly conduct him to happiness. From this, it will appear, that *reason* is man's nature, modified by experience, moulded by judgment, regulated by reflection: it supposes a moderate, sober temperament; a just, a sound mind; a well-regulated, orderly imagination; a knowledge of truth, grounded upon tried, upon reiterated experience; in fact, prudence and foresight: this will serve to prove, that although nothing is more commonly asserted, although the phrase is repeated daily, nay, hourly, that *man is a reasonable being*, yet there are but a very small number of the individuals who compose the human species, of whom it can with truth be said; who really enjoy the faculty of reason, or who combine the dispositions, the experience, by which it is constituted. It ought not, then to excite surprise, that the individuals of the human race, who are in a capacity to make true experience, are so few in number. Man, when he is born, brings with him into the world organs susceptible of receiving impulse, amassing ideas, of collecting experience; but whether it be from the vice of his system, the imperfection of his organization, or from those causes by which it is modified, his experience is false, his ideas are confused, his images are badly associated, his judgment is erroneous, his brain is saturated with vicious, with wicked systems, which necessarily have an influence over his conduct, which are continually disturbing his mind, and confounding his reason.

Man's senses, as it has been shewn, are the only means by which he is enabled to ascertain whether his opinions are true or false, whether his conduct is useful to himself and beneficial to others, whether it is advantageous or disadvantageous. But that his senses may be competent to make a faithful relation—that they may be in a capacity to impress true ideas on his brain, it is requisite they should be sound; that is to say, in the state necessary to maintain his existence; in that order which is suitable to his preservation—that condition which is calculated to ensure his permanent felicity. It is also indispensable that his brain itself should be healthy, or in the proper circumstances to enable it to fulfil its functions with precision, to exercise its faculties with vigour. It is necessary that memory should faithfully delineate its anterior sensations, should accurately retrace its former ideas; to the end, that he may be competent to judge, to foresee the effects he may have to hope, the consequences he may have to fear, from those actions to which he may be determined by his will. If his organic system be vicious, if his interior or exterior organs be defective, whether by their natural conformation or from those causes by which they are regulated, he feels but imperfectly—in a manner less distinct than is requisite; his ideas are either false or suspicious, he judges badly, he is in a delusion, in a state of ebriety, in a sort of intoxication that prevents his grasping the true relation of things. In short, if his memory is faulty, if it is treacherous, his reflection is void, his imagination leads him astray, his mind deceives him, whilst the sensibility of his organs, simultaneously assailed by a crowd of impressions, shocked by a variety of impulsions, oppose him to prudence, to foresight, to the exercise of his reason. On the other hand, if the conformation of his organs, as it happens with those of a phlegmatic temperament, of a dull habit, does not permit him to move, except with feebleness, in a sluggish manner, his experience is slow, frequently unprofitable. The tortoise and the butterfly are alike incapable of preventing their destruction. The stupid man, equally with him who is intoxicated, are in that state which renders it impossible for them to arrive at or attain the end they have in view.

But what is the end? What is the aim of man in the sphere he occupies? It is to preserve himself; to render his existence happy. It becomes then of the utmost importance, that he should understand the true means which reason points out, which prudence teaches him to use, in order that he may with certainty, that he may constantly arrive at the end which he proposes to himself. These he will find are his natural faculties—his mind—his talents—his industry—his actions, determined by those passions of which his nature renders him susceptible, which give more or less activity to his will. Experience and reason again shew him, that the men with whom he is associated are necessary to him, are capable of contributing to his happiness, are in a capacity to administer to his pleasures, are competent to assist him by those faculties which are peculiar to them; experience teaches him the mode he must adopt to induce them to concur in his designs, to determine them to will and incline them to act in his favour. This points out to him the actions they approve—those which displease them—the conduct which attracts them—that which repels them—the judgment by which they are swayed—the advantages that occur—the prejudicial effects that result to him from their various modes of existence and from their diverse manner of acting. This experience furnishes him with the ideas of virtue and of vice, of justice and of injustice, of goodness and of wickedness, of decency and of indecency, of probity and of knavery: In short, he learns to form a judgment of men—to estimate their actions—to distinguish the various sentiments excited in them, according to the diversity of those effects which they make him experience. It is upon the necessary diversity of these effects that is founded the discrimination between good and evil—between virtue and vice; distinctions which do not rest, as some thinkers have believed, on the conventions made between men; still less, as some metaphysicians have asserted, upon the chimerical will of supernatural beings: but upon the solid, the invariable, the eternal relations that subsist between beings of the human species congregated together, and living in society: which relations will have existence as long as man shall remain, as long as society shall continue to exist.

Thus *virtue* is every thing that is truly beneficial, every thing that is constantly useful to the individuals of the human race, living together in society; *vice* every thing that is really prejudicial, every thing that is permanently injurious to them. The greatest virtues are those which procure for man the most durable advantages, from which he derives the most solid happiness, which preserves the greatest degree of order in his association: the greatest vices, are those which most disturb his tendency to happiness, which perpetuate error, which most interrupt the necessary order of society.

The *virtuous man*, is he whose actions tend uniformly to the welfare, constantly to the happiness, of his fellow creatures. The *vicious man*, is he whose conduct tends to the misery, whose propensities form the unhappiness of those with whom he lives; from whence his own peculiar misery most commonly results.

Every thing that procures for a man true and permanent happiness is reasonable; every thing that disturbs his individual felicity, or that of the beings necessary to his happiness, is foolish and unreasonable. The man who injures others, is wicked; the man who injures himself, is an imprudent being, who neither has a knowledge of reason, of his own peculiar interests, nor of truth.

Man's *duties* are the means pointed out to him by experience, the circle which reason describes for him, by which he is to arrive at that goal he proposes to himself; these duties are the necessary consequence of the relations subsisting between mortals, who equally desire happiness, who are equally anxious to preserve their existence. When it is said these duties *compel him*, it signifies nothing more than that, without taking these means, he could not reach the end proposed to him by his nature. Thus, *moral obligation* is the necessity of employing the natural means to render the beings with whom he lives happy; to the end that he may determine them in turn to contribute to his own individual happiness: his obligation toward himself, is the necessity he is under to take those means, without which he would be incapable to conserve himself, or render his existence solidly and permanently happy. Morals, like the universe, is founded upon necessity, or upon the eternal relation of things.

Happiness is a mode of existence of which man naturally wishes the duration, or in which he is willing to continue. It is measured by its duration, by its vivacity. The greatest happiness is that which has the longest continuance: transient happiness, or that which has only a short duration, is called *Pleasure*; the more lively it is, the more fugitive, because man's senses are only susceptible of a certain quantum of motion. When pleasure exceeds this given quantity, it is changed into *anguish*, or into that painful mode of existence, of which he ardently desires the cessation: this is the reason why pleasure and pain frequently so closely approximate each other as scarcely to be discriminated. Immoderate pleasure is the forerunner of regret. It is succeeded by ennui, it is followed by weariness, it ends in disgust: transient happiness frequently converts itself into durable misfortune. According to these principles it will be seen that man, who in each moment of his duration seeks necessarily after happiness, ought, when he is reasonable, to manage, to husband, to regulate his pleasures; to refuse himself to all those of which the indulgence would be succeeded by regret; to avoid those which can convert themselves into pain; in order that he may procure for himself the most permanent felicity.

Happiness cannot be the same for all the beings of the human species; the same pleasures cannot equally affect men whose conformation is different, whose modification is diverse. This no doubt, is the true reason why the greater number of moral philosophers are so little in accord upon those objects in which they have made man's happiness consist, as well as on the means by which it may be obtained. Nevertheless, in general, happiness appears to be a state, whether momentary or durable, in which man readily acquiesces, because he finds it conformable to his being. This state results from the accord, springs out of the conformity, which is found between himself and those circumstances in which he has been placed by Nature; or, if it be preferred, *happiness is the co-ordination of man, with the causes that give him impulse.*

The ideas which man forms to himself of happiness depend not only on his temperament, on his individual conformation, but also upon the habits he has contracted. *Habit* is, in man, a mode of existence—of thinking—of acting, which his organs, as well interior as exterior, contract, by the frequent reiteration of the same motion; from whence results the faculty of performing these actions with promptitude, of executing them with facility.

If things be attentively considered, it will be found that almost the whole conduct of man—the entire system of his actions—his occupations—his connexions—his studies—his amusements—his manners—his customs—his very garments—even his aliments, are the effect of habit. He owes equally to habit, the facility with which he exercises his mental faculties of thought—of judgment—of wit—of reason—of taste, &c. It is to habit he owes the greater part of his inclinations—of his desires—of his opinions—of his prejudices—of the ideas, true or false, he forms to himself of his welfare. In short, it is to habit, consecrated by time, that he owes those errors into which everything strives to precipitate him; from which every thing is calculated to prevent him emancipating himself. It is habit that attaches him either to virtue or to vice: experience proves this: observation teaches incontrovertibly that the first crime is always accompanied by more pangs of remorse than the second; this again, by more than the third; so on to those that follow. A first action is the commencement of a habit; those which succeed confirm it: by force of combatting the obstacles that prevent the commission of criminal actions, man arrives at the power of vanquishing them with ease; of conquering them with facility. Thus he frequently becomes wicked from habit.

Man is so much modified by habit, that it is frequently confounded with his nature: from hence results, as will presently be seen, those opinions or those ideas, which he has called *innate*: because he has been unwilling to recur back to the source from whence they sprung: which has, as it were, identified itself with his brain. However this may be, he adheres with great strength of attachment to all those things to which he is habituated; his mind experiences a sort of violence, an incommodious revulsion, a troublesome distaste, when it is endeavoured to make him change the course of his ideas: a fatal predilection frequently conducts him back to the old track in despite of reason.

It is by a pure mechanism that may be explained the phenomena of habit, as well physical as moral; the soul, notwithstanding its spirituality, is modified exactly in the same manner as the body. Habit, in man, causes the organs of voice to learn the mode of expressing quickly the ideas consigned to his brain, by means of certain motion, which, during his infancy, the tongue acquires the power of executing with facility: his tongue, once habituated to move itself in a certain manner, finds much trouble, has great pain, to move itself after another mode; the throat yields with difficulty to those inflections which are exacted by a language different from that to which he has, been accustomed. It is the same with regard to his ideas; his brain, his interior organ, his soul, inured to a given manner of modification, accustomed to attach certain ideas to certain objects, long used to form to itself a system connected with certain opinions, whether true or false, experiences a painful sensation, whenever he undertakes to give it a new impulse, or alter the direction of its habitual motion. It is nearly as difficult to make him change his opinions as his language.

Here, then, without doubt, is the cause of that almost invincible attachment which man displays to those customs—those prejudices—those institutions of which it is in vain that reason, experience, good sense prove to him the inutility, or even the danger. Habit opposes itself to the clearest, the most evident demonstrations; these can avail nothing against those passions, those vices, which time has rooted in him—against the most ridiculous systems—against the most absurd notions—against the most extravagant hypotheses—against the strangest customs: above all, when he has learned to attach to them the ideas of utility, of common interest, of the welfare of society. Such is the source of that obstinacy, of that stubbornness, which man evinces for his religion, for ancient usages, for unreasonable customs, for laws so little accordant with justice, for abuses, which so frequently make him suffer, for prejudices of which he sometimes acknowledges the absurdity, yet is unwilling to divest himself of them. Here is the reason why nations contemplate the most useful novelties as mischievous innovations—why they believe they would be lost, if they were to remedy those evils to which they have become habituated; which they have learned to consider as necessary to their repose; which they have been taught to consider dangerous to be cured.

Education is only the art of making man contract, in early life, that is to say, when his organs are extremely flexible, the habits, the opinions, the modes of existence, adopted by the society in which he is placed. The first moments of his infancy are employed in collecting experience; those who are charged with the care of rearing him, or who are entrusted to bring him up, teach him how to apply it: it is they who develope reason in him: the first impulse they give him commonly decides upon his condition, upon his passions, upon the ideas he forms to himself of happiness, upon the means he shall employ to procure it, upon his virtues, and upon his vices. Under the eyes of his masters, the infant acquires ideas: under their tuition he learns to associate them,—to think in a certain manner,—to judge well or ill. They point out to him various objects, which they accustom him either to love or to hate, to desire or to avoid, to esteem or to despise. It is thus opinions are transmitted from fathers, mothers, nurses, and masters, to man in his infantine state. It is thus, that his mind by degrees saturates itself with truth, or fills itself with error; after which he regulates his conduct, which renders him either happy or miserable, virtuous or vicious, estimable or hateful. It is thus he becomes either contented or discontented with his destiny, according to the objects towards which they have directed his passions—towards which they have bent the energies of his mind; that is to say, in which they have shewn him his interest, in which they have taught him to place his felicity: in consequence, he loves and searches after that which they have taught him to revere—that which they have made the object of his research; he has those tastes, those inclinations, those phantasms, which, during the whole course of his life, he is forward to indulge, which he is eager to satisfy, in proportion to the activity they have excited in him, and the capacity with which he has been provided by Nature.

Politics ought to be the art of regulating the passions of man—of directing them to the welfare of society—of diverting them into a genial current of happiness—of making them flow gently to the general benefit of all: but too frequently it is nothing more than the detestible art of arming the passions of the various members of society against each other,—of making them the engines to accomplish their mutual destruction,—of converting them into agents which embitter their existence, create jealousies among them, and fill with rancorous animosities that association from which, if properly managed, man ought to derive his felicity. Society is commonly so vicious because it is not founded upon Nature, upon experience, and upon general utility; but on the contrary, upon the passions, upon the caprices, and upon the particular interests of those by whom it is governed. In short, it is for the most part the advantage of the few opposed to the prosperity of the many.

Politics, to be useful, should found its principles upon Nature; that is to say, should conform itself to the essence of man, should mould itself to the great end of society: but what is society? and what is its end? It is a whole, formed by the union of a great number of families, or by a collection of individuals, assembled from a reciprocity of interest, in order that they may satisfy with greater facility their reciprocal wants—that they may, with more certainty, procure the advantages they desire—that they may obtain mutual succours—above all, that they may gain the faculty of enjoying, in security, those benefits with which Nature and industry may furnish them: it follows, of course, that politics, which are intended to maintain society, and to consolidate the interests of this congregation, ought to enter into its views, to facilitate the means of giving them efficiency, to remove all those obstacles that have a tendency to counteract the intention with which man entered into association.

Man, in approximating to his fellow man, to live with him in society, has made, either formally or tacitly, a covenant; by which he engages to render mutual services, to do nothing that can be prejudicial to his neighbour. But as the nature of each individual impels him each instant to seek after his own welfare, which he has mistaken to consist in the gratification of his passions, and the indulgence of his transitory caprices, without any regard to the convenience of his fellows; there needed a power to conduct him back to his duty, to oblige him to conform himself to his obligations, and to recall him to his engagements, which the hurry of his passions frequently make him forget. This power is the *law*; it is, or ought to be, the collection of the will of society, reunited to fix the conduct of its members, to direct their action in such a mode, that it may concur to the great end of his association—the general good.

But as society, more especially when very numerous, is incapable of assembling itself, unless with great difficulty, as it cannot with tumult make known its intentions, it is obliged to choose citizens in whom it places a confidence, whom it makes the interpreter of its will, whom it constitutes the depositaries of the power requisite to carry it into execution. Such is the origin of all *government*, which to be legitimate can only be founded on the free consent of society. Those who are charged with the care of governing, call themselves sovereigns, chiefs, legislators: according to the form which society has been willing to give to its government: these sovereigns are styled monarchs, magistrates, representatives, &c. Government only borrows its power from society: being established for no other purpose than its welfare, it is evident society can revoke this power whenever its interest shall exact it; change the form of its government; extend or limit the power which it has confided to its chiefs, over whom, by the immutable laws of Nature, it always conserves a supreme authority: because these laws enjoin, that the part shall always remain subordinate to the whole.

Thus sovereigns are the ministers of society, its interpreters, the depositaries of a greater or of a less portion of its power; but they are not its absolute masters, neither are they the proprietors of nations. By a *covenant*, either expressed or implied, they engage themselves to watch over the maintenance, to occupy themselves with the welfare of society; it is only upon these conditions society consents to obey them. The price of obedience is protection. There is or ought to be a reciprocity of interest between the governed and the governor: whenever this reciprocity is wanting, society is in that state of confusion of which we spoke in the fifth chapter: it is verging on destruction. No society upon earth was ever willing or competent to confer irrevocably upon its chiefs the power, the right, of doing it injury. Such a concession, such a compact, would be annulled, would be rendered void by Nature; because she wills that each society, the same as each individual of the human species shall tend to its own conservation; it has not therefore the capacity to consent to its permanent unhappiness. *Laws*, in order that they may be just, ought invariably to have for their end, the general interest of society; that is to say, to assure to the greater number of citizens those advantages for which man originally associated. These advantages are *liberty, property, security*.

Liberty, to man, is the faculty of doing, for his own peculiar happiness, every thing which does not injure or diminish the happiness of his associates: in associating, each individual renounced the exercise of that portion of his natural liberty which would be able to prejudice or injure the liberty of his fellows. The exercise of that liberty which is injurious to society is called *licentiousness*.

Property, to man, is the faculty of enjoying those advantages which spring from labour; those benefits which industry or talent has procured to each member of society.

Security, to man, is the certitude, the assurance, that each individual ought to have, of enjoying in his person, of finding for his property the protection of the laws, as long as he shall faithfully observe, as long as he shall punctually perform, his engagements with society.

Justice, to man, assures to all the members of society, the possession of these advantages, the enjoyment of those rights, which belong to them. From this, it will appear, that without justice, society is not in a condition to procure the happiness of any man. Justice is also called *equity*, because by the assistance of the laws made to command the whole, she reduces all its members to a state of equality; that is to say, she prevents them from prevailing one over the other, by the inequality which Nature or industry may have made between their respective powers.

Rights, to man, are every thing which society, by equitable laws, permits each individual to do for his own peculiar felicity. These rights are evidently limited by the invariable end of all association: society has, on its part, rights over all its members, by virtue of the advantages which it procures for them; all its members, in turn, have a right to claim, to exact from society, or secure from its ministers those advantages for the procuring of which they congregated, in favour of which they renounced a portion of their natural liberty. A society, of which the chiefs, aided by the laws, do not procure any good for its members, evidently loses its right over them: those chiefs who injure society lose the right of commanding. It is not our country, without it secures the welfare of its inhabitants; a society without equity contains only enemies; a society oppressed is composed only of tyrants and slaves; slaves are incapable of being citizens; it is liberty, property, and security, that render our country dear to us; it is the true love of his country that forms the citizen.

For want of having a proper knowledge of these truths, or for want of applying them when known, some nations have become unhappy—have contained nothing but a vile heap of slaves, separated from each other, detached from society, which neither procures for them any good, nor secures to them any one advantage. In consequence of the imprudence of some nations, or of the craft, cunning, and violence of those to whom they have confided the power of making laws, and carrying them into execution, their sovereigns have rendered themselves absolute masters of society. These, mistaking the true source of their power, pretended to hold it from heaven, to be accountable for their actions to God alone, to owe nothing, not to have any obligation to society, in a word, to be gods upon earth, to possess the right of governing arbitrarily. From thence politics became corrupted: they were only a mockery. Such nations, disgraced and grown contemptible, did not dare resist the will of their chiefs; their laws were nothing more than the expression of the caprice of these chiefs; public welfare was sacrificed to their peculiar interests; the force of society was turned against itself; its members withdrew to attach themselves to its oppressors, to its tyrants; these to seduce them, permitted them to injure it with impunity and to profit by its misfortunes. Thus liberty, justice, security, and virtue, were banished from many nations; politics was no longer any thing more than the art of availing itself of the forces of a people and of the treasure of society; of dividing it on the subject of its interest, in order to subjugate it by itself; at length a stupid, a mechanical habit, made them cherish their oppressors, and love their chains.

Man when he has nothing to fear, presently becomes wicked; he who believes he has not occasion for his fellow, persuades himself he may follow the inclinations of his heart without caution or discretion. Thus fear is the only obstacle society can effectually oppose to the passions of its chiefs; without it they will quickly become corrupt, and will not scruple to avail themselves of the means society has placed in their hands, to make them accomplices in their iniquity. To prevent these abuses, it is requisite society should set bounds to its confidence; should limit the power which it delegates to its chiefs; should reserve to itself a sufficient portion of authority to prevent them from injuring it; it must establish prudent checks: it must cautiously divide the power it confers, because re-united, it will by such reunion be infallibly oppressed. The slightest reflection, the most scanty review, will make men feel that the burthen of governing and weight of administration, is too ponderous and overpowering to be borne by an individual; that the scope of his jurisdiction, that the range of his surveillance, and multiplicity of his duties must always render him negligent; that the extent of his power has ever a tendency to render him mischievous. In short, the experience of all ages will convince nations that man is continually tempted to the abuse of power: that as an abundance of strong liquor intoxicates his brain, so unlimited power corrupts his heart; that therefore the sovereign ought to be subject to the law, not the law to the sovereign.

Government has necessarily an equal influence over the philosophy, as over the morals of nations. In the same manner that its care produces labour, activity, abundance, salubrity and justice; its negligence induces idleness, sloth, discouragement, penury, contagion, injustice, vices and crimes. It depends upon government either to foster industry, mature genius, give a spring to talents, or stifle them. Indeed government, the disturber of dignities, of riches, of rewards, and punishments; the master of those objects in which man from his infancy has learned to place his felicity, and contemplate as the means of his happiness; acquires a necessary influence over his conduct: it kindles his passions; gives them direction; makes him instrumental to whatever purpose it pleases; it modifies him; determines his manners; which in a whole people, as in the individual, is nothing more than the conduct, the general system of wills, of actions that necessarily result from his education, government, laws, and religious opinions—his institutions, whether rational or irrational. In short, manners are the habits of a people: these are good whenever society draws from them true felicity and solid happiness; they are bad, they are detestable in the eye of reason, when the happiness of society does not spring from them; they are unwholesome when they have nothing more in their favour than the suffrage of time, and the countenance of prejudice which rarely consults experience, which is almost ever at variance with good sense: notwithstanding they may have the sanction of the law, custom, religion, public opinion, or example, they may be unworthy and may be disgraceful, provided society is in disorder; that crime abounds; that virtue shrinks beneath the basilisk eye of triumphant vice; they may then be said to resemble the UPAS, whose luxuriant yet poisonous foliage, the produce of a rank soil, becomes more baneful to those who are submitted to its vortex, in proportion as it extends its branches. If experience he consulted, it will be found there is no action, however abominable, that has not received the applause, that has not obtained the approbation of some people. Parricide, the sacrifice of children, robbery, usurpation, cruelty, intolerance, and prostitution, have all in their turn been licensed actions; have been advocated; have been deemed laudable and meritorious deeds with some nations of the earth. Above all, *superstition* has consecrated the most unreasonable, the most revolting customs.

Man's passions result from and depend on the motion of attraction or repulsion, of which he is rendered susceptible by Nature; who enables him, by his peculiar essence, to be attracted by those objects which appear useful to him, to be repelled by those which he considers prejudicial; it follows that government, by holding the magnet, can put these passions into activity, has the power either of restraining them, or of giving them a favorable or an unfavorable direction. All his passions are constantly limited by either loving or hating, seeking or avoiding, desiring or fearing. These passions, so necessary to the conservation of man, are a consequence of his organization; they display themselves with more or less energy, according to his temperament; education and habit develope them; government gives them play, conducts them towards those objects, which it believes itself interested in making desirable to its subjects. The various names which have been given to these passions, are relative to the different objects by which they are excited, such as pleasure, grandeur, or riches, which produce voluptuousness, ambition, vanity and avarice. If the source of those passions which predominate in nations be attentively examined it will be commonly found in their governments. It is the impulse received from their chiefs that renders them sometimes warlike, sometimes superstitious, sometimes aspiring after glory, sometimes greedy after wealth, sometimes rational, and sometimes unreasonable; if sovereigns, in order to enlighten and render happy their dominions, were to employ only the *tenth* part of the vast expenditures which they lavish, only a *tythe* of the pains which they employ to render them brutish, to stupify them, to deceive them, and to afflict them; their subjects would presently be as wise, would quickly be as happy, as they are now remarkable for being blind, ignorant, and miserable.

Let the vain project of destroying, the delusive attempt at rooting his passions from the heart of man, he abandoned; let an effort be made to direct them towards objects that may be useful to himself, beneficial to his associates. Let education, let government, let the laws, habituate him to restrain his passions within those just bounds that experience fixes and reason prescribes. Let the ambitious have honours, titles, distinctions, and power, when they shall have usefully served their country; let riches be given to those who covet them, when they shall have rendered themselves necessary to their fellow citizens; let commendations, let eulogies, encourage those who shall be actuated by the love of glory. In short, let the passions of man have a free, an uninterrupted course, whenever there shall result from their exercise, real, substantial, and durable advantages to society. Let education kindle only those, which are truly beneficial to the human species; let it favour those alone which are really necessary to the maintenance of society. The passions of man are dangerous, only because every thing conspires to give them an evil direction.

Nature does not make man either good or wicked: she combines machines more or less active, mobile, and energetic; she furnishes him with organs and temperament, of which his passions, more or less impetuous, are the necessary consequence; these passions have always his happiness for their object, his welfare for their end: in consequence they are legitimate, they are natural, they can only be called bad or good, relatively, to the influence they have on the beings of his species. Nature gives man legs proper to sustain his weight, and necessary to transport him from one place to another; the care of those who rear them strengthens them, habituates him to avail himself of him, accustoms him to make either a good or a bad use of them. The arm which he has received from Nature is neither good nor bad; it is necessary to a great number of the actions of life; nevertheless, the use of this arm becomes criminal, if he has contracted the habit of using it to rob, to assassinate, with a view to obtain that money which he has been taught from his infancy to desire, and which the society in which he lives renders necessary to him, but which his industry will enable him to obtain without doing injury to his fellow man.

The heart of man is a soil which Nature has made equally suitable to the production of brambles, or of useful grain—of deleterous poison, or of refreshing fruit, by virtue of the seeds which may be sown in it—by the cultivation that may be bestowed upon it, In his infancy, those objects are pointed out to him which he is to estimate or to despise, to seek after or to avoid, to love or to hate. It is his parents, his instructors, who render him either virtuous or wicked, wise or unreasonable, studious or dissipated, steady or trifling, solid or vain. Their example, their discourse, modify him through his whole life, teaching him what are the things he ought either to desire or to avoid; what the objects he ought to fear or to love: he desires them, in consequence; and he imposes on himself the task of obtaining them, according to the energy of his temperament, which ever decides the force of his passions. It is thus that education, by inspiring him with opinions, by infusing into him ideas, whether true or false, gives him those primitive impulsions after which he acts, in a manner either advantageous or prejudicial both to himself and to others. Man, at his birth, brings with him into the world nothing but the necessity of conserving himself, of rendering his existence happy: instruction, example, the customs of the world, present him with the means, either real or imaginary, of achieving it; habit procures for him the facility of employing these means: he attaches himself strongly to those he judges best calculated, most proper to secure to him the possession of those objects which they have taught him, which he has learned to desire as the preferable good attached to his existence. Whenever his education—whenever the examples which have been afforded him—whenever the means with which he has been provided, are approved by reason, are the result of experience, every thing concurs to render him virtuous; habit strengthens these dispositions in him; he becomes, in consequence, a useful member of society; to the interests of which, every thing ought to prove to him his own permanent well-being, his own durable felicity, is necessarily allied. If, on the contrary, his education—his institutions—the examples which are set before him—the opinions which are suggested to him in his infancy, are of a nature to exhibit to his mind virtue as useless and repugnant—vice as useful and congenial to his own individual happiness, he will become vicious; he will believe himself interested in injuring society, in rendering his associates unhappy; he will be carried along by the general current: he will renounce virtue, which to him will no longer be any thing more than a vain idol, without attractions to induce him to follow it; without charms to tempt his adoration; because it will appear to exact, that he should immolate at its shrine, that he should sacrifice at its altar all those objects which he has been constantly taught to consider the most dear to himself; to contemplate as benefits the most desirable.

In order that man may become virtuous, it is absolutely requisite that he should have an interest, that he should find advantages in practising virtue. For this end, it is necessary that education should implant in him reasonable ideas; that public opinion should lean towards virtue, as the most desirable good; that example should point it out as the object most worthy esteem;

that government should faithfully recompense, should regularly reward it; that honor should always accompany its practice; that vice should constantly be despised; that crime should invariably be punished. Is virtue in this situation amongst men? does the education of man infuse into him just, faithful ideas of happiness—true notions of virtue—dispositions really favourable to the beings with whom he is to live? The examples spread before him, are they suitable to innocence and manners? are they calculated to make him respect decency—to cause him to love probity—to practice honesty—to value good faith—to esteem equity—to revere conjugal fidelity—to observe exactitude in fulfilling his duties? Religion, which alone pretends to regulate his manners, does it render him sociable—does it make him pacific—does it teach him to be humane? The arbiters, the sovereigns of society, are they faithful in recompensing, punctual in rewarding, those who have best served their country? in punishing those who have pillaged, who have robbed, who have plundered, who have divided, who have ruined it? Justice, does she hold her scales with a firm, with an even hand, between all the citizens of the state? The laws, do they never support the strong against the weak—favor the rich against the poor—uphold the happy against the miserable? In short, is it an uncommon spectacle to behold crime frequently justified, often applauded, sometimes crowned with success, insolently triumphing, arrogantly striding over that merit which it disdains, over that virtue which it outrages? Well then, in societies thus constituted, virtue can only be heard by a very small number of peaceable citizens, a few generous souls, who know how to estimate its value, who enjoy it in secret. For the others, it is only a disgusting object; they see in it nothing but the supposed enemy to their happiness, or the censor of their individual conduct.

If man, according to his nature, is necessitated to desire his welfare, he is equally obliged to love and cherish the means by which he believes it is to be acquired: it would be useless, it would perhaps be unjust, to demand that a man should be virtuous, if he could not be so without rendering himself miserable. Whenever he thinks vice renders him happy, he must necessarily love vice; whenever he sees inutility recompensed, crime rewarded—whenever he witnesses either or both of them honored,—what interest will he find in occupying himself with the happiness of his fellow-creatures? what advantage will he discover in restraining the fury of his passions? Whenever his mind is saturated with false ideas, filled with dangerous opinions, it follows, of course, that his whole conduct will become nothing more than a long chain of errors, a tissue of mistakes, a series of depraved actions.

We are informed, that the savages, in order to flatten the heads of their children, squeeze them between two boards, by that means preventing them from taking the shape designed for them by Nature. It is pretty nearly the same thing with the institutions of man; they commonly conspire to counteract Nature, to constrain and divert, to extinguish the impulse Nature has given him, to substitute others which are the source of all his misfortunes. In almost all the countries of the earth, man is bereft of truth, is fed with falsehoods, and amused with marvellous chimeras: he is treated like those children whose members are, by the imprudent care of their nurses, swathed with little fillets, bound up with rollers, which deprive them of the free use of their limbs, obstruct their growth, prevent their activity, and oppose themselves to their health.

Most of the superstitious opinions of man have for their object only to display to him his supreme felicity in those illusions for which they kindle his passions: but as the phantoms which are presented to his imagination are incapable of being considered in the same light by all who contemplate them, he is perpetually in dispute concerning these objects; he hates his fellow, he persecutes his neighbour, his neighbour in turn persecutes him, and he believes that in doing this he is doing well: that in committing the greatest crimes to sustain his opinions he is acting right. It is thus superstition infatuates man from his infancy, fills him with vanity, and enslaves him with fanaticism: if he has a heated imagination, it drives him on to fury; if he has activity, it makes him a madman, who is frequently as cruel himself, as he is dangerous to his fellow-creatures, as he is incommodious to others: if, on the contrary, he be phlegmatic, and of a slothful habit, he becomes melancholy and useless to society.

Public opinion every instant offers to man's contemplation false ideas of honor, and wrong notions of glory: it attaches his esteem not only to frivolous advantages, but also to prejudicial interests and injurious actions; which example authorizes, which prejudice consecrates, which habit precludes him from viewing with the disgust and horror which they merit. Indeed, habit familiarizes his mind with the most absurd ideas, the most unreasonable customs, the most blameable actions; with prejudices the most contrary to his own interests, and detrimental to the society in which he lives. He finds nothing strange, nothing singular, nothing despicable, nothing ridiculous, except those opinions and objects to which he is himself unaccustomed. There are countries in which the most laudable actions appear very blameable and ridiculous—where the foulest and most diabolical actions pass for very honest and perfectly rational conduct. In some nations they kill the old men; in some the children strangle their fathers. The Phoenicians and Carthaginians immolated their children to their gods. Europeans approve duels; he who refuses to cut the throat of another, or to blow out the brains of his neighbour, is contemplated by them as dishonoured. The Spaniards and Portuguese think it meritorious to burn an heretic. In some countries women prostitute themselves without dishonour; in others it is the height of hospitality for a man to present his wife to the embraces of the stranger: the refusal to accept this, excites his scorn and calls forth his resentment.

Authority commonly believes itself interested in maintaining the received opinions: those prejudices and errors which it considers requisite to the maintenance of its power and the consolidation of its interests, are sustained by force, which is never rational. Princes themselves, filled with deceptive images of happiness, mistaken notions of power, erroneous opinions of grandeur, and false ideas of glory, are surrounded with flattering courtiers, who are interested in keeping up the delusion of their masters: these contemptible men have acquired ideas of virtue, only that they may outrage it: by degrees they corrupt the people, these become depraved, lend themselves to their debaucheries, pander to the vices of the great, then make a merit of imitating them in their irregularities. A court is too frequently the true focus of the corruption of a people.

This is the true source of moral evil. It is thus that every thing conspires to render man vicious, and give a fatal impulse to his soul: from whence results the general confusion of society, which becomes unhappy, from the misery of almost every one of its members. The strongest motive-powers are put in action to inspire man with a passion for futile objects which are indifferent to him; which make him become dangerous to his fellow man, by the means which he is compelled to employ, in order to obtain them. Those who have the charge of guiding his steps, either impostors themselves, or the dupes to their own prejudices, forbid him to hearken to reason; they make truth appear dangerous to him; they exhibit error as requisite to his welfare, not only in this world, but in the next. In short, habit strongly attaches him to his irrational opinions, to his perilous inclinations, and to his blind passion for objects either useless or dangerous. Here, then, is the reason why for the most part man finds himself necessarily determined to evil; the reason why the passions, inherent in his Nature and necessary to his conservation, become the instruments of his destruction, and the bane of that society, which properly conducted, they ought to preserve; the reason why society becomes a state of warfare; why it does nothing but assemble enemies, who are envious of each other, and are always rivals for the prize. If some virtuous beings are to be found in these societies, they must be sought for in the very small number of those, who born with a phlegmatic temperament have moderate passions, who therefore, either do not desire at all, or desire very feebly, those objects with which their associates are continually inebriated.

Man's nature, diversely cultivated, decides upon his faculties, as well corporeal as intellectual; upon his qualities, as well moral as physical. The man who is of a sanguine, robust constitution, must necessarily have strong passions; he who is of a bilious, melancholy habit, will as necessarily have fantastical and gloomy passions; the man of a gay turn, of a sprightly imagination, will have cheerful passions; while the man in whom phlegm abounds, will have those which are gentle, or which have a very slight degree of violence. It appears to be upon the equilibrium of the humours, that depends the state of the man who is called *virtuous*; his temperament seems to be the result of a combination, in which the elements or principles are balanced with such precision that no one passion predominates over another, or carries into his machine more disorder than its neighbour.

Habit, as we have seen, is man's nature modified: this latter furnishes the matter; education, domestic example, national manners, give it the form: these, acting on his temperament, make him either reasonable, or irrational—enlightened, or stupid—a fanatic, or a hero—an enthusiast for the public good, or an unbridled criminal—a wise man, smitten with the advantages of virtue, or a libertine, plunged into every kind of vice. All the varieties of the moral man, depend on the diversity of his ideas; which are themselves arranged and combined in his brain by the intervention of his senses. His temperament is the produce of physical substances, his habits are the effect of physical modifications; the opinions, whether good or bad, injurious or beneficial, true or false, which form themselves in his mind, are never more than the effect of those physical impulsions which the brain receives by the medium of the senses.

CHAP. X.

The Soul does not derive its ideas from itself—It has no innate Ideas.

What has preceded suffices to prove, that the interior organ of man, which is called his *soul*, is purely material. He will be enabled to convince himself of this truth, by the manner in which he acquires his ideas,—from those impressions which material objects successively make on his organs, which are themselves acknowledged to be material. It has been seen, that the faculties which are called intellectual, are to be ascribed to that of feeling; the different qualities of those faculties which are called moral, have been explained after the necessary laws of a very simple mechanism: it now remains, to reply to those who still obstinately persist in making the soul a substance distinguished from the body, or who insist on giving it an essence totally distinct. They seem to found their distinction upon this, that this interior organ has the faculty of drawing its ideas from within itself; they will have it, that man, at his birth, brings with him ideas into the world, which, according to this wonderful notion, they have called *innate*. The Jews have a similar doctrine which they borrowed from the Chaldeans: their rabbins taught, that each soul, before it was united to the seed that must form an infant in the womb of a woman, is confided to the care of an angel, which causes him to behold heaven, earth, and hell: this, they pretend, is done by the assistance of a lamp, which extinguishes itself as soon as the infant comes into the world. Some ancient philosophers have held, that the soul originally contains the principles of several notions or doctrines: the Stoics designated this by the term PROLEPSIS, *anticipated opinions*; the Greek mathematicians, KOINAS ENNOIAS, *universal ideas.* They have believed that the soul, by a special privilege, in a nature where every thing is connected, enjoyed the faculty of moving itself without receiving any impulse; of creating to itself ideas, of thinking on a subject, without being determined to such action, by any exterior object; which by moving its organs should furnish it with an image of the subject of its thoughts. In consequence of these gratuitous suppositions, of these extraordinary pretensions, which it is only requisite to expose, in order to confute some very able speculators, who were prepossessed by their superstitious prejudices; have ventured the length to assert, that without model, without prototype to act on the senses, the soul is competent to delineate to itself, the whole universe with all the beings it contains. DESCARTES and his disciples have assured us, that the body went absolutely for nothing, in the sensations, in the perceptions, in the ideas of the soul; that it can feel, that it can perceive, that it can understand, that it can taste, that it can touch, even when there should exist nothing that is corporeal or material exterior to ourselves. But what shall be said of a BERKELEY, who has endeavoured, who has laboured to prove to man, that every thing in this world is nothing more than a chimerical illusion; that the universe exists nowhere but in himself; that it has no identity but in his imagination; who has rendered the existence of all things problematical by the aid of sophisms, insolvable even to those who maintain the doctrine of the spirituality of the soul.

Extravagant as this doctrine of the BISHOP OF CLOYNE may appear, it cannot well be more so than that of MALEBRANCHE, the champion of innate ideas; who makes the divinity the common bond between the soul and the body: or than that of those metaphysicians, who maintain that the soul is a substance heterogeneous to the body; who by ascribing to this soul the thoughts of man, have in fact rendered the body superfluous. They have not perceived they were liable to one solid objection, which is, that if the ideas of man are innate, if he derives them from a superior being, independent of exterior causes, if he sees every thing in God; how comes it that so many false ideas are afloat, that so many errors prevail, with which the human mind is saturated? From whence comes these opinions, which according to the theologians are so displeasing to God? Might it not be a question to the Malebranchists, was it in the Divinity that SPINOZA beheld his system?

Nevertheless, to justify such monstrous opinions, they assert that ideas are only the objects of thought. But according to the last analysis, these ideas can only reach man from exterior objects, which in giving impulse to his senses modify his brain; or from the material beings contained within the interior of his machine, who make some parts of his body experience those sensations which he perceives, which furnish him with ideas, which he relates, faithfully or otherwise, to the cause that moves him. Each idea is an effect, but however difficult it may be to recur to the cause, can we possibly suppose it is not ascribable to a cause? If we can only form ideas of material substances, how can we suppose the cause of our ideas can possibly be immaterial? To pretend that man without the aid of exterior objects, without the intervention of his senses, is competent to form ideas of the universe, is to assert, that a blind man is in a capacity to form a true idea of a picture, that represents some fact of which he has never heard any one speak.

It is very easy to perceive the source of those errors, into which men, otherwise extremely profound and very enlightened have fallen, when they have been desirous to speak of the soul: to describe its operations. Obliged either by their own prejudices, or by the fear of combatting the opinions of some imperious theologian, they have become the advocates of the principle, that the soul was a pure spirit: an immaterial substance; of an essence directly different from that of the body; from every thing we behold: this granted, they have been incompetent to conceive how material objects could operate, in what manner gross and corporeal organs were enabled to act on a substance, that had no kind of analogy with them; how they were in a capacity to modify it by conveying its ideas; in the impossibility of explaining this phenomenon, at the same time perceiving that the soul had ideas, they concluded that it must draw them from itself, and not from those beings, which according to their own hypothesis, were incapable of acting on it, or rather, of which they could not conceive the manner of action; they therefore imagined that all the modifications, all the actions of this soul, sprung from its own peculiar energy, were imprinted on it from its first formation, by the Author of Nature: that these did not in any manner depend upon the beings of which we have a knowledge, or which act upon it, by the gross means of our senses.

There are, however, some phenomena, which, considered superficially, appear to support the opinion of these philosophers; to announce a faculty in the human soul of producing ideas within itself, without any exterior aid; these are *dreams*, in which the interior organ of man, deprived of objects that move it visibly, does not, however, cease to have ideas—to be set in activity—to be modified in a manner that is sufficiently sensible—to have an influence upon his body. But if a little reflection be called in, the solution to this difficulty will be found: it will be perceived that, even during sleep, his brain is supplied with a multitude of ideas, with which the eye or time before has stocked it; these ideas were communicated to it by exterior or corporeal objects, by which they have been modified: it will be found that these modifications renew themselves, not by any spontaneous, not by any voluntary motion on its part, but by a chain of involuntary movements which take place in his machine, which determine, which excite those that give play to the brain; these modifications renew themselves with more or less fidelity, with a greater or lesser degree of conformity to those which it has anteriorly experienced. Sometimes in dreaming, he has memory, then he retraces to himself the objects which have struck him faithfully;—at other times, these modifications renew themselves without order, and without connection, very differently from those, which real objects have before excited in his interior organ. If in a dream he believes he sees a friend, his brain renews in itself the modifications or the ideas which this friend had formerly excited—in the same order that they arranged themselves when his eyes really beheld him—this is nothing more than an effect of memory. If in his dream he fancies he sees a monster which has no model in nature, his brain is then modified in the same manner that it was by the particular, by the detached ideas, with which it then does nothing more than compose an ideal whole; by assembling, and associating, in a ridiculous manner, the scattered ideas that were consigned to its keeping; it is then, that in dreaming he has imagination.

Those dreams that are troublesome, extravagant, whimsical, or unconnected, are commonly the effect of some confusion in his machine; such as painful indigestion—an overheated blood—a prejudicial fermentation, &c.—these material causes excite in his body a disorderly motion, which precludes the brain from being modified in the same manner it was on the day before; in consequence of this irregular motion the brain is disturbed, it only represents to itself confused ideas that want connection. When in a dream, he believes he sees a Sphinx, a being supposed by the poets to have a head and face like a woman, a body like a dog, wings like a bird, and claws like a lion, who put forth riddles and killed those who could not expound them; either, he has seen the representation of one when he was awake, or else the disorderly motion of the brain is such that it causes it to combine ideas, to connect parts, from which there results a whole without model, of which the parts were not formed to be united. It is thus, that his brain combines the head of a woman, of which it already has the idea, with the body of a lioness, of which it also has the image. In this his head acts in the same manner, as when by any defect in the interior organ, his disordered imagination paints to him some objects, notwithstanding he is awake. He frequently dreams, without being asleep: his dreams never produce any thing so strange but that they have some resemblance, with the objects which have anteriorly acted on his senses; which have already communicated ideas to his brain. The watchful theologians have composed, at their leisure, in their waking hours, those phantoms, of which they avail themselves, to terrify or frighten man; they have done nothing more than assemble the scattered traits which they have found in the most terrible beings of their own species; by exaggerating the powers, by enlarging the rights claimed by tyrants, they have formed ideal beings, before whom man trembles, and is afraid.

Thus, it is seen, that dreams, far from proving that the soul acts by its own peculiar energy, that it draws its ideas from its own recesses; prove, on the contrary, that in sleep it is intirely passive, that it does not even renew its modifications, but according to the involuntary confusion, which physical causes produce in the body, of which every thing tends to shew the identity, the consubstantiality with the soul. What appears to have led those into a mistake, who maintained that the soul drew its ideas from itself, is this, they have contemplated these ideas, as if they were real beings, when, in point of fact, they are nothing more than the modifications produced in the brain of man, by objects to which this brain is a stranger; they are these objects, who are the true models, who are the real archetypes to which it is necessary to recur: here is the source of all their errors.

In the individual who dreams, the soul does not act more from itself, than it does in the man who is drunk, that is to say, who is modified by some spirituous liquor: or than it does in the sick man, when he is delirious, that is to say, when he is modified by those physical causes which disturb his machine, which obstruct it in the performance of its functions; or than it, does in him, whose brain is disordered: dreams, like these various states, announce nothing more than a physical confusion in the human machine, under the influence of which the brain ceases to act, after a precise and regular manner: this disorder may be traced to physical causes, such as the aliments—the humours—the combinations—the fermentations, which are but little analogous to the salutary state of man; from hence it will appear, that his brain is necessarily confused, whenever his body is agitated in an extraordinary manner.

Do not let him, therefore, believe that his soul acts by itself, or without a cause, in any one moment of his existence; it is, conjointly with the body, submitted to the impulse of beings, who act on him necessarily, according to their various properties. Wine taken in too great a quantity, necessarily disturbs his ideas, causes confusion in his corporeal functions, occasions disorder in his mental faculties.

If there really existed a being in Nature, with the capability of moving itself by its own peculiar energies, that is to say, able to produce motion, independent of all other causes, such a being would have the power of arresting itself, or of suspending the motion of the universe; which is nothing more than an immense chain of causes linked one to another, acting and re-acting by necessary immutable laws, and which cannot be changed, which are incapable of being suspended, unless the essences of every thing in it were changed, without the properties of every thing were annihilated. In the general system of the world, nothing more can be perceived than a long series of motion, received and communicated in succession, by beings capacitated to give impulse to each other: it is thus, that each body is moved by the collision of some other body. The invisible motion of some soul is to be attributed to causes concealed within himself; he believes that it is moved by itself, because he does not see the springs which put it in motion, or because he conceives those powers are incapable of producing the effects he so much admires: but, does he more clearly conceive, how a spark in exploding gunpowder, is capable of producing the terrible effects he witnesses? The source of his errors arise from this, that he regards his body as gross and inert, whilst this body is a sensible machine, which has necessarily an instantaneous conscience the moment it receives an impression; which is conscious of its own existence by the recollection of impressions successively experienced; memory by resuscitating an impression anteriorly received, by detaining it, or by causing an impression which it receives to remain, whilst it associates it with another, then with a third, gives all the mechanism of *reasoning*.

An idea, which is only an imperceptible modification of the brain, gives play to the organ of speech, which displays itself by the motion it excites in the tongue: this, in its turn, breeds ideas, thoughts, and passions, in those beings who are provided with organs susceptible of receiving analagous motion; in consequence of which, the wills of a great number of men are influenced, who, combining their efforts, produce a revolution in a state, or even have an influence over the entire globe. It is thus, that an ALEXANDER decided the fate of Asia, it is thus, that a MAHOMET changed the face of the earth; it is thus, that imperceptible causes produce the most terrible, the most extended effects, by a series of necessary motion imprinted on the brain of man.

The difficulty of comprehending the effects produced on the soul of man, has made him attribute to it those incomprehensible qualities which have been examined. By the aid of imagination, by the power of thought, this soul appears to quit his body, to carry itself with the greatest ease, to transport itself with the utmost facility towards the most distant objects; to run over, to approximate in the twinkling of an eye, all the points of the universe: he has therefore believed, that a being who is susceptible of such rapid motion, must be of a nature very distinguished from all others; he has persuaded himself that this soul in reality does travel, that it actually springs over the immense space necessary to meet these various objects; he did not perceive, that to do it in an instant, it had only to run over itself to approximate the ideas consigned to its keeping, by means of the senses.

Indeed, it is never by any other means than by his senses, that beings become known to man, or furnish him with ideas; it is only in consequence of the impulse given to his body, that his brain is modified, or that his soul thinks, wills, and acts. If, as ARISTOTLE asserted more than two thousand years ago,—"*nothing enters the mind of man but through the medium of his senses,*"— it follows as a consequence, that every thing that issues from it must find some sensible object to which it can attach its ideas, whether immediately, as a man, a tree, a bird, &c. or in the last analysis or decomposition, such as pleasure, happiness, vice, virtue, &c. This principle, so true, so luminous, so important in its consequence, has been set forth in all its lustre, by a great number of philosophers; among the rest, by the great LOCKE. Whenever, therefore, a word or its idea does not connect itself with some sensible object to which it can be related, this word or this idea is unmeaning, and void of sense; it were better for man that the idea was banished from his mind, struck out of his language: this principle is only the converse of the axiom of ARISTOTLE,—"*if the direct be evident, the inverse must be so likewise.*" How has it happened, that the profound LOCKE, who, to the great mortification of the metaphysicians, has placed this principle of ARISTOTLE in the clearest point of view? how is it, that all those who, like him, have recognized the absurdity of the system of innate ideas, have not drawn the immediate, the necessary consequences? How has it come to pass, that they have not had sufficient courage to apply so clear a principle to all those fanciful chimeras with which the human mind has for such a length of time been so vainly occupied? did they not perceive that their principle sapped the very foundations of those metaphysical speculations, which never occupy man but with those objects of which, as they are inaccessible to his senses, he consequently can never form to himself any accurate idea? But prejudice, when it is generally held sacred, prevents him from seeing the most simple application of the most self-evident principles. In metaphysical researches, the greatest men are frequently nothing more than children, who are incapable of either foreseeing or deducing the consequence of their own data.

LOCKE, as well as all those who have adopted his system, which is so demonstrable,—or to the axiom of ARISTOTLE, which is so clear, ought to have concluded from it that all those wonderful things with which metaphysicians have amused themselves, are mere chimeras; mere wanderings of the imagination; that an immaterial spirit or substance, without extent, without parts, is, in fact, nothing more than an absence of ideas; in short, they ought to have felt that the ineffable intelligence which they have supposed to preside at the helm of the world, is after all nothing more than a being of their own imagination, on which man has never been in accord, whom he has pictured under all the variety of forms, to which he has at different periods, in different climes, ascribed every kind of attribute, good or bad; but of which it is impossible his senses can ever prove either the existence or the qualities.

For the same reason, moral philosophers ought to have concluded, that what is called moral sentiment, *moral instinct*, that is, innate ideas of virtue, anterior to all experience of the good or bad effects resulting from its practice, are mere chimerical notions, which, like a great many others, have for their guarantee and base only metaphysical speculation. Before man can judge, he must feel; before he can distinguish good from evil, he must compare. *Morals*, is a science of facts: to found them, therefore, on an hypothesis inaccessible to his senses, of which he has no means of proving the reality, is to render them uncertain; it is to cast the log of discord into his lap, to cause him unceasingly to dispute upon that which he can never understand. To assert that the ideas of morals are *innate*, or the effect of *instinct*, is to pretend that man knows how to read before he has learned the letters of the alphabet; that he is acquainted with the laws of society before they are either made or promulgated.

To undeceive him, with respect to innate ideas or modifications, imprinted on his soul, at the moment of his birth, it is simply requisite to recur to their source; he will then see that those with which he is familiar, which have, as it were, identified themselves with his existence, have all come to him through the medium of some of his senses; that they are sometimes engraven on his brain with great difficulty,—that they have never been permanent,—that they have perpetually varied in him: he will see that these pretended inherent ideas of his soul, are the effect of education, of example, above all, of habit, which by reiterated motion has taught his brain to associate his ideas either in a confused or a perspicuous manner; to familiarize itself with systems either rational or absurd. In short, he takes those for innate ideas of which he has forgotten the origin; he no longer recals to himself, either the precise epoch, or the successive circumstances when these ideas were first consigned to his brain: arrived at a certain age he believes he has always had the same notions; his memory, crowded with experience, loaded with a multitude of facts, is no longer able to distinguish the particular circumstances which have contributed to give his brain its present modifications; its instantaneous mode of thinking; its actual opinions. For example, not one of his race, perhaps, recollects the first time the word God struck his ears—the first ideas that it formed in him—the first thoughts that it produced in him; nevertheless, it is certain that from thence he has searched for some being with whom to connect the idea which he has either formed to himself, or which has been suggested to him: accustomed to hear God continually spoken of, he has, when in other respects, the most enlightened, regarded this idea as if it were infused into him by Nature; whilst it is visibly to be attributed to those delineations of it, which his parents or his instructors have made to him; which he has, in consequence, modified according to his own particular organization, and the circumstances in which he has been placed; it is thus, that each individual forms to himself a God, of which he is himself the model, or which he modifies after his own fashion.

His ideas of morals, although more real than those of metaphysics, are not however innate: the moral sentiments he forms on the will, or the judgment he passes on the actions of man, are founded on experience; which alone can enable him to discriminate those which are either useful or prejudicial, virtuous or vicious, honest or dishonest, worthy his esteem, or deserving his censure. His moral sentiments are the fruit of a multitude of experience that is frequently very long and very complicated. He gathers it with time; it is more or less faithful, by reason of his particular organization and the causes by which he is modified; he ultimately applies this experience with greater or less facility; to this is to be attributed his habit of judging. The celerity with which he applies his experience when he judges of the moral actions of his fellow man, is what has been termed *moral instinct*.

That which in natural philosophy is called *instinct*, is only the effect of some want of the body, the consequence of some attraction or some repulsion in man or animals. The child that is newly born, sucks for the first time; the nipple of the breast is put into his mouth: by the natural analogy, that is found between the conglomerate glands, filled with nerves; which line his mouth, and the milk which flows from the bosom of the nurse, through the medium of the nipple, causes the child to press it with his mouth, in order to express the fluid appropriate to nourish his tender age; from all this the infant gathers experience; by degrees the idea of a nipple, of milk, of pleasure, associate themselves in his brain: every time he sees the nipple, he seizes it, promptly conveys it to his mouth, and applies it to the use for which it is designed.

What has been said, will enable us to judge of those prompt and sudden sentiments, which have been designated *the force of blood*. Those sentiments of love, which fathers and mothers have for their children—those feelings of affection, which children, with good inclinations, bear towards their parents, are by no means *innate sentiments*; they are nothing more, than the effect of experience, of reflection, of habit, in souls of sensibility. These sentiments do not even exist in a great number of human beings. We but too often witness tyrannical parents, occupied with making enemies of their children, who appear to have been formed, only to be the victims of their irrational caprices or their unreasonable desires.

From the instant in which man commences, until that in which he ceases to exist, he feels—he is moved either agreeably or unpleasantly—he collects facts—he gathers experience; these produce ideas in his brain, that are either cheerful or gloomy. Not one individual has all this experience present to his memory at the same time, it does not ever represent to him the whole clew at once: it is, however, this experience that mechanically directs him, without his knowledge, in all his actions; it was to designate the rapidity with, which he applied this experience, of which he so frequently loses the connection—of which he is so often at a loss to render himself an account, that he imagined the word *instinct*: it appears to be the effect of magic, the operation of a supernatural power, to the greater number of individuals: it is a word devoid of sense to many others; but to the philosopher it is the effect of a very lively feeling to him it consists in the faculty of combining, promptly, a multitude of experience—of arranging with facility—of comparing with quickness, a long and numerous train of extremely complicated ideas. It is want that causes the inexplicable instinct we behold in animals which have been denied souls without reason, whilst they are susceptible of an infinity of actions that prove they think—judge—have memory—are capable of experience—can combine ideas—can apply them with more or less facility to satisfy the wants engendered by their particular organization; in short, that prove they have passions that are capable of being modified. Nothing but the height of folly can refuse intellectual faculties to animals; they feel, choose, deliberate, express love, show hatred; in many instances their senses are much keener than those of man. Fish will return periodically to the spot where it is the custom to throw them bread.

It is well known the embarrassments which animals have thrown in the way of the partizans of the doctrine of spirituality; they have been fearful, if they allowed them to have a spiritual soul, of elevating them to the condition of human creatures; on the other hand, in not allowing them to have a soul, they have furnished their adversaries with authority to deny it in like manner to man, who thus finds himself debased to the condition of the animal. Metaphysicians have never known how to extricate themselves from this difficulty. DESCARTES fancied he solved it by saying that beasts have no souls, but are mere machines. Nothing can be nearer the surface, than the absurdity of this principle. Whoever contemplates Nature without prejudice, will readily acknowledge that there is no other difference between the man and the beast, than that which is to be attributed to the diversity of his organization.

In some beings of the human species, who appear to be endowed with a greater sensibility of organs than others, may be seen an instinct, by the assistance of which they very promptly judge of the concealed dispositions of their fellows, simply by inspecting the lineaments of their face. Those who are denominated *physiognomists*, are only men of very acute feelings; who have gathered an experience of which others, whether from the coarseness of their organs, from the little attention they have paid, or from some defect in their senses, are totally incapable: these last do not believe in the science of physiognomy, which appears to them perfectly ideal. Nevertheless, it is certain, that the action of this soul, which has been made spiritual, makes impressions that are extremely marked upon the exterior of the body; these impressions, continually reiterated, their image remains: thus the habitual passions of man paint themselves on his countenance; by which the attentive observer, who is endowed with acute feeling, is enabled to judge with great rapidity of his mode of existence, and even to foresee his actions, his inclinations, his desires, his predominant passions, &c. Although the science of physiognomy appears chimerical to a great number of persons, yet there are few who have not a clear idea of a tender regard— of a cruel eye—of an austere aspect—of a false, dissimulating look—of an open countenance, &c. Keen practised optics acquire without doubt the faculty of penetrating the concealed motion of the soul, by the visible traces it leaves upon features that it has continually modified. Above all, the eyes of man very quickly undergo changes according to the motion which is excited in him: these delicate organs are visibly altered by the smallest shock communicated to his brain. Serene eyes announce a tranquil soul; wild eyes indicate a restless mind; fiery eyes pourtray a choleric, sanguine temperament; fickle or inconstant eyes give room to suspect a soul either alarmed or dissimulating. It is the study of this variety of shades that renders man practised and acute: upon the spot he combines a multitude of acquired experience, in order to form his judgment of the person he beholds. His judgment, thus rapidly formed, partakes in nothing of the supernatural, in nothing of the wonderful: such a man is only distinguished by the fineness of his organs, and by the celerity with which his brain performs its functions.

It is the same with some beings of the human species, in whom may be discovered an extraordinary sagacity, which, to the uninformed, appears miraculous. The most skilful practitioners in medicine, are, no doubt, men endowed with very acute feelings, similar to that of the physiognomists, by the assistance of which they judge with great facility of diseases, and very promptly draw their prognostics. Indeed, we see men who are capable of appreciating in the twinkling of an eye a multitude of circumstances, who have sometimes the faculty of foreseeing the most distant events; yet, this species of prophetic talent has nothing in it of the supernatural; it indicates nothing more than great experience, with an extremely delicate organization, from which they derive the faculty of judging with extreme faculty of causes, of foreseeing their very remote effects. This faculty, however, is also found in animals, who foresee much better than man, the variations of the atmosphere with the various changes of the weather. Birds have long been the prophets, and even the guides of several nations who pretend to be extremely enlightened.

It is, then, to their organization, exercised after a particular manner, that must be attributed those wonderous faculties which distinguish some beings, that astonish others. To have *instinct*, only signifies to judge quickly, without requiring to make a long, reasoning on the subject. Man's ideas upon vice and upon virtue, are by no means innate; they are, like all others, acquired: the judgment he forms, is founded upon experience, whether true or false,—this depends upon his conformation, and upon the habits that have modified him. The infant has no ideas either of the Divinity or of virtue; it is from those who instruct him that he receives these ideas; he makes more or less use of them, according to his natural organization, or as his dispositions have been more or less exercised. Nature gives man legs, the nurse teaches him their use, his agility depends upon their natural conformation, and the manner in which he exercises them.

What is called *taste*, in the fine arts, is to be attributed, in the same manner, only to the acuteness of man's organs, practised by the habit of seeing, of comparing, of judging certain objects; from whence results, to some of his species, the faculty of judging with great rapidity, in the twinkling of an eye, the whole with its various relations. It is by the force of seeing, of feeling, of experiencing objects, that he attains to a knowledge of them; it is in consequence of reiterating this experience, that he acquires the power, that he gains the habit of judging with celerity. But this experience is by no means innate, he did not possess it before he was born; he is neither able to think, to judge, nor to have ideas, before he has feeling; he is neither in a capacity to love, nor to hate; to approve, nor to blame, before he has been moved, either agreeably or disagreeably. Nevertheless, this is precisely what must be supposed by those who are desirous to make man admit of innate ideas, of opinions; infused by Nature, whether in morals, metaphysics, or any other science. That his mind should have the faculty of thought, that it should occupy itself with an object, it is requisite it should be acquainted with its qualities; that it may have a knowledge of these qualities, it is necessary some of his senses should have been struck by them: those objects, therefore, of which he does not know any of the qualities, are nullities; or at least they do not exist for him.

It will be asserted, perhaps, that the universal consent of man, upon certain propositions, such as *the whole is greater than its part*, upon all geometrical demonstrations, appear to warrant the supposition of certain primary notions that are innate, not acquired. It may be replied, that these notions are always acquired; that they are the fruit of an experience more or less prompt; that it is requisite to have compared the whole with its part, before conviction can ensue, that the whole is the greater of the two. Man when he is born, does not bring with him the idea that two and two make four; but he is, nevertheless, speedily convinced of its truth. Before forming any judgment whatever, it is absolutely necessary to have compared facts.

It is evident, that those who have gratuitously supposed innate ideas, or notions inherent in man, have confounded his organization, or his natural dispositions, with the habit by which he is modified; with the greater or less aptitude he has of making experience, and of applying it in his judgment. A man who has taste in painting, has, without doubt, brought with him into the world eyes more acute, more penetrating than another; but these eyes would by no means enable him to judge with promptitude, if he had never had occasion to exercise them; much less, in some respects, can those dispositions which are called *natural*, be regarded as innate. Man is not, at twenty years of age, the same as he was when he came into the world; the physical causes that are continually acting upon him, necessarily have an influence upon his organization, and so modify it, that his natural dispositions themselves are not at one period what they are at another. La Motte Le Vayer says, "We think quite otherwise of things at one time than at another; when young than when old—when hungry than when our appetite is satisfied—in the night than in the day—when peevish than when cheerful. Thus, varying every hour, by a thousand other circumstances, which keep us in a state of perpetual inconstancy and instability." Every day may be seen children, who, to a certain age—display a great deal of ingenuity, a strong aptitude for the sciences, who finish by falling into stupidity. Others may be observed, who, during their infancy, have shown dispositions but little favourable to improvement, yet develope themselves in the end, and astonish us by an exhibition of those qualities of which we hardly thought them susceptible: there arrives a moment in which the mind takes a spring, makes use of a multitude of experience which it has amassed, without its having been perceived; and, if I may be allowed the expression, without their own knowledge.

Thus, it cannot be too often repeated, all the ideas, all the notions, all the modes of existence, and all the thoughts of man, are acquired. His mind cannot act, cannot exercise itself, but upon that of which it has knowledge; it can understand either well or ill, only those things which it has previously felt. Such of his ideas that do not suppose some exterior material object for their model, or one to which he is able to relate them, which are therefore called *abstract ideas*, are only modes in which his interior organ considers its own peculiar modifications, of which it chooses some without respect to others. The words which he uses to designate these ideas, such as *bounty, beauty, order, intelligence, virtue*, &c. do not offer any one sense, if he does not relate them to, or if he does not explain them by, those objects which his senses have shewn him to be susceptible of those qualities, or of those modes of existence, of that manner of acting, which is known to him. What is it that points out to him the vague idea of *beauty*, if he does not attach it to some object that has struck his senses in a peculiar manner, to which, in consequence, he attributes this quality? What is it that represents the word *intelligence*, if he does not connect it with a certain mode of being and of acting? Does the word *order* signify any thing, if he does not relate it to a series of actions, to a chain of motion, by which he is affected in a certain manner? Is not the word *virtue* void of sense, if he does not apply it to those dispositions of his fellows which produce known effects, different from those which result from contrary inclinations? What do the words *pain* and *pleasure* offer to his mind in the moment when his organs neither suffer nor enjoy, if it be not the modes in which he has been affected, of which his brain conserves the remembrance, of those impressions, which experience has shewn him to be either useful or prejudicial? But when he bears the words spirituality, immateriality, incorporeality, &c. pronounced, neither his senses nor his memory afford him any assistance; they do not furnish him with any means by which he can form an idea of their qualities, or of the objects to which he ought to apply them; in that which is not matter he can only see vacuum and emptiness, which as long as he remains what he is, cannot, to his mind, be susceptible of any one quality.

All the errors, all the disputes of men, have their foundation in this, that they have renounced experience, have surrendered the evidence of their senses, to give themselves up to the guidance of notions which they have believed infused or innate; although in reality they are no more than the effect of a distempered imagination, of prejudices, in which they have been instructed from their infancy, with which habit has familiarized them, which authority has obliged them to conserve. Languages are filled with abstract words, to which are attached confused and vague ideas; of which, when they come to be examined, no model can be found in Nature; no object to which they can be related. When man gives himself the trouble to analyze things, he is quite surprised to find, that those words which are continually in the mouths of men, never present any fixed or determinate idea: he hears them unceasingly speaking of spirits—of the soul and its faculties—of duration—of space—of immensity—of infinity—of perfection—of virtue—of reason—of sentiment—of instinct—of taste, &c. without his being able to tell precisely, what they themselves understand by these words. Nevertheless, they do not appear to have been invented, but for the purpose of representing the images of things; or to paint, by the assistance of the senses, those known objects on which the mind is able to meditate, which it is competent to appreciate, to compare, and to judge.

For man to think of that which has not acted on any of his senses, is to think on words; it is for his senses to dream; it is to seek in his own imagination for objects to which he can attach his wandering ideas: to assign qualities to these objects is, unquestionably, to redouble his extravagance, to set no limits to his folly. If a word be destined to represent to him an object that has not the capacity to act on any one of his organs; of which, it is impossible for him to prove either the existence or the qualities; his imagination, by dint of racking itself, will nevertheless, in some measure, supply him with the ideas he wants; he composes some kind of a picture, with the images or colours he is always obliged to borrow, from the objects of which he has a knowledge: thus the Divinity has been represented by some under the character of a venerable old man; by others, under that of a puissant monarch; by others, as an exasperated, irritated being, &c. It is evident, however, that man, with some of his qualities, has served for the model of these pictures: but if he be informed of objects that are represented as pure spirits—that have neither body nor extent—that are not contained in space—that are beyond nature,—here then he is plunged into emptiness; his mind no longer has any ideas—it no longer knows upon what it meditates. This, as will be seen in the sequel, no doubt, is the source of those unformed notions which some men have formed of the Divinity; they themselves frequently annihilate him, by assembling incompatible and contradictory attributes. In giving him morals—in composing him of known qualities,—they make him a man;—in assigning him the negative attributes of every thing they know, they render him inaccessible to their senses—they destroy all antecedent ideas—they make him a mere nothing. From this it will appear, that those sublime sciences which are called *Theology, Psychology, Metaphysics*, have been mere sciences of words: morals and politics, with which they very frequently mix, have, in consequence, become inexplicable enigmas, which there is nothing short of the study of Nature can enable us to expound.

Man has occasion for truth; it consists in a knowledge of the true relations he has with those beings competent to have an influence on his welfare; these relations are to be known only by experience: without experience there can be no reason; without reason man is only a blind creature, who conducts himself by chance. But, how is he to acquire experience upon ideal objects, which his senses neither enable him to know nor to examine? How is he to assure himself of the existence, how ascertain the qualities of beings he is not able to feel? How can he judge whether there objects be favorable or prejudicial to him? How is he to know, without the evidence of his senses, what he ought to love, what he should hate, what to seek after, what to shun, what to do, what to leave undone? It is, however, upon this knowledge that his condition in this world rests; it is upon this knowledge that morals is founded. From whence it may be seen, that, by causing him to blend vague metaphysical notions with morals, or the science of the certain and invariable relations which subsist between mankind; or by weakly establishing them upon chimerical ideas, which have no existence but in his imagination; these morals, upon which the welfare of society so much depends, are rendered uncertain, are made arbitrary, are abandoned to the caprices of fancy, are not fixed upon any solid basis.

Beings essentially different by their natural organization, by the modifications they experience, by the habits they contract, by the opinions they acquire, must of necessity think differently. His temperament, as we have seen, decides the mental qualities of man: this temperament itself is diversely modified in him: from whence it consecutively follows, his imagination cannot possibly be the same; neither can it create to him the same images. Each individual is a connected whole, of which all the parts have a necessary correspondence. Different eyes must see differently, must give extremely varied ideas of the objects they contemplate, even when these objects are real. What, then, must be the diversity of these ideas, if the objects meditated upon do not act upon the senses? Mankind have pretty nearly the same ideas, in the gross, of those substances that act upon his organs with vivacity; he is sufficiently in unison upon some qualities which he contemplates very nearly in the same manner; I say, very nearly, because the intelligence, the notion, the conviction of any one proposition, however simple, however evident, however clear it may be supposed, is not, nor cannot be, strictly the same, in any two men. Indeed, one man not being another man, the first cannot, for example, have rigorously and mathematically the same notion of unity as the second; seeing that an identical effect cannot be the result of two different causes. Thus, when men are in accord in their ideas, in their modes of thinking, in their judgment, in their passions, in their desires, in, their tastes, their consent does not arise from their seeing or feeling the same objects precisely in the same manner, but pretty nearly; language is not, nor cannot be, sufficiently copious to designate the vast variety of shades, the multiplicity of imperceptible differences, which is to be found in their modes of seeing and thinking. Each man, then, has, to say thus, a language which is peculiar to himself alone, and this language is incommunicable to others. What harmony, what unison, then, can possibly exist between them, when they discourse with each other, upon objects only known to their imagination? Can this imagination in one individual ever be the same as in another? How can they possibly understand each other, when they assign to those objects qualities that can only be attributed to the particular manner in which their brain is affected.

For one man to exact from another that he shall think like himself, is to insist that he shall be organized precisely in the same manner—that he shall have been modified exactly the same in every moment of his existence: that he shall have received the same temperament, the same nourishment, the same education: in a word, that he shall require that other to be himself. Wherefore is it not exacted that all men shall have the same features? Is man more the master of his opinions? Are not his opinions the necessary consequence of his Nature, and of those peculiar circumstances which, from his infancy, have necessarily had an influence upon his mode of thinking, and his manner of acting? If man be a connected whole, whenever a single feature differs from his own, ought he not to conclude that it is not possible his brain can either think, associate ideas, imagine, or dream precisely in the same manner with that other.

The diversity in the temperament of man, is the natural, the necessary source of the diversity of his passions, of his taste, of his ideas of happiness, of his opinions of every kind. Thus, this same diversity will be the fatal source of his disputes, of his hatreds, of his injustice, every time he shall reason upon unknown objects, but to which he shall attach the greatest importance. He will never understand either himself or others, in speaking of a spiritual soul, or of immaterial substances distinguished from Nature; he will, from that moment, cease to speak the same language, and he will never attach the same ideas to the same words. What, then, shall be, the common standard that shall decide which is the man that thinks with the greatest justice? What the scale by which to measure who has the best regulated imagination? What balance shall be found sufficiently exact to determine whose knowledge is most certain, when he agitates subjects, which experience cannot enable him to examine, that escape all his senses, that have no model, that are above reason? Each individual, each legislator, each speculator, each nation, has ever formed to himself different ideas of these things; each believes, that his own peculiar reveries ought to be preferred to those of his neighbours; which always appear to him an absurd, ridiculous, and false as his own can possibly have appeared to his fellow; each clings to his own opinion, because each retains his own peculiar mode of existence; each believes his happiness depends upon his attachment to his prejudices, which he never adopts but because he believes them beneficial to his welfare. Propose to a man to change his religion for yours, he will believe you a madman; you will only excite his indignation, elicit his contempt; he will propose to you, in his turn, to adopt his own peculiar opinions; after much reasoning, you will treat each other as absurd beings, ridiculously opiniated, pertinaciously stubborn: and he will display the least folly, who shall first yield. But if the adversaries become heated in the dispute, which always happens, when they suppose the matter important, or when they would defend the cause of their own self-love; from thence their passions sharpen, they grow angry, quarrels are provoked, they hate each other, and end by reciprocal injury. It is thus, that for opinions, which no man can demonstrate, we see the Brahmin despised; the Mahommedan hated; the Pagan held in contempt; that they oppress and disdain each with the most rancorous animosity: the Christian burns the Jew at what is called an *auto-de-fe*, because he clings to the faith of his fathers: the Roman Catholic condemns the Protestant to the flames, and makes a conscience of massacring him in cold blood: this re-acts in his turn; sometimes the various sects of Christians league together against the incredulous Turk, and for a moment suspend their own bloody disputes that they may chastise the enemies to the true faith: then, having glutted their revenge, return with redoubled fury, to wreak over again their infuriated vengeance on each other.

If the imaginations of men were the same, the chimeras which they bring forth would be every where the same; there would be no disputes among them on this subject, if they all dreamt in the same manner; great numbers of human beings would be spared, if man occupied his mind with objects capable of being known, of which the existence was proved, of which he was competent to discover the true qualities, by sure, by reiterated experience. *Systems of Philosophy* are not subject to dispute but when their principles are not sufficiently proved; by degrees experience, in pointing out the truth and detecting their errors, terminates these quarrels. There is no variance among *geometricians* upon the principles of their science; it is only raised, when their suppositions are false, or their objects too much complicated. *Theologians* find so much difficulty in agreeing among themselves, simply, because, in their contests, they divide without ceasing, not known and examined propositions, but prejudices with which they have been imbued in their youth—in the schools—by each other's books, &c. They are perpetually reasoning, not upon real objects, of which the existence is demonstrated, but upon imaginary systems of which they have never examined the reality; they found these disputes, not upon averred experience, or constant facts, but upon gratuitious suppositions, which each endeavours to convince the other are without solidity. Finding these ideas of long standing, that few people, refuse to admit them, they take them for incontestible truths, that ought to be received merely upon being announced; whenever they attach great importance to them, they irritate themselves against the temerity of those who have the audacity to doubt, or even to examine them.

If prejudice had been laid aside, it would perhaps have been discovered that many of those objects, which have given birth to the most shocking, the most sanguinary disputes among men, were mere phantoms; which a little examination would have shown to be unworthy their notice: *the priests of Apollo* would have been harmless, if man had examined for himself, without prejudice, the tenets they held forth: he would have found, that he was fighting, that he was cutting his neighbour's throat, for words void of sense; or, at the least, he would have learned to doubt his right to act in the manner he did; he would have renounced that dogmatical, that imperious tone he assumed, by which he would oblige his fellow to unite with him in opinion. The most trifling reflection would have shewn him the necessity of this diversity in his notions, of this contrariety in his imagination, which depends upon his Natural conformation diversely modified: which necessarily has an influence over his thoughts, over his will, and over his actions. In short, if he had consulted morals, if he had fallen back upon reason, every thing would have conspired to prove to him, that beings who call themselves rational, were made to think variously; on that account were designed to live peaceable with each other, to love each other, to lend each other mutual succours whatever may be their opinions upon subjects, either impossible to be known, or to be contemplated under the same point of view: every thing would have joined in evidence to convince him of the unreasonable tyranny, of the unjust violence, of the useless cruelty of those men of blood, who persecute, who destroy mankind, in order that they may mould him to their own peculiar opinions; every thing would have conducted mortals to *mildness*, to *indulgence*, to *toleration*; virtues, unquestionably of more real importance, much more necessary to the welfare of society, than the marvellous speculations by which it is divided, by which it is frequently hurried on to sacrifice to a maniacal fury, the pretended enemies to these revered flights of the imagination.

From this it must be evident, of what importance it is to *morals* to examine the ideas, to which it has been agreed to attach so much worth; to which man is continually sacrificing his own peculiar happiness; to which he is immolating the tranquillity of nations, at the irrational command of fanatical cruel guides. Let him fall back on his experience; let him return to Nature; let him occupy himself with reason; let him consult those objects that are real, which are useful to his permanent felicity; let him study Nature's laws; let him study himself; let him consult the bonds which unite him to his fellow mortals; let him examine the fictitious bonds that enchain him to the most baneful prejudices. If his imagination must always feed itself with illusions, if he remains steadfast in his own opinions, if his prejudices are dear to him, let him at least permit others to ramble in their own manner, or seek after truth as best suits their inclination; but let him always recollect, that all the opinions—all the ideas—all the systems—all the wills—all the actions of man, are the necessary consequence of his nature, of his temperament, of his organization, and of those causes, either transitory or constant, which modify hint: in short, that *man is not more a free agent to think than to act:* a truth that will be again proved in the following chapter.

CHAP. XI

Of the System of Man's free agency.

Those who have pretended that the *soul* is distinguished from the body, is immaterial, draws its ideas from its own peculiar source, acts by its own energies without the aid of any exterior object; by a consequence of their own system, have enfranchised it from those physical laws, according to which all beings of which we have a knowledge are obliged to act. They have believed that the foul is mistress of its own conduct, is able to regulate its own peculiar operations; has the faculty to determine its will by its own natural energy; in a word, they have pretended man is a *free agent*.

It has been already sufficiently proved, that the soul is nothing more than the body, considered relatively to some of its functions, more concealed than others: it has been shewn, that this soul, even when it shall be supposed immaterial, is continually modified conjointly with the body; is submitted to all its motion; that without this it would remain inert and dead: that, consequently, it is subjected to the influence of those material, to the operation those physical causes, which give impulse to the body; of which the mode of existence, whether habitual or transitory, depends upon the material elements by which it is surrounded; that form its texture; that constitute its temperament; that enter into it by the means of the aliments; that penetrate it by their subtility; the faculties which are called intellectual, and those qualities which are styled moral, have been explained in a manner purely physical; entirely natural: in the last place, it has been demonstrated, that all the ideas, all the systems, all the affections, all the opinions, whether true or false, which man forms to himself, are to be attributed to his physical powers; are to be ascribed to his material senses. Thus man is a being purely physical; in whatever manner he is considered, he is connected to universal Nature: submitted to the necessary, to the immutable laws that she imposes on all the beings she contains, according to their peculiar essences; conformable to the respective properties with which, without consulting them, she endows each particular species. Man's life is a line that Nature commands him to describe upon the surface of the earth: without his ever being able to swerve from it even for an instant. He is born without his own consent; his organizations does in no wise depend upon himself; his ideas come to him involuntarily; his habits are in the power of those who cause him to contract them; he is unceasingly modified by causes, whether visible or concealed, over which he has no controul; give the hue to his way of thinking, and determine his manner of acting. He is good or bad—happy or miserable—wise or foolish—reasonable or irrational, without his will going for anything in these various states. Nevertheless, in despite of the shackles by which he is bound, it is pretended he is a free agent, or that independent of the causes by which he is moved, he determines his own will; regulates his own condition.

However slender the foundation of this opinion, of which every thing ought to point out to him the error; it is current at this day for an incontestible truth, and believed enlightened; it is the basis or religion, which has been incapable of imagining how man could either merit reward or deserve punishment if he was not a free agent. Society has been believed interested in this system, because an idea has gone abroad, that if all the actions of man were to be contemplated as necessary, the right of punishing those who injure their associates would no longer exist. At length human vanity accommodated itself to an hypothesis which, unquestionable, appears to distinguish man from all other physical beings, by assigning to him the special privilege of a total independence of all other causes; but of which a very little reflection would have shewn him the absurdity or even the impossibility.

As a part, subordinate to the great whole, man is obliged to experience its influence. To be a free agent it were needful that each individual was of greater strength than the entire of Nature; or, that he was out of this Nature: who, always in action herself, obliges all the beings she embraces, to act, and to concur to her general motion; or, as it has been said elsewhere, to conserve her active existence, by the motion that all beings produce in consequence of their particular energies, which result from their being submitted to fixed, eternal, and immutable laws. In order that man might be a free agent, it were needful that all beings should lose their essences; it is equally necessary that he himself should no longer enjoy physical sensibility; that he should neither know good nor evil; pleasure nor pain; but if this was the case, from that moment he would no longer be in a state to conserve himself, or render his existence happy; all beings would become indifferent to him; he would no longer have any choice; he would cease to know what he ought to love; what it was right he should fear; he would not have any acquaintance with that which he should seek after; or with that which it is requisite he should avoid. In short, man would be an unnatural being; totally incapable of acting in the manner we behold. It is the actual essence of man to tend to his well-being; to be desirous to conserve his existence; if all the motion of his machine springs as a necessary consequence from this primitive impulse; if pain warns him of that which he ought to avoid; if pleasure announces to him that which he should desire; if it is in his essence to love that which either excites delight, or, that from which he expects agreeable sensations; to hate that which makes him either fear contrary impressions; or, that which afflicts him with uneasiness; it must necessarily be, that he will be attracted by that which he deems advantageous; that his will shall be determined by those objects which he judges useful; that he will be repelled by those beings which he believes prejudicial, either to his habitual, or to his transitory mode of existence; by that which he considers disadvantageous. It is only by the aid of experience, that man acquires the faculty of understanding what he ought to love; of knowing what he ought to fear. Are his organs sound? his experience will be true: are they unsound? it will be false: in the first instance he will have reason, prudence, foresight; he will frequently foresee very remote effects; he will know, that what he sometimes contemplates as a good, may possibly become an evil, by its necessary or probable consequences: that what must be to him a transient evil, may by its result procure him a solid and durable good. It is thus experience enables him to foresee that the amputation of a limb will cause him painful sensation, he consequently is obliged to fear this operation, and he endeavours to avoid the pain; but if experience has also shewn him, that the transitory pain this amputation will cause him may be the means of saving his life; the preservation, of his existence being of necessity dear to him, he is obliged to submit himself to the momentary pain with a view to procuring a permanent good, by which it will be overbalanced.

The will, as we have elsewhere said, is a modification of the brain, by which it is disposed to action or prepared to give play to the organs. This will is necessarily determined by the qualities, good or bad, agreeable or painful, of the object or the motive that acts upon his senses; or of which the idea remains with him, and is resuscitated by his memory. In consequence, he acts necessarily; his action is the result of the impulse he receives either from the motive, from the object, or from the idea, which has modified his brain, or disposed his will. When he does not act according to this impulse, it is because there comes some new cause, some new motive, some new idea, which modifies his brain in a different manner, gives him a new impulse, determines his will in another way; by which the action of the former impulse is suspended: thus, the sight of an agreeable object, or its idea, determines his will to set him in action to procure it; but if a new object or a new idea more powerfully attracts him, it gives a new direction to his will, annihilates the effect of the former, and prevents the action by which it was to be procured. This is the mode in which reflection, experience, reason, necessarily arrests or suspends the action of man's will; without this, he would, of necessity, have followed the anterior impulse which carried him towards a then desirable object. In all this he always acts according to necessary laws, from which he has no means of emancipating himself.

If, when tormented with violent thirst, he figures to himself an idea, or really perceives a fountain, whose limpid streams might cool his feverish habit, is he sufficient master of himself to desire or not to desire the object competent to satisfy so lively a want? It will no doubt be conceded, that it is impossible he should not be desirous to satisfy it; but it will be said,—If at this moment it is announced to him, the water he so ardently desires is poisoned, he will, notwithstanding his vehement thirst, abstain from drinking it; and it has, therefore, been falsely concluded that he is a free agent. The fact, however, is, that the motive in either case is exactly the same: his own conservation. The same necessity that determined him to drink, before he knew the water was deleterious, upon this new discovery, equally determines him not to drink; the desire of conserving himself, either annihilates or suspends the former impulse; the second motive becomes stronger than the preceding; that is, the fear of death, or the desire of preserving himself, necessarily prevails over the painful sensation caused by his eagerness to drink. But, (it will be said) if the thirst is very parching, an inconsiderate man, without regarding the danger, will risque swallowing the water. Nothing is gained by this remark: in this case, the anterior impulse only regains the ascendency; he is persuaded, that life may possibly be longer preserved, or that he shall derive a greater good by drinking the poisoned water, than by enduring the torment, which, to his mind, threatens instant dissolution: thus, the first becomes the strongest, and necessarily urges him on to action. Nevertheless, in either case, whether he partakes of the water, or whether he does not, the two actions will be equally necessary; they will be the effect of that motive which finds itself most puissant; which consequently acts in a most coercive manner upon his will.

This example will serve to explain the whole phaenomena of the human will. This will, or rather the brain, finds itself in the same situation as a bowl, which although it has received an impulse that drives it forward in a straight line, is deranged in its course, whenever a force, superior to the first, obliges it to change its direction. The man who drinks the poisoned water, appears a madman; but the actions of fools are as necessary as those of the most prudent individuals. The motives that determine the voluptuary, that actuate the debauchee to risk their health, are as powerful, their actions are as necessary, as those which decide the wise man to manage his. But, it will be insisted, the debauchee may be prevailed on to change his conduct; this does not imply that he is a free agent; but, that motives may be found sufficiently powerful to annihilate the effect of those that previously acted upon him; then these new motives determine his will to the new mode of conduct he may adopt, as necessarily as the former did to the old mode.

Man is said to *deliberate* when the action of the will is suspended; this happens when two opposite motives act alternately upon him. To deliberate, is to hate and to love in succession; it is to be alternately attracted and repelled; it is to be moved sometimes by one motive, sometimes by another. Man only deliberates when he does not distinctly understand the quality of the objects from which he receives impulse, or when experience has not sufficiently apprised him of the effects, more or less remote, which his actions will produce. He would take the air, but the weather is uncertain; he deliberates in consequence; he weighs the various motives that urge his will to go out or to stay at home; he is at length determined by that motive which is most probable; this removes his indecision, which necessarily settles his will either to remain within or to go abroad: this motive is always either the immediate or ultimate advantage he finds or thinks he finds in the action to which he is persuaded.

Man's will frequently fluctuates between two objects, of which either the presence or the ideas move him alternately: he waits until he has contemplated the objects or the ideas they have left in his brain; which solicit him to different actions; he then compares these objects or ideas: but even in the time of deliberation, during the comparison, pending these alternatives of love and hatred, which succeed each other sometimes with the utmost rapidity, he is not a free agent for a single instant; the good or the evil which he believes he finds successively in the objects, are the necessary motives of these momentary wills; of the rapid motion of desire or fear that he experiences as long as his uncertainty continues. From this it will be obvious, that deliberation is necessary; that uncertainty is necessary; that whatever part he takes, in consequence of this deliberation, it will always necessarily be that which he has judged, whether well or ill, is most probable to turn to his advantage.

When the soul is assailed by two motives that act alternately upon it, or modify it successively, it deliberates; the brain is in a sort of equilibrium, accompanied with perpetual oscillations, sometimes towards one object, sometimes towards the other, until the most forcible carries the point, and thereby extricates it, from this state of suspense, in which consists the indecision of his will. But when the brain is simultaneously assailed by causes equally strong, that move it in opposite directions; agreeable to the general law of all bodies, when they are struck equally by contrary powers, it stops, it is in *nisu*; it is neither capable to will nor to act; it waits until one of the two causes has obtained sufficient force to overpower the other, to determine its will, to attract it in such a manner that it may prevail over the efforts of the other cause.

This mechanism, so simple, so natural, suffices to demonstrate, why uncertainty is painful; why suspense is always a violent state for man. The brain, an organ so delicate, so mobile, experiences such rapid modifications, that it is fatigued; or when it is urged in contrary directions, by causes equally powerful, it suffers a kind of compression, that prevents the activity which is suitable to the preservation of the whole, which is necessary to procure what is advantageous to its existence. This mechanism will also explain the irregularity, the indecision, the inconstancy of man; and account for that conduct, which frequently appears an inexplicable mystery, which indeed it is, under the received systems. In consulting experience, it will be found that the soul is submitted to precisely the same physical laws as the material body. If the will of each individual, during a given time, was only moved by a single cause or passion, nothing would be more easy than to foresee his actions; but his heart is frequently assailed by contrary powers, by adverse motives, which either act on him simultaneously or in succession; then his brain, attracted in opposite directions, is either fatigued, or else tormented by a state of compression, which deprives it of activity. Sometimes it is in a state of incommodious inaction; sometimes it is the sport of the alternate shocks it undergoes. Such, no doubt, is the state in which man finds himself, when a lively passion solicits him to the commission of crime, whilst fear points out to him the danger by which it is attended: such, also, is the condition of him whom remorse, by the continued labour of his distracted soul, prevents from enjoying the objects he has criminally obtained.

If the powers or causes, whether exterior or interior, acting on the mind of man, tend towards opposite points, his soul, is well as all other bodies, will take a mean direction between the two; in consequence of the violence with which his soul is urged, his condition becomes sometimes so painful that his existence is troublesome: he has no longer a tendency to his own peculiar conservation; he seeks after death, as a sanctuary against himself— as the only remedy to his despair: it is thus we behold men, miserable and discontented, voluntarily destroy themselves, whenever life becomes insupportable. Man is competent to cherish his existence, no longer than life holds out charms to him; when he is wrought upon by painful sensations, or drawn by contrary impulses, his natural tendency is deranged, he is under the necessity to follow a new route; this conducts him to his end, which it even displays to him as the most desirable good. In this manner may be explained, the conduct of those melancholy beings, whose vicious temperaments, whose tortured consciences, whose chagrin, whose *ennui*, sometimes determine them to renounce life.

The various powers, frequently very complicated, that act either successively or simultaneously upon the brain of man, which modify him so diversely in the different periods of his existence, are the true causes of that obscurity in morals, of that difficulty which is found, when it is desired to unravel the concealed springs of his enigmatical conduct. The heart of man is a labyrinth, only because it very rarely happens that we possess the necessary gift of judging it; from whence it will appear, that his circumstances, his indecision, his conduct, whether ridiculous, or unexpected, are the necessary consequences of the changes operated in him; are nothing but the effect of motives that successively determine his will; which are dependent on the frequent variations experienced by his machine. According to these variations, the same motives have not, always, the same influence over his will, the same objects no longer enjoy the faculty of pleasing him; his temperament has changed, either for the moment, or for ever. It follows as a consequence, that his taste, his desires, his passions, will change; there can be no kind of uniformity in his conduct, nor any certitude in the effects to be expected.

Choice by no means proves the free-agency of man; he only deliberates when he does not yet know which to choose of the many objects that move him, he is then in an embarrassment, which does not terminate, until his will as decided by the greater advantage he believes be shall find in the object he chooses, or the action he undertakes. From whence it may be seen that choice is necessary, because he would not determine for an object, or for an action, if he did not believe that he should find in it some direct advantage. That man should have free-agency, it were needful that he should be able to will or choose without motive; or, that he could prevent motives coercing his will. Action always being the effect of his will once determined, as his will cannot be determined but by a motive, which is not in his own power, it follows that he is never the master of the determination of his own peculiar will; that consequently he never acts as a free agent. It has been believed that man was a free agent, because he had a will with the power of choosing; but attention has not been paid to the fact, that even his will is moved by causes independent of himself, is owing to that which is inherent in his own organization, or which belongs to the nature of the beings acting on him. Indeed, man passes a great portion of his life without even willing. His will attends the motive by which it is determined. If he was to render an exact account of every thing he does in the course of each day, from rising in the morning to lying down at night, he would find, that not one of his actions have been in the least voluntary; that they have been mechanical, habitual, determined by causes he was not able to foresee, to which he was either obliged to, yield, or with which he was allured to acquiesce; he would discover, that all the motives of his labours, of his amusements, of his discourses, of his thoughts, have been necessary; that they have evidently either seduced him or drawn him along. Is he the master of willing, not to withdraw his hand from the fire when he fears it will be burnt? Or has he the power to take away from fire the property which makes him fear it? Is he the master of not choosing a dish of meat which he knows to be agreeable, or analogous to his palate; of not preferring it to that which he knows to be disagreeable or dangerous? It is always according to his sensations, to his own peculiar experience, or to his suppositions, that he judges of things either well or ill; but whatever way be his judgment, it depends necessarily on his mode of feeling, whether habitual or accidental, and the qualities he finds in the causes that move him, which exist in despite of himself.

All the causes which by his will is actuated, must act upon him in a manner sufficiently marked, to give him some sensation, some perception, some idea, whether complete or incomplete, true or false; as soon as his will is determined, he must have felt, either strongly or feebly; if this was not the case he would have determined without motive: thus, to speak correctly, there are no causes which are truly indifferent to the will: however faint the impulse he receives, whether on the part of the objects themselves, or on the part of their images or ideas, as soon as his will acts, the impulse has been competent to determine him. In consequence of a slight, of a feeble impulse, the will is weak, it is this weakness of the will that is called *indifference*. His brain with difficulty perceives the sensation, it has received; it consequently acts with less vigour, either to obtain or remove the object or the idea that has modified it. If the impulse is powerful, the will is strong, it makes him act vigorously, to obtain or to remove the object which appears to him either very agreeable or very incommodious.

It has been believed man was a free agent, because it has been imagined that his soul could at will recall ideas, which sometimes suffice to check his most unruly desires. Thus, the idea of a remote evil frequently prevents him from enjoying a present and actual good: thus, remembrance, which is an almost insensible, a slight modification of his brain, annihilates, at each instant, the real objects that act upon his will. But he is not master of recalling to himself his ideas at pleasure; their association is independent of him; they are arranged in his brain, in despite of him, without his own knowledge, where they have made an impression more or less profound; his memory itself depends upon his organization; its fidelity depends upon the habitual or momentary state in which he finds himself; when his will is vigorously determined to some object or idea that excites a very lively passion in him, those objects or ideas that would be able to arrest his action no longer present themselves to his mind; in those moments his eyes are shut to the dangers that menace him, of which the idea ought to make him forbear; he marches forward headlong towards the object by whose image he is hurried on; reflection cannot operate upon him in any way; he sees nothing but the object of his desires; the salutary ideas which might be able to arrest his progress disappear, or else display themselves either too faintly or too late to prevent his acting. Such is the case with all those who, blinded by some strong passion, are not in a condition to recal to themselves those motives, of which the idea alone, in cooler moments, would be sufficient to deter them from proceeding; the disorder in which they are, prevents their judging soundly; render them incapable of foreseeing the consequence of their actions; precludes them from applying to their experience; from making use of their reason; natural operations, which suppose a justness in the manner of associating their ideas; but to which their brain is then not more competent, in consequence of the momentary delirium it suffers, than their hand is to write whilst they are taking violent exercise.

Man's mode of thinking is necessarily determined by his manner of being; it must, therefore, depend on his natural organization, and the modification his system receives independently of his will. From this we are obliged to conclude, that his thoughts, his reflections, his manner of viewing things, of feeling, of judging, of combining ideas, is neither voluntary nor free. In a word, that his soul is neither mistress of the motion excited in it, nor of representing to itself, when wanted, those images or ideas that are capable of counterbalancing the impulse it receives. This is the reason why man, when in a passion, ceases to reason; at that moment reason is as impossible to be heard, as it is during an extacy, or in a fit of drunkenness. The wicked are never more than men who are either drunk or mad: if they reason, it is not until tranquillity is re-established in their machine; then, and not till then, the tardy ideas that present themselves to their mind, enable them to see the consequence of their actions, and give birth to ideas, that bring on them that trouble, which is designated *shame, regret, remorse*.

The errors of philosophers on the free-agency of man, have arisen from their regarding his will as the *primum mobile*, the original motive of his actions; for want of recurring back, they have not perceived the multiplied, the complicated causes, which, independently of him, give motion to the will itself, or which dispose and modify his brain, whilst he himself is purely passive in the motion he receives. Is he the master of desiring or not desiring an object that appears desirable to him? Without doubt it will be answered, No: but he is the master of resisting his desire, if he reflects on the consequences. But, I ask, is he capable of reflecting on these consequences when his soul is hurried along by a very lively passion, which entirely depends upon his natural organization, and the causes by which he is modified? Is it in his power to add to these consequences all the weight necessary to counterbalance his desire? Is he the master of preventing the qualities which render an object desirable from residing in it? I shall be told, he ought to have learned to resist his passions; to contract a habit of putting a curb on his desires. I agree to it without any difficulty: but in reply, I again ask, Is his nature susceptible of this modification? Does his boiling blood, his unruly imagination, the igneous fluid that circulates in his veins, permit him to make, enable him to apply true experience in the moment when it is wanted? And, even when his temperament has capacitated him, has his education, the examples set before him, the ideas with which he has been inspired in early life, been suitable to make him contract this habit of repressing his desires? Have not all these things rather contributed to induce him to seek with avidity, to make him actually desire those objects which you say he ought to resist.

The *ambitious man* cries out,—You will have me resist my passion, but have they not unceasingly repeated to me, that rank, honours, power, are the most desirable advantages in life? Have I not seen my fellow-citizens envy them—the nobles of my country sacrifice every thing to obtain them? In the society in which I live, am I not obliged to feel, that if I am deprived of these advantages, I must expect to languish in contempt, to cringe under the rod of oppression?

The *miser* says,—You forbid me to love money, to seek after the means of acquiring it: alas! does not every thing tell me, that in this world money is the greatest blessing; that it is amply sufficient to render me happy? In the country I inhabit, do I not see all my fellow-citizens covetous of riches? but do I not also witness that they are little scrupulous in the means of obtaining wealth? As soon as they are enriched by the means which you censure, are they not cherished, considered, and respected? By what authority, then, do you object to my amassing treasure? what right have you to prevent my using means, which although you call them sordid and criminal, I see approved by the sovereign? Will you have me renounce my happiness?

The *voluptuary* argues,—You pretend that I should resist my desires; but was I the maker of my own temperament, which unceasingly invites me to pleasure? You call my pleasures disgraceful; but in the country in which I live, do I not witness the most dissipated men enjoying the most distinguished rank? Do I not behold, that no one is ashamed of adultery but the husband it has outraged? do not I see men making trophies of their debaucheries, boasting of their libertinism, rewarded, with applause?

The *choleric* man vociferates,—You advise me to put a curb on my passions; to resist the desire of avenging myself: but can I conquer my nature? Can I alter the received opinions of the world? Shall I not be for ever disgraced, infallibly dishonoured in society, if I do not wash out, in the blood of my fellow-creature, the injuries I have received?

The *zealous enthusiast* exclaims,—You recommend to me mildness, you advise me to be tolerant, to be indulgent to the opinions of my fellow-men; but is not my temperament violent? Do I not ardently love my God? Do they not assure me that zeal is pleasing to him; that sanguinary inhuman persecutors have been his friends? That those who do not think as I do are his enemies? I wish to render myself acceptable in his sight, I therefore adopt the means you reprobate.

In short, the actions of man are never free; they are always the necessary consequence of his temperament, of the received ideas, of the notions, either true or false, which he has formed to himself of happiness: of his opinions, strengthened by example, forfeited by education, consolidated by daily experience. So many crimes are witnessed on the earth, only because every thing conspires to render man vicious, to make him criminal; very frequently, the superstitions he has adopted, his government, his education, the examples set before him, irresistibly drive him on to evil: under these circumstances morality preaches virtue to him in vain. In those societies where vice is esteemed, where crime is crowned, where venality is constantly recompenced, where the most dreadful disorders are punished, only in those who are too weak to enjoy the privilege of committing them with impunity; the practice of virtue is considered nothing more than a painful sacrifice of fancied happiness. Such societies chastise, in the lower orders, those excesses which they respect in the higher ranks; and frequently have the injustice to condemn those in penalty of death, whom public prejudices, maintained by constant example, have rendered criminal.

Man, then, is not a free agent in any one instant of his life; he is necessarily guided in each step by those advantages, whether real or fictitious, that he attaches to the objects by which his passions are roused: these passions themselves are necessary in a being who, unceasingly tends towards his own happiness; their energy is necessary, since that depends on his temperament; his temperament is necessary, because it depends on the physical elements which enter into his composition; the modification of this temperament is necessary, as it is the infallible result, the inevitable consequence of the impulse he receives from the incessant action of moral and physical beings.

In despite of these proofs of the want of free-agency in man, so clear to unprejudiced minds, it will, perhaps, be insisted upon with no small feeling of triumph, that if it be proposed to any one to move or not to move his hand, an action in the number of those called *indifferent*, he evidently appears to be the master of choosing; from which it is concluded, evidence has been offered of his free-agency. The reply is, this example is perfectly simple; man in performing some action which he is resolved on doing, does not by any means prove his free-agency: the very desire of displaying this quality, excited by the dispute, becomes a necessary motive which decides his will either for the one or the other of these actions: what deludes him in this instance, or that which persuades him he is a free agent at this moment, is, that he does not discern the true motive which sets him in action; which is neither more nor less than the desire of convincing his opponent: if in the heat of the dispute he insists and asks, "Am I not the master of throwing myself out of the window?" I shall answer him, no; that whilst he preserves his reason, there is not even a probability that the desire of proving his free-agency, will become a motive sufficiently powerful, to make him sacrifice his life to the attempt; if, notwithstanding this, to prove he is a free agent, he should actually precipitate himself from the window, it would not be a sufficient warrantry to conclude he acted freely, but rather that it was the violence of his temperament which spurred him on to this folly. Madness is a state that depends upon the heat of the blood, not upon the will. A fanatic or a hero, braves death as necessarily as a more phlegmatic man or a coward flies from it. There is, in point of fact, no difference between the man who is cast out of the window by another, and the man who throws himself out of it, except that the impulse in the first instance comes immediately from without, whilst that which determines the fall in the second case, springs from within his own peculiar machine, having its more remote cause also exterior. When Mutius Scaevola held his hand in the fire, he was as much acting under the influence of necessity, caused by interior motives, that urged him to this strange action, as if his arm had been held by strong men; pride, despair, the desire of braving his enemy, a wish to astonish him, an anxiety to intimidate him, &c. were the invisible chains that held his hand bound to the fire. The love of glory, enthusiasm for their country, in like manner, caused Codrus and Decius to devote themselves for their fellow citizens. The Indian Calanus and the philosopher Peregrinus were equally obliged to burn themselves, by the desire of exciting the astonishment of the Grecian assembly.

It is said that free-agency is the absence of those obstacles competent to oppose themselves to the actions of man, or to the exercise of his faculties: it is pretended that he is a free agent, whenever, making use of these faculties, he produces the effect he has proposed to himself. In reply to this reasoning, it is sufficient to consider that it in no wise depends upon himself to place or remove the obstacles that either determine or resist him; the motive that causes his action is no more in his own power than the obstacle that impedes him, whether this obstacle or motive be within his own machine or exterior of his person: he is not master of the thought presented to his mind which determines his will; this thought is excited by some cause independent of himself.

To be undeceived on the system of his free-agency, man has simply to recur to the motive by which his will is determined, he will always find this motive is out of his own controul. It is said, that in consequence of an idea to which the mind gives birth, man acts freely if he encounters no obstacle.

But the question is, what gives birth to this idea in his brain? has he the power either to prevent it from presenting itself, or from renewing itself in his brain? Does not this idea depend either upon objects that strike him exteriorly and in despite of himself, or upon causes that without his knowledge act within himself and modify his brain? Can he prevent his eyes, cast without design upon any object whatever, from giving him an idea of this object, from moving his brain? He is not more master of the obstacles; they are the necessary effects of either interior or exterior causes, which always act according to their given properties. A man insults a coward, who is necessarily irritated against his insulter, but his will cannot vanquish the obstacle that cowardice places to the object of his desire, which is, to resent the insult; because his natural conformation, which does not depend upon himself, prevents his having courage. In this case the coward is insulted in despite of himself, and against his will is obliged patiently to brook the insult he has received.

The partizans of the system of free-agency appear ever to have confounded constraint with necessity. Man believes he acts as a free agent, every time he does not see any thing that places obstacles to his actions; he does not perceive that the motive which causes him to will is always necessary, is ever independent of himself. A prisoner loaded with chains is compelled to remain in prison, but he is not a free agent, he is not able to resist the desire to emancipate himself; his chains prevent him from acting, but they do not prevent him from willing; he would save himself if they would loose his fetters, but he would not save himself as a free agent, fear or the idea of punishment would be sufficient motives for his action.

Man may therefore cease to be restrained, without, for that reason, becoming a free agent: in whatever manner he acts, he will act necessarily; according to motives by which he shall be determined. He may be compared to a heavy body, that finds itself arrested in its descent by any obstacle whatever: take away this obstacle, it will gravitate or continue to fall; but who shall say this dense body is free to fall or not? Is not its descent the necessary effect of its own specific gravity? The virtuous Socrates submitted to the laws of his country, although they were unjust; notwithstanding the doors of his gaol were left open to him he would not save himself; but in this he did not act as a free agent; the invisible chains of opinion, the secret love of decorum, the inward respect for the laws, even when they were iniquitous, the fear of tarnishing his glory, kept him in his prison: they were motives sufficiently powerful, with this enthusiast for virtue, to induce him to wait death with tranquillity; it was not in his power to save himself, because he could find no potential motive to bring him to depart, even for an instant, from those principles to which his mind was accustomed.

Man, says he, frequently acts against his inclination, from whence he has falsely concluded he is a free agent; when he appears to act contrary to his inclination, he is determined to it by some motive sufficiently efficacious to vanquish this inclination. A sick man, with a view to his cure, arrives at conquering his repugnance to the most disgusting remedies: the fear of pain, the dread of death, then become necessary and intelligent motives; consequently, this sick man cannot be said, with truth, by any means, to act freely.

When it is said, that man is not a free agent, it is not pretended to compare him to a body moved by a simple impulsive cause: he contains within himself causes inherent to his existence; he is moved by an interior organ, which has its own peculiar laws; which is itself necessarily determined, in consequence of ideas formed from perceptions, resulting from sensations, which it receives from exterior objects. As the mechanism of these sensations, of these perceptions, and the manner they engrave ideas on the brain of man, are not known to him, because he is unable to unravel all these motions; because he cannot perceive the chain of operations in his soul, or the motive-principle that acts within him, he supposes himself a free agent; which, literally translated, signifies that he moves himself by himself; that he determines himself without cause; when he rather ought to say, he is ignorant how or for why he acts in the manner he does. It is true the soul enjoys an activity peculiar to itself, but it is equally certain that this activity would never be displayed if some motive or some cause did not put it in a condition to exercise itself, at least it will not be pretended that the soul is able either to love or to hate without being moved, without knowing the objects, without having some idea of their qualities. Gunpowder has unquestionably a particular activity, but this activity will never display itself, unless fire be applied to it; this, however, immediately sets in motion.

It is the great complication of motion in man, it is the variety of his action, it is the multiplicity of causes that move him, whether simultaneously or in continual succession, that persuades him he is a free agent: if all his motions were simple, if the causes that move him did not confound themselves with each other, if they were distinct, if his machine was less complicated, he would perceive that all his actions were necessary, because he would be enabled to recur instantly to the cause that made him act. A man who should be always obliged to go towards the west would always go on that side, but he would feel extremely well, that in so going he was not a free agent: if he had another sense, as his actions or his motion augmented by a sixth would be still more varied, much more complicated, he would believe himself still more a free agent than he does with his five senses.

It is, then, for want of recurring to the causes that move him, for want of being able to analyse, from not being competent to decompose the complicated motion of his machine, that man believes himself a free agent; it is only upon his own ignorance that he founds the profound yet deceitful notion he has of his free-agency, that he builds those opinions which he brings forward as a striking proof of his pretended freedom of action. If, for a short time, each man was willing to examine his own peculiar actions, to search out their true motives, to discover their concatenation, he would remain convinced that the sentiment he has of his natural free-agency is a chimera that must speedily be destroyed by experience.

Nevertheless, it must be acknowledged that the multiplicity, the diversity of the causes which continually act upon man, frequently without even his knowledge, render it impossible, or at least extremely difficult, for him to recur to the true principles of his own peculiar actions, much less the actions of others; they frequently depend upon causes so fugitive, so remote from their effects, and which, superficially examined, appear to have so little analogy, so slender a relation with them, that it requires singular sagacity to bring them into light. This is what renders the study of the moral man a task of such difficulty; this is the reason why his heart is an abyss, of which it is frequently impossible for him to fathom the depth. He is, then, obliged to content himself with a knowledge of the general and necessary laws by which the human heart is regulated; for the individuals of his own species these laws are pretty nearly the same, they vary only in consequence of the organization that is peculiar to each, and of the modification it undergoes; this, however, is not, cannot be rigorously the same in any two. It suffices to know that by his essence man tends to conserve himself, to render his existence happy: this granted, whatever may be his actions, if he recurs back to this first principle, to this general, this necessary tendency of his will, he never can be deceived with regard to his motives. Man, without doubt, for want of cultivating reason, being destitute of experience, frequently deceives himself upon the means of arriving at this end; sometimes the means he employs are unpleasant to his fellows, because they are prejudicial to their interests; or else those of which he avails himself appear irrational, because they remove him from the end to which he would approximate: but whatever may be these means, they have always necessarily and invariably for object, either an existing or imaginary happiness; are directed to preserve himself in a state analogous to his mode of existence, to his manner of feeling, to his way of thinking; whether durable or transitory. It is from having mistaken this truth, that the greater number of moral philosophers have made rather the romance, than the history of the human heart; they have attributed the actions of man to fictitious causes; at least they have not sought out the necessary motives of his conduct. Politicians and legislators have been in the same state of ignorance; or else impostors have found it much shorter to employ imaginary motive-powers, than those which really have existence: they have rather chosen to make man wander out of his way, to make him tremble under incommodious phantoms, than guide him to virtue by the direct road to happiness; notwithstanding the conformity of the latter with the natural desires of his heart. So true it is, that *error can never possibly be useful, to the human species.*

However this may be, man either sees or believes he sees, much more distinctly, the necessary relation of effects with their causes in natural philosophy than in the human heart; at least he sees in the former sensible causes constantly produce sensible effects, ever the same, when the circumstances are alike. After this, he hesitates not to look upon physical effects as necessary, whilst he refuses to acknowledge necessity in the acts of the human will; these he has, without any just foundation, attributed to a motive-power that acts independently by its own peculiar energy, that is capable of modifying itself without the concurrence of exterior causes, and which is distinguished from all material or physical beings. *Agriculture* is founded upon the assurance afforded by experience, that the earth, cultivated and sown in a certain manner, when it has otherwise the requisite qualities, will furnish grain, fruit, and flowers, either necessary for subsistence or pleasing to the senses. If things were considered without prejudice, it would be perceived, that in morals education is nothing more than *the agriculture of the mind*; that like the earth, by reason of its natural disposition, of the culture bestowed upon it, of the seeds with which it is sown, of the seasons, more or less favorable, that conduct it to maturity, we may be assured that the soul will produce either virtue or vice; *moral fruit* that will be either salubrious for man or baneful to society. *Morals* is the science of the relations that subsist between the minds, the wills, and the actions of men; in the same manner that *geometry* is the science of the relations that are found between bodies. Morals would be a chimera, it would have no certain principles, if it was not founded upon the knowledge of the motives which must necessarily have an influence upon the human will, and which must necessarily determine the actions of human beings.

If in the moral as well as in the physical world, a cause of which the action is not interrupted be necessarily followed by a given effect, it flows consecutively that a *reasonable education*, grafted upon truth, founded upon wise laws,—that honest principles instilled during youth, virtuous examples continually held forth, esteem attached solely to merit, recompense awarded to none but good actions, contempt regularly visiting vice, shame following falsehood as its shadow, rigorous chastisements applied without distinction to crime, are causes that would necessarily act on the will of man; that would determine the greater number of his species to exhibit virtue, to love it for its own sake, to seek after it as the most desirable good, as the surest road to the happiness he so ardently desires. But if, on the contrary, superstition, politics, example, public opinion, all labour to countenance wickedness, to train man viciously; if, instead of fanning his virtues, they stifle good principles; if, instead of directing his studies to his advantage, they render his education either useless or unprofitable; if this education itself, instead of grounding him in virtue, only inoculates him with vice; if, instead of inculcating reason, it imbues him with prejudice; if, instead of making him enamoured of truth, it furnishes him with false notions; if, instead of storing his mind with just ideas drawn from experience, it fills him with dangerous opinions; if, instead of fostering mildness and forbearance, it kindles in his breast only those passions which are incommodious to himself and hurtful to others; it must be of necessity, that the will of the greater number shall determine them to evil; shall render them unworthy, make them baneful to society. Many authors have acknowledged the importance of a good education, that youth was the season to feed the human heart with wholesome diet; but they have not felt, that a good education is incompatible, nay, impossible, with the superstition of man, since this commences with giving his mind a false bias: that it is equally inconsistent with arbitrary government, because this always dreads lest he should become enlightened, and is ever sedulous to render him servile, mean, contemptible, and cringing; that it is incongruous with laws that are not founded in equity, that are frequently bottomed on injustice; that it cannot obtain with those received customs that are opposed to good sense; that it cannot exist whilst public opinion is unfavourable to virtue; above all, that it is absurd to expect it from incapable instructors, from masters with weak minds, who have only the ability to infuse into their scholars those false ideas with which they are themselves infected. Here, without doubt, is the real source from whence springs that universal corruption, that wide-spreading depravity, of which moralists, with great justice, so loudly complain; without, however, pointing out those causes of the evil, which are true as they are necessary: instead of this, they search for it in human nature, say it is corrupt, blame man for loving himself, and for seeking after his own happiness, insist that he must have supernatural assistance, some marvellous interference, to enable him to become good: this is a very prejudicial doctrine for him, it is directly subversive of his true happiness; by teaching him to hold himself in contempt, it tends necessarily to discourage him; it either makes him sluggish, or drives him to despair whilst waiting for this grace: is it not easy to be perceived, that he would always have it if he was well educated; if he was honestly governed? There cannot well exist a wilder or a stranger system of morals, than that of the theologians who attribute all moral evil to an original sin, and all moral good to the pardon of it. It ought not to excite surprise if such a system is of no efficacy; what can reasonably be the result of such an hypothesis? Yet, notwithstanding the supposed, the boasted free-agency of man, it is insisted that nothing less than the Author of Nature himself is necessary to destroy the wicked desires of his heart: but, alas! no power whatever is found sufficiently efficacious to resist those unhappy propensities, which, under the fatal constitution of things, the most vigorous motives, as before observed, are continually infusing into the will of man; no agency seems competent to turn the course of that unhappy direction these are perpetually giving to the stream of his natural passions. He is, indeed, incessantly exhorted to resist these passions, to stifle them, and to root them out of his heart; but is it not evident they are necessary to his welfare? Can it not be perceived they are inherent in his nature? Does not experience prove them to be useful to his conservation, since they have for object, only to avoid that which may be injurious to him; to procure that which may be advantageous to his mode of existence? In short, is it not easy to be seen, that these passions, well directed, that is to say, carried towards objects that are truly useful, that are really interesting to himself, which embrace the happiness of others, would necessarily contribute to the substantial, to the permanent well-being of society? Theologians themselves have felt, they have acknowledged the necessity of the passions: many of the fathers of the church have broached this doctrine; among the rest Father Senault has written a book expressly on the subject: the passions of man are like fire, at once necessary to the wants of life, suitable to ameliorate the condition of humanity, and equally capable of producing the most terrible ravages, the most frightful devastation.

Every thing becomes an impulse to the will; a single word frequently suffices to modify a man for the whole course of his life, to decide for ever his propensities; an infant who has burned his finger by having approached it too near the flame of a lighted taper, is warned from thence, that he ought to abstain from indulging a similar temptation; a man, once punished and despised for having committed a dishonest action, is not often tempted to continue so unfavourable a course. Under whatever point of man is considered, he never acts but after the impulse given to his will, whether it be by the will of others, or by more perceptible physical causes. The particular organization decides the nature of the impulse; souls act upon souls that are analogous; inflamed, fiery imaginations, act with facility upon strong passions; upon imaginations easy to be inflamed, the surprising progress of enthusiasm; the hereditary propagation of superstition; the transmission of religious errors from race to race, the excessive ardour with which man seizes on the marvellous, are effects as necessary as those which result from the action and re-action of bodies.

In despite of the gratuitous ideas which man has formed to himself on his pretended free-agency; in defiance of the illusions of this suppose intimate sense, which, contrary to his experience, persuades him that he is master of his will,—all his institutions are really founded upon necessity: on this, as on a variety of other occasions, practice throws aside speculation. Indeed, if it was not believed that certain motives embraced the power requisite to determine the will of man, to arrest the progress of his passions, to direct them towards an end, to modify him; of what use would be the faculty of speech? What benefit could arise from education itself? What does education achieve, save give the first impulse to the human will, make man contract habits, oblige him to persist in them, furnish him with motives, whether true or false, to act after a given manner? When the father either menaces his son with punishment, or promises him a reward, is he not convinced these things will act upon his will? What does legislation attempt, except it be to present to the citizens of a state those motives which are supposed necessary to determine them to perform some actions that are considered worthy; to abstain from committing others that are looked upon as unworthy? What is the object of morals, if it be not to shew man that his interest exacts he should suppress the momentary ebullition of his passions, with a view to promote a more certain happiness, a more lasting well-being, than can possibly result from the gratification of his transitory desires? Does not the religion of all countries suppose the human race, together with the entire of Nature, submitted to the irresistible will of a necessary being, who regulates their condition after the eternal laws of immutable wisdom? Is not God the absolute master of their destiny? Is it not this divine being who chooses and rejects? The anathemas fulminated by religion, the promises it holds forth, are they not founded upon the idea of the effects they will necessarily produce upon mankind? Is not man brought into existence without his own knowledge? Is he not obliged to play a part against his will? Does not either his happiness or his misery depend on the part he plays?

All religion has been evidently founded upon *Fatalism*. Among the Greeks they supposed men were punished for their necessary faults, as may be seen in Orestes, in Oedipus, &c. who only committed crimes predicted by the oracles. It is rather singular that the theological defenders of the doctrine of *free-agency*, which they endeavour to oppose to that of *predestination*,—which according to them is irreconcileable with *Christianity*, inasmuch as it is a false and dangerous system,—should not have been aware that the doctrines of *the fall of angels, original sin, the small number of the elect, the system of grace, &c.* were most incontestibly supporting, by the most cogent arguments, a *true system of fatalism*.

Education, then, is only necessity shewn to children: *legislation* is necessity shewn to the members of the body politic: *morals* is the necessity of the relations subsisting between men, shewn to reasonable beings: in short, man grants *necessity* in every thing for which he believes he has certain, unerring experience: that of which he does not comprehend the necessary connection of causes with their effects he styles *probability*: he would not act as he does, if he was not convinced, or, at least, if he did not presume he was, that certain effects will necessarily follow his actions. The *moralist* preaches reason, because he believes it necessary to man: the *philosopher* writes, because he believes truth must, sooner or later, prevail over falsehood: *tyrants* and *fanatical priests* necessarily hate truth, despise reason, because they believe them prejudicial to their interests: the *sovereign*, who strives to terrify crime by the severity of his laws, but who nevertheless, from motives of state policy sometimes renders it useful and even necessary to his purposes, presumes the motives he employs will be sufficient to keep his subjects within bounds. All reckon equally upon the power or upon the necessity of the motives they make use of; each individual flatters himself, either with or without reason, that these motives will have an influence on the conduct of mankind. The education of man is commonly so defective, so inefficacious, so little calculated to promote the end he has in view, because it is regulated by prejudice: even when this education is good, it is but too often speedily counteracted, by almost every thing that takes place in society. Legislation and politics are very frequently iniquitous, and serve no better purpose than to kindle passions in the bosom of man, which once set afloat, they are no longer competent to restrain. The great art of the moralist should be, to point out to man, to convince those who are entrusted with the sacred office of regulating his will, that their interests are identified; that their reciprocal happiness depends upon the harmony of their passions; that the safety, the power, the duration of empires, necessarily depend on the good sense diffused among the individual members; on the truth of the notions inculcated in the mind of the citizens, on the moral goodness that is sown in their hearts, on the virtues that are cultivated in their breasts; religion should not be admissible, unless it truly fortified, unless it really strengthened these motives. But in the miserable state into which error has plunged a considerable portion of the human species, man, for the most part, is seduced to be wicked: he injures his fellow-creature as a matter of conscience, because the strongest motives are held out to him to be persecuting; because his institutions invite him to the commission of evil, under the lure of promoting his own immediate happiness. In most countries superstition renders him a useless being, makes him an abject slave, causes him to tremble under its terrors, or else turns him into a furious fanatic, who is at once cruel, intolerant, and inhuman: in a great number of states arbitrary power crushes him, obliges him to become a cringing sycophant, renders him completely vicious: in those despotic states the law rarely visits crime with punishment, except in those who are too feeble to oppose its course? or when it has become incapable of restraining the violent excesses to which a bad government gives birth. In short, rational education is neglected; a prudent culture of the human mind is despised; it depends, but too frequently, upon bigotted, superstitious priests, who are interested in deceiving man, and who are sometimes impostors; or else upon parents or masters without understanding, who are devoid of morals, who impress on the ductile mind of their scholars those vices with which they are themselves tormented; who transmit to them the false opinions, which they believe they have an interest in making them adopt.

All this proves the necessity of falling back to man's original errors, and recurring to the primitive source of his wanderings, if it be seriously intended to furnish him with suitable remedies for such enormous maladies: it is useless to dream of correcting his mistakes, of curing him of his depravity, until the true causes that move his will are unravelled; until more real, more beneficial, more certain motives are substituted for those which are found so inefficacious; which prove so dangerous both to society and to himself. It is for those who guide the human will, who regulate the condition of nations, who hold the real happiness of man in their grasp, to seek after these motives,—with which reason will readily furnish them—which experience will enable them to apply with success: even a good book, by touching the heart of a great prince, may become a very powerful cause that shall necessarily have an influence over the conduct of a whole people, and decide upon the felicity of a portion of the human race.

From all that has been advanced in this chapter, it results, that in no one moment of his existence man is a free agent: he is not the architect of his own conformation; this he holds from Nature, he has no controul over his own ideas, or over the modification of his brain; these are due to causes, that, in despite of him, very frequently without his own knowledge, unceasingly act upon him; he is not the master of not loving that which he finds amiable; of not coveting that which appears to him desirable; he is not capable of refusing to deliberate, when he is uncertain of the effects certain objects will produce upon him; he cannot avoid choosing that which he believes will be most advantageous to him: in the moment when his will is determined by his choice, he is not competent to act otherwise than he does: in what instance, then, is he the master of his own actions? In what moment is he a free agent?

That which a man is about to do is always a consequence of that which he has been—of that which he is—of that which he has done up to the moment of the action: his total and actual existence, considered under all its possible circumstances, contains the sum of all the motives to the action he is about to commit; this is a principle, the truth of which no thinking, being will be able to refuse accrediting: his life is a series of necessary moments; his conduct, whether good or bad, virtuous or vicious, useful or prejudicial, either to himself or to others, is a concatenation of action, a chain of causes and effects, as necessary as all the moments of his existence. To *live*, is to exist in a necessary mode during the points of its duration, which succeed each other necessarily: to *will*, is to acquiesce or not in remaining such as he is: to be *free*, is to yield to the necessary motives that he carries within himself.

If he understood the play of his organs, if he was able to recal to himself all the impulsions they have received, all the modifications they have undergone, all the effects they have produced, he would perceive, that all his actions are submitted to that *fatality* which regulates his own particular system, as it does the entire system of the universe: no one effect in him, any more than in Nature, produce itself by *chance*; this, as has been before proved, is a word void of sense. All that passes in him, all that is done by him, as well as all that happens in Nature, or that is attributed to her, is derived from necessary laws, which produce necessary effects; from whence necessarily flow others.

Fatality is the eternal, the immutable, the necessary order established in Nature, or the indispensible connection of causes that act with the effects they operate. Conforming to this order, heavy bodies fall, light bodies rise; that which is analogous in matter, reciprocally attracts; that which is heterogeneous, mutually repels; man congregates himself in society, modifies each his fellow, becomes either virtuous or wicked; either contributes to his mutual happiness, or reciprocates his misery; either loves his neighbour, or hates his companion necessarily; according to the manner in which the one acts upon the other. From whence it may be seen, that the same necessity which regulates the physical, also regulates the moral world: in which every thing is in consequence submitted to fatality. Man, in running over, frequently without his own knowledge, often in despite of himself, the route which Nature has marked out for him, resembles a swimmer who is obliged to follow the current that carries him along; he believes himself a free agent, because he sometimes consents, sometimes does not consent, to glide with the stream; which, notwithstanding, always hurries him forward; he believes himself the master of his condition, because he is obliged to use his arms under the fear of sinking.

The false ideas he has formed to himself upon free-agency, are in general thus founded: there are certain events which he judges *necessary*; either because he sees they are effects that are constantly, are invariably linked to certain causes, which nothing seems to prevent; or because he believes he has discovered the chain of causes and effects that is put in play to produce those events: whilst he contemplates as *contingent*, other events, of whose causes he is ignorant; the concatenation of which he does not perceive; with whose mode of acting he is unacquainted: but in Nature, where every thing is connected by one common bond, there exists no effect without a cause. In the moral as well as in the physical world, every thing that happens is a necessary consequence of causes, either visible or concealed; which are, of necessity, obliged to act after their peculiar essences. *In man, free-agency is nothing more than necessity contained within himself.*

CHAP. XII.

An examination of the Opinion which pretends that the System of Fatalism is dangerous.

For a being whose essence obliges him to have a constant tendency to his own conservation, to continually seek to render himself happy, experience is indispensible: without it he cannot discover truth, which is nothing more, as has been already said, than a knowledge of the constant relations which subsist between man, and those objects that act upon him; according to his experience he denominates those that contribute to his permanent welfare useful and salutary; those that procure him pleasure, more or less durable, he calls agreeable. Truth itself becomes the object of his desires, only when he believes it is useful; he dreads it, whenever he presumes it will injure him. But has truth the power to injure him? Is it possible that evil can result to man from a correct understanding of the relations he has with other beings? Can it be true, that he can be harmed by becoming acquainted with those things, of which, for his own happiness, he is interested in having a knowledge? No: unquestionably not. It is upon its utility that truth founds its worth; upon this that it builds its rights; sometimes it may be disagreeable to individuals—it may even appear contrary to their interests—but it will ever be beneficial to them in the end; it will always be useful to the whole human species; it will eternally benefit the great bulk of mankind; whose interests must for ever remain distinct from those of men, who, duped by their own peculiar passions, believe their advantage consists in plunging others into error.

Utility, then, is the touchstone of his systems, the test of his opinions, the criterion of the actions of man; it is the standard of the esteem, the measure of the love he owes to truth itself: the most useful truths are the most estimable: those truths which are most interesting for his species, he styles *eminent*; those of which the utility limits itself to the amusement of some individuals who have not correspondent ideas, similar modes of feeling, wants analogous to his own, he either disdains, or else calls them *barren*.

It is according to this standard, that the principles laid down in this work, ought to be judged. Those who are acquainted with the immense chain of mischief produced on the earth by erroneous systems of superstition, will acknowledge the importance of opposing to them systems more accordant with truth, schemes drawn from Nature, sciences founded on experience. Those who are, or believe they are, interested in maintaining the established errors, will contemplate, with horror, the truths here presented to them: in short, those infatuated mortals, who do not feel, or who only feel very faintly, the enormous load of misery brought upon mankind by metaphysical speculation; the heavy yoke of slavery under which prejudice makes him groan, will regard all our principles as useless; or, at most, as sterile truths, calculated to amuse the idle hours of a few speculators.

No astonishment, therefore, need be excited at the various judgments formed by man: his interests never being the same, any more than his notions of utility, he condemns or disdains every thing that does not accord with his own peculiar ideas. This granted, let us examine, if in the eyes of the disinterested man, who is not entangled by prejudice—who is sensible to the happiness of his species—who delights in truth—the *doctrine of fatalism* be useful or dangerous? Let us see if it is a barren speculation, that his not any influence upon the felicity of the human race? At has been already shewn, that it will furnish morals with efficacious arguments, with real motives to determine the will, supply politics with the true lever to raise the proper activity in the mind of man. It will also be seen that it serves to explain in a simple manner the mechanism of man's actions; to develope in an easy way the arcana of the most striking phenomena of the human heart: on the other hand, if his ideas are only the result of unfruitful speculations, they cannot interest the happiness of the human species. Whether he believes himself a free agent, or whether he acknowledges the necessity of things, he always equally follows the desires imprinted on his soul; which are to preserve his existence and render himself happy. A rational education, honest habits, wise systems, equitable laws, rewards uprightly distributed, punishments justly inflicted, will conduct man to happiness by making him virtuous; while thorny speculations, filled with difficulties, can at most only have an influence over persons unaccustomed to think.

After these reflections, it will be very easy to remove the difficulties that are unceasingly opposed to the system of fatalism, which so many persons, blinded by their superstitious prejudices, are desirous to have considered as dangerous—as deserving of punishment—as calculated to disturb public tranquility—as tending to unchain the passions—to undermine the opinions man ought to have; and to confound his ideas of vice and of virtue.

The opposers of necessity, say, that if all the actions of man are necessary, no right whatever exists to punish bad ones, or even to he angry with those who commit them: that nothing ought to be imputed to them; that the laws would be unjust if they should decree punishment for necessary actions; in short, that under this system man could neither have merit nor demerit. In reply, it may be argued, that, to impute an action to any one, is to attribute that action to him; to acknowledge him for the author: thus, when even an action was supposed to be the effect of an agent, and that agent *necessity*, the imputation would lie: the merit or demerit, that is ascribed to an action are ideas originating in the effects, whether favourable or pernicious, that result to those who experience its operation; when, therefore, it should be conceded, that the agent was necessity, it is not less certain, that the action would be either good or bad; estimable or contemptible, to those who must feel its influence; in short that it would be capable of either eliciting their love, or exciting their anger. Love and anger are modes of existence, suitable to modify, beings of the human species: when, therefore, man irritates himself against his fellow, he intends to excite his fear, or even to punish him, in order to deter him from committing that which is displeasing to him. Moreover his anger is necessary; it is the result of his Nature; the consequence of his temperament. The painful sensation produced by a stone that falls on the arm, does not displease the less, because it comes from a cause deprived of will; which acts by the necessity of its Nature. In contemplating man as acting necessarily, it is impossible to avoid distinguishing that mode of action or being which is agreeable, which elicits approbation, from that which is afflicting, which irritates, which Nature obliges him to blame and to prevent. From this it will be seen, that the system of fatalism, does not in any manner change the actual state of things, and is by no means calculated to confound man's ideas of virtue and vice.

Man's Nature always revolts against that which opposes it: there are men so choleric, that they infuriate themselves even against insensible and inanimate objects; reflection on their own impotence to modify these objects ought to conduct them back to reason. Parents are frequently very much to be blamed for correcting their children with anger: they should be contemplated as beings who are not yet modified; or who have, perhaps, been very badly modified by themselves: nothing is more common in life, than to see men punish faults of which they are themselves the cause.

Laws are made with a view to maintain society; to uphold its existence; to prevent man associated, from injuring his neighbour; they are therefore competent to punish those who disturb its harmony, or those who commit actions that are injurious to their fellows; whether these associates may be the agents of necessity, or whether they are free agents, it suffices to know they are susceptible of modification, and are therefore submitted to the operation of the law. Penal laws are, or ought to be, those motives which experience has shewn capable of restraining the inordinate passions of man, or of annihilating the impulse these passions give to his will; from whatever necessary cause man may derive these passions, the legislator proposes to arrest their effect, when he takes suitable means, when he adopts proper methods, he is certain of success. The Judge, in decreeing to crime, gibbets, tortures, or any other chastisement whatever, does nothing more than is done by the architect, who in building a house, places gutters to carry off the rain, and prevent it from sapping the foundation.

Whatever may be the cause that obliges man to act, society possesses the right to crush the effects, as much as the man whose land would be ruined by a river, has to restrain its waters by a bank: or even, if he is able, to turn its course. It is by virtue of this right that society has the power to intimidate, the faculty to punish, with a view to its own conservation, those who may be tempted to injure it; or those who commit actions which are acknowledged really to interrupt its repose; to be inimical to its security; repugnant to its happiness.

It will, perhaps, be argued, that society does not, usually, punish those faults in which the will has no share; that, in fact, it punishes the will alone; that this it is which decides the nature of the crime, and the degree of its atrocity; that if this will be not free, it ought not to be punished. I reply, that society is an assemblage of sensible beings, susceptible of reason, who desire their own welfare; who fear evil, and seek after good. These dispositions enable their will to be so modified or determined, that they are capable of holding such a conduct as will conduce to the end they have in view. Education, the laws, public opinion, example, habit, fear, are the causes that must modify associated man, influence his will, regulate his passions, restrain the actions of him who is capable of injuring the end of his association, and thereby make him concur to the general happiness. These causes are of a nature to make impressions on every man, whose organization, whose essence, whose sanity, places him in a capacity to contract the habits, to imbibe the modes of thinking, to adopt the manner of acting, with which society is willing to inspire him. All the individuals of the human species are susceptible of fear, from whence it flows as a natural consequence, that the fear of punishment, or the privation of the happiness he desires, are motives that must necessarily more or less influence his will, and regulate his actions. If the man is to be found who is so badly constituted as to resist, whose organization is so vicious as to be insensible to those motives which operate upon all his fellows, he is not fit to live in society; he would contradict the very end of his association: he would be its enemy; he would place obstacles to its natural tendency; his rebellious disposition, his unsociable will, not being susceptible of that modification which is convenient to his own true interests and to the interests of his fellow-citizens; these would unite themselves against such an enemy; and the law which is, or ought to be the expression of the general will, would visit with condign punishment that refractory individual upon whom the motives presented to him by society, had not the effect which it had been induced to expect: in consequence, such an unsociable man would be chastised; he would be rendered miserable, and according to the nature of his crime he would be excluded from society as a being but little calculated to concur in its views.

If society has the right to conserve itself, it has also the right to take the means: these means are the laws which present or ought to present to the will of man those motives which are most suitable to deter him from committing injurious actions. If these motives fail of the proper effect, if they are unable to influence him, society, for its own peculiar good, is obliged to wrest from him the power of doing it further injury. From whatever source his actions may arise, therefore, whether they are the result of free-agency, or whether they are the offspring of necessity, society coerces him if, after having furnished him with motives, sufficiently powerful to act upon reasonable beings, it perceives that these motives have not been competent to vanquish his depraved nature. It punishes him with justice, when the actions from which it dissuades him are truly injurious to society; it has an unquestionable right to punish, when it only commands those things that are conformable to the end proposed by man in his association; or defends the commission of those acts, which are contrary to this end; which are hostile to the nature of beings associated for their reciprocal advantage. But, on the other hand, the law has not acquired the right to punish him: if it has failed to present to him the motives necessary to have an influence over his will, it has not the right to coerce him if the negligence of society has deprived him of the means of subsisting; of exercising his talents; of exerting his industry; of labouring for its welfare. It is unjust, when it punishes those to whom it has, neither given an education, nor honest principles; whom it has not enabled to contract habits necessary to the maintenance of society: it is unjust when it punishes them for faults which the wants of their nature, or the constitution of society has rendered necessary to them: it is unjust, it is irrational, whenever it chastises them for having followed those propensities, which example, which public opinion, which the institutions, which society itself conspires to give them. In short, the law is defective when it does not proportion the punishment to the real evil which society has sustained. The last degree of injustice, the acme of folly is, when society is so blinded as to inflict punishment on those citizens who have served it usefully.

The *penal* laws, in exhibiting terrifying objects to man, who must be supposed susceptible of fear, presents him with motives calculated to have an influence over his will. The idea of pain, the privation of liberty, the fear of death, are, to a being well constituted, in the full enjoyment of his faculties, very puissant obstacles, that strongly oppose themselves to the impulse of his unruly desires: when these do not coerce his will, when they fail to arrest his progress, he is an irrational being; a madman; a being badly organized; against whom society has the right to guarantee itself; against whom it has a right to take measures for its own security. Madness is, without doubt, an involuntary, a necessary state; nevertheless, no one feels it unjust to deprive the insane of their liberty, although their actions can only be imputed to the derangement of their brain. The wicked are men whose brain is either constantly or transitorily disturbed; still they must be punished by reason of the evil they commit; they must always be placed in the impossibility of injuring society: if no hope remains of bringing them back to a reasonable conduct—if every prospect of recalling them to their duty has vanished—if they cannot be made to adopt a mode of action conformable to the great end of association—they must be for ever excluded its benefits.

It will not be requisite to examine here, how far the punishments which society inflicts upon those who offend against it, may be reasonably carried. Reason should seem to indicate that the law ought to shew to the necessary crimes of man, all the indulgence that is compatible with the conservation of society. The system of fatalism, as we have seen, does not leave crime unpunished; but it is, at least, calculated to moderate the barbarity with which a number of nations punish the victims to their anger. This cruelty becomes still more absurd, when experience has shewn its inutility: the habit of witnessing ferocious punishments familiarizes criminals with the idea. If it be true that society possesses the right of taking away the life of its members—if it be really a fact, that the death of a criminal, thenceforth useless, can be advantageous for society, which it will be necessary to examine, humanity, at least, exacts that this death should not be accompanied with useless tortures; with which laws, perhaps in this instance too rigorous, frequently seem to delight in overwhelming their victim. This cruelty seems to defeat its own end, it only serves to make the culprit, who is immolated to the public vengeance, suffer without any advantage to society; it moves the compassion of the spectator, interests him in favor of the miserable offender who groans under its weight; it impresses nothing upon the wicked, but the sight of those cruelties destined for himself; which but too frequently renders him more ferocious, more cruel, more the enemy of his associates: if the example of death was less frequent, even without being accompanied with tortures, it would be more efficacious. If experience was consulted, it would be found that the greater number of criminals only look upon death as a *bad quarter of an hour*. It is an unquestionable fact, that a thief seeing one of his comrades, display a want of firmness under the punishment, said to him: *"Is not this what I have often told you, that in our business, we have one evil more than the rest of mankind?"* Robberies are daily committed, even at the foot of the scaffolds where criminals are punished. In those nations, where the penalty of death is so lightly inflicted, has sufficient attention been paid to the fact, that society is yearly deprived of a great number of individuals who would be able to render it very useful service, if made to work, and thus indemnify the community for the injuries they have committed? The facility with which the lives of men are taken away, proves the incapacity of counsellors; is an evidence of the negligence of legislators: they find it a much shorter road, that it gives them less trouble to destroy the citizens than to seek after the means to render them better.

What shall be said for the unjust cruelty of some nations, in which the law, that ought to have for its object the advantage of the whole, appears to be made only for the security of the most powerful? How shall we account for the inhumanity of those societies, in which punishments the most disproportionate to the crime, unmercifully take away the lives of men, whom the most urgent necessity, the dreadful alternative of famishing in a land of plenty, has obliged to become criminal? It is thus that in a great number of civilized nations, the life of the citizen is placed in the same scales with money; that the unhappy wretch who is perishing from hunger, who is writhing under the most abject misery, is put to death for having taken a pitiful portion of the superfluity of another whom he beholds rolling in abundance! It is this that, in many otherwise very enlightened societies, is called *justice*, or making the punishment commensurate with the crime.

Let the man of humanity, whose tender feelings are alive to the welfare of his species—let the moralist, who preaches virtue, who holds out forbearance to man—let the philosopher, who dives into the secrets of Nature—let the theologian himself say, if this dreadful iniquity, this heinous sin, does not become yet more crying, when the laws decree the most cruel tortures for crimes to which the most irrational customs gave birth—which bad institutions engender—which evil examples multiply? Is not this something like building a sorry, inconvenient hovel, and then punishing the inhabitant, because he does not find all the conveniences of the most complete mansion, of the most finished structure? Man, as at cannot be too frequently repeated, is so prone to evil, only because every thing appears to urge him on to the commission of it, by too frequently shewing him vice triumphant: his education is void in a great number of states, perhaps defective in nearly all; in many places he receives from society no other principles, save those of an unintelligible superstition; which make but a feeble barrier against those propensities that are excited by dissolute manners; which are encouraged by corrupt examples: in vain the law cries out to him: "abstain from the goods of thy neighbour;" his wants, more powerful, loudly declare to him that he must live: unaccustomed to reason, having never been submitted to a wholesome discipline, he conceives he must do it at the expence of a society who has done nothing for him: who condemns him to groan in misery, to languish in indigence: frequently deprived of the common necessaries requisite to support his existence, which his essence, of which he is not the master, compels him to conserve. He compensates himself by theft, he revenges himself by assassination, he becomes a plunderer by profession, a murderer by trade; he plunges into crime, and seeks at the risque of his life, to satisfy those wants, whether real or imaginary, to which every thing around him conspires to give birth. Deprived of education, he has not been taught to restrain the fury of his temperament—to guide his passions with discretion—to curb his inclinations. Without ideas of decency, destitute of the true principles of honour, he engages in criminal pursuits that injure his country: which at the same time has been to him nothing more than a step-mother. In the paroxysm of his rage, in the exacerbation of his mind, he loses sight of his neighbour's rights, he overlooks the gibbet, he forgets the torture; his unruly desires have become too potent—they have completely absorbed his mind; by a criminal indulgence they have given an inveteracy to his habits which preclude him from changing them; laziness has made him torpid: remorse has gnawed his peace; despair has rendered him blind; he rushes on to death; and society is compelled to punish him rigorously, for those fatal, those necessary dispositions, which it has perhaps itself engendered in his heart by evil example: or which at least, it has not taken the pains seasonably to root out; which it has neglected to oppose by suitable motives—by those calculated to give him honest principles—to excite him to industrious habits, to imbue him with virtuous inclinations. Thus, society frequently punishes those propensities of which it is itself the author, or which its negligence has suffered to spring up in the mind of man: it acts like those unjust fathers, who chastise their children for vices which they have themselves made them contract.

However unjust, however unreasonable this conduct may be, or appear to be, it is not the less necessary: society, such as it is, whatever may be its corruption, whatever vices may pervade its institutions, like every thing else in Nature, is willing to subsist; tends to conserve itself: in consequence, it is obliged to punish those excesses which its own vicious constitution has produced: in despite of its peculiar prejudices, notwithstanding its vices, it feels cogently that its own immediate security demands that it should destroy the conspiracies of those who make war against its tranquillity: if these, hurried on by the foul current of their necessary propensities, disturb its repose—if, borne on the stream of their ill-directed desires, they injure its interests, this following the natural law, which obliges it to labour to its own peculiar conservation, removes them out of its road; punishes them with more or less rigor, according to the objects to which it attaches the greatest importance, or which it supposes best suited to further its own peculiar welfare: without doubt, it deceives itself frequently, both upon these objects and the means; but it deceives itself necessarily, for want of the knowledge calculated to enlighten it, with regard to its true interests; for want of those, who regulate its movements possessing proper vigilance—suitable talents—the requisite virtue. From this it will appear, that the injustice of a society badly constituted, and blinded by its prejudices, is as necessary, as the crimes of those by whom it is hostilely attacked—by whose vices it is distracted. The body politic, when in a state of insanity, cannot act more consistently with reason, than one of its members whose brain is disturbed by madness.

It will still be said that these maxims, by submitting every thing to necessity, must confound, or even destroy the notions man forms of justice and injustice; of good and evil; of merit and demerit: I deny it. Although man, in every thing he does, acts necessarily, his actions are good, they are just, they are meritorious, every time they tend to the real utility of his fellows; of the society of which he makes a part: they are, of necessity, distinguished from those which are really prejudicial to the welfare of his associates. Society is just, it is good, it is worthy our reverence, when it procures for all its members, their physical wants, when it affords them protection, when it secures their liberty, when it puts them in possession of their natural rights. It is ill this that consists all the happiness of which the social compact is susceptible: society is unjust, it is bad, it is unworthy our esteem, when it is partial to a few, when it is cruel to the greater number: it is then that it multiplies its enemies, obliges them to revenge themselves by criminal actions which it is under the necessity to punish. It is not upon the caprices of political society that depend the true notions of justice and injustice—the right ideas of moral good and evil—a just appreciation of merit and demerit; it is upon *utility*, upon the necessity of things, which always forces man to feel that there exists a mode of acting on which he implicitly relies, which he is obliged to venerate, which he cannot help approving either in his fellows, in himself, or in society: whilst there is another mode to which he cannot lend his confidence, which his nature makes him to hate, which his feelings compel him to condemn. It is upon his own peculiar essence that man founds his ideas of pleasure and of pain—of right and of wrong—of vice and of virtue: the only difference between these is, that pleasure and pain make them instantaneously felt in his brain; he becomes conscious of their existence upon the spot; in the place of which, the advantages that accrue to him from justice, the benefit that he derives from virtue, frequently do not display themselves but after a long train of reflections—after multiplied experience and complicated attention; which many, either from a defect in their conformation, or from the peculiarity of the circumstances under which they are placed, are prevented from making, or at least from making correctly.

By a necessary consequence of this truism, the system of fatalism, although it has frequently been so accused, does not tend to encourage man in crime, to make remorse vanish from his mind. His propensities are to be ascribed to his nature; the use he makes of his passions depends upon his habits, upon his opinions, upon the ideas he has received in his education; upon the examples held forth by the society in which he lives. These things are what necessarily decide his conduct. Thus, when his temperament renders him susceptible of strong passions, he is violent in his desires, whatever may be his speculations.

Remorse is the painful sentiment excited in him by grief, caused either by the immediate or probable future effect of his indulged passions: if these effects were always useful to him, he would not experience remorse; but, as soon as he is assured that his actions render him hateful, that his passions make him contemptible; or, as soon as he fears he shall be punished in some mode or other, he becomes restless, discontented with himself—he reproaches himself with his own conduct—he feels ashamed—he fears the judgement of those beings whose affection he has learned to esteem—in whose good-will he finds his own comfort deeply interested. His experience proves to him that the wicked man is odious to all those upon whom his actions have any influence: if these actions are concealed at the moment of commission, he knows it very rarely happens they remain so for ever. The smallest reflection convinces him that there is no wicked man who is not ashamed of his own conduct—who is truly contented with himself—who does not envy the condition of the good man—who is not obliged to acknowledge that he has paid very dearly for those advantages he is never able to enjoy, without experiencing the most troublesome sensations, without making the most bitter reproaches against himself; then he feels ashamed, despises himself, hates himself, his conscience becomes alarmed, remorse follows in it train. To be convinced of the truth of this principle it is only requisite to cast our eyes on the extreme precautions that tyrants and villains, who are otherwise sufficiently powerful not to dread the punishment of man, take to prevent exposure;—to what lengths they push their cruelties against some, to what meannesses they stoop to others of those who are able to hold them up to public scorn. Have they not, then, a consciousness of their own iniquities? Do they not know that they are hateful and contemptible? Have they not remorse? Is their condition happy? Persons well brought up acquire these sentiments in their education; which are either strengthened or enfeebled by public opinion, by habit, or by the examples set before them. In a depraved society, remorse either does not exist, or presently disappears; because, in all his actions, it is ever the judgment of his fellow-man that man is obliged necessarily to regard. He never feels either shame or remorse for actions he sees approved, that are practised by the world. Under corrupt governments, venal souls, avaricious being, mercenary individuals, do not blush either at meanness, robbery, or rapine, when it is authorized by example; in licentious nations, no one blushes at adultery except the husband, at whose expence it is committed; in superstitious countries, man does not blush to assassinate his fellow for his opinions. It will be obvious, therefore, that his remorse, as well as the ideas, whether right or wrong, which man has of decency, virtue, justice, &c. are the necessary consequence of his temperament, modified by the society in which he lives: assassins and thieves, when they live only among themselves, have neither shame nor remorse.

Thus, I repeat, all the actions of man are necessary those which are always useful, which constantly contribute to the real, tend to the permanent happiness of his species, are called *virtues*, and are necessarily pleasing to all who experience their influence; at least, if their passions or false opinions do not oblige them to judge in that manner which is but little accordant with the nature of things: each man acts, each individual judges, necessarily, according to his own peculiar mode of existence—after the ideas, whether true or false, which he has formed with regard to his happiness. There are necessary actions which man is obliged to approve; there are others, that, in despite of himself, he is compelled to censure; of which the idea generates shame when his reflection permits him to contemplate them under the same point of view that they are regarded by his associates. The virtuous man and the wicked man act from motives equally necessary: they differ simply in their organization—in the ideas they form to themselves of happiness: we love the one necessarily—we detest the other from the same necessity. The law of his nature, which wills that a sensible being shall constantly labour to preserve himself, has not left to man the power to choose, or the free-agency to prefer pain to pleasure—vice to utility—crime to virtue. It is, then, the essence of man himself that obliges him to discriminate those actions which are advantageous to him, form those which are prejudicial to his interest, from those which are baneful to his felicity.

This distinction subsists even in the most corrupt societies, in which the ideas of virtue, although completely effaced from their conduct, remain the same in their mind. Let us suppose a matt, who had decidedly determined for villainy, who should say to himself—"It is folly to be virtuous in a society that is depraved, in a community that is debauched." Let us suppose also, that he has sufficient address, the unlooked-for good fortune to escape censure or punishment, during a long series of years; I say, that in despite of all these circumstances, apparently so advantageous for himself, such a man has neither been happy nor contented with his own conduct, He has been in continual agonies—ever at war with his own actions—in a state of constant agitation. How much pain, how much anxiety, has he not endured in this perpetual conflict with himself? How many precautions, what excessive labour, what endless solicitude, has he not been compelled to employ in this continued struggle; how many embarrassments, how many cares, has he not experienced in this eternal wrestling with his associates, whose penetration he dreads, whose scorn he fears will follow a true knowledge of his pursuits. Demand of him what he thinks of himself, he will shrink from the question. Approach the bedside of this villain at the moment he is dying; ask him if he would be willing to recommence, at the same price, a life of similar agitation? If he is ingenuous, he will avow that he has tasted neither repose nor happiness; that each crime filled him with inquietude—that reflection prevented him from sleeping—that the world has been to him only one continued scene of alarm—an uninterrupted concatenation of terror—an everlasting, anxiety of mind;—that to live peaceably upon bread and water, appears to him to be a much happier, a more easy condition, than to possess riches, credit, reputation, honours, on the same terms that he has himself acquired them. If this villain, notwithstanding all his success, finds his condition so deplorable, what must be thought of the feelings of those who have neither the same resources nor the same advantages to succeed in their criminal projects.

Thus, the system of necessity is a truth not only founded upon certain experience, but, again, it establishes morals upon an immoveable basis. Far from sapping the foundations of virtue, it points out its necessity; it clearly shows the invariable sentiments it must excite—sentiments so necessary, so strong, so congenial to his existence, that all the prejudices of man—all the vices of his institutions—all the effect of evil example, have never been able entirely to eradicate them from his mind. When he mistakes the advantages of virtue, it ought to be ascribed to the errors that are infused into him—to the irrationality of his institutions: all his wanderings are the fatal consequences of error,—the necessary result of prejudices which have identified themselves with his existence. Let it not, therefore, any longer be imputed to his nature that he has become wicked, but to those baneful opinions which he has imbibed with his mother's milk,—that have rendered him ambitious, avaricious, envious, haughty, arrogant, debauched, intolerant, obstinate, prejudiced, incommodious to his fellows, mischievous to himself. It is education that carries into his system the germ of those vices which necessarily torment him during the whole course of his life.

Fatalism is reproached with discouraging man—with damping the ardour of his soul—with plunging him into apathy—with destroying the bonds that should connect him with society. Its opponents say, "If every thing is necessary, we must let things go on, and not be disturbed by any thing." But does it depend on man to be sensible or not? Is he master of feeling or not feeling pain? If Nature has endowed him with a humane, with a tender soul, is it possible he should not interest himself in a very lively manner, in the welfare of beings whom he knows are necessary to his own peculiar happiness? His feelings are necessary: they depend on his own peculiar nature, cultivated by education. His imagination, prompt to concern itself with the felicity of his race, causes his heart to be oppressed at the sight of those evils his fellow-creature is obliged to endure,—makes his soul tremble in the contemplation of the misery arising from the despotism that crushes him—from the superstition that leads him astray—from the passions that distract him in a state of warfare against his neighbour. Although he knows that death is the fatal, the necessary period to the form of all beings, his soul is not affected in a less lively manner at the loss of a beloved wife,—at the demise of a child calculated to console his old age,—at the final separation from an esteemed friend who had become dear to his heart. Although he is not ignorant that it is the essence of fire to burn, he does not believe he is dispensed from using his utmost efforts to arrest the progress of a conflagration. Although he is intimately convinced that the evils to which he is a witness, are the necessary consequence of primitive errors with which his fellow-citizens are imbued, he feels he ought to display truth to them, if Nature has given him the necessary courage; under the conviction, that if they listen to it, it will, by degrees, become a certain remedy for their sufferings, that it will produce those necessary effects which it is of its essence to operate.

If the speculations of man modify his conduct, if they change his temperament, he ought not to doubt that the system of necessity would have the most advantageous influence over him; not only is it suitable to calm the greater part of his inquietude, but it will also contribute to inspire him with a useful submission, a rational resignation, to the decrees of a destiny with which his too great sensibility frequently causes him to be overwhelmed. This happy apathy, without doubt, would be, desirable to those whose souls, too tender to brook the inequalities of life, frequently render them the deplorable sport of their fate; or whose organs, too weak to make resistance to the buffettings of fortune, incessantly expose them to be dashed in pieces under the rude blows of adversity.

But, of all the important advantages the human race would be enabled to derive from the doctrine of fatalism, if man was to apply it to his conduct, none would be of greater magnitude, none of more happy consequence, none that would more efficaciously corroborate his happiness, than that general indulgence, that universal toleration, that must necessarily spring from the opinion, that *all is necessary*. In consequence, of the adoption of this principle, the fatalist, if he had a sensible soul, would commisserate the prejudices of his fellow-man—would lament over his wanderings—would seek to undeceive him—would try by gentleness to lead him into the right path, without ever irritating himself against his weakness, without ever insulting his misery. Indeed, what right have we to hate or despise man for his opinions? His ignorance, his prejudices, his imbecility, his vices, his passions, his weakness, are they not the inevitable consequence of vicious institutions? Is he not sufficiently punished by the multitude of evils that afflict him on every side? Those despots who crush him with an iron sceptre, are they not continual victims to their own peculiar restlessness—mancipated to their perpetual diffidence—eternal slaves to their suspicions? Is there one wicked individual who enjoys a pure, an unmixed, a real happiness? Do not nations unceasingly suffer from their follies? Are they not the incessant dupes to their prejudices? Is not the ignorance of chiefs, the ill-will they bear to reason, the hatred they have for truth, punished by the imbecility of their citizens, by the ruin of the states they govern? In short, the fatalist would grieve to witness necessity each moment exercising its severe decrees upon mortals who are ignorant of its power, or who feel its castigation, without being willing to acknowledge the hand from whence it proceeds; he will perceive that ignorance is necessary, that credulity is the necessary result of ignorance—that slavery and bondage are necessary consequences of ignorant credulity—that corruption of manners springs necessarily from slavery—that the miseries of society, the unhappiness of its members, are the necessary offspring of this corruption. The fatalist, in consequence, of these ideas, will neither be a gloomy misanthrope, nor a dangerous citizen; he will pardon in his brethren those wanderings, he will forgive them those errors—which their vitiated nature, by a thousand causes, has rendered necessary—he will offer them consolation—he will endeavour to inspire them with courage—he will be sedulous to undeceive them in their idle notions, in their chimerical ideas; but he will never display against them bitterness of soul—he will never show them that rancorous animosity which is more suitable, to make them revolt from his doctrines, than to attract them to reason;—he will not disturb the repose of society—he will not raise the people to insurrection against the sovereign authority; on the contrary, he will feel that the miserable blindness of the great, and the wretched perverseness, the fatal obstinacy of so many conductors of the people, are the necessary consequence of that flattery that is administered to them in their infancy—that feeds their hopes with allusive falsehoods—of the depraved malice of those who surround them—who wickedly corrupt them, that they may profit by their folly—that they may take advantage of their weakness: in short, that these things are the inevitable effect of that profound ignorance of their true interest, in which every thing strives to keep them.

 The fatalist has no right to be vain of his peculiar talents; no privilege to be proud of his virtues; he knows that these qualities are only the consequence of his natural organization, modified by circumstances that have in no wise depended upon himself. He will neither have hatred nor feel contempt for those whom Nature and circumstances have not favoured in a similar manner. It is the fatalist who ought to be humble, who should be modest from principle: is he not obliged to acknowledge, that he possesses nothing that he has not previously received?

In fact, will not every thing conduct to indulgence the fatalist whom experience has convinced of the necessity of things? Will he not see with pain, that it is the essence of a society badly constituted, unwisely governed, enslaved to prejudice, attached to unreasonable customs, submitted to irrational laws, degraded under despotism, corrupted by luxury, inebriated by false opinions, to be filled with trifling members; to be composed of vicious citizens; to be made up of cringing slaves, who are proud of their chains; of ambitious men, without idea of true glory; of misers and prodigals; of fanatics and libertines! Convinced of the necessary connection of things, he will not be surprised to see that the supineness of their chiefs carries discouragement into their country, or that the influence of their governors stirs up bloody wars by which it is depopulated, and causes useless expenditures that impoverish it; that all these excesses united, is the reason why so many nations contain only men wanting happiness, without understanding to attain it; who are devoid of morals, destitute of virtue. In all this he will contemplate nothing more than the necessary action and re-action of physics upon morals, of morals upon physics. In short, all who acknowledge fatality, will remain persuaded that a nation badly governed is a soil very fruitful in venomous reptiles—very abundant in poisonous plants; that these have such a plentiful growth as to crowd each other and choak themselves. It is in a country cultivated by the hands of a Lycurgus, that he will witness the production of intrepid citizens, of noble-minded individuals, of disinterested men, who are strangers to irregular pleasures. In a country cultivated by a Tiberius, he will find nothing but villains with depraved hearts, men with mean contemptible souls, despicable informers, execrable traitors. It is the soil, it is the circumstances in which man finds himself placed, that renders him either a useful object or a prejudicial being: the wise man avoids the one, as he would those dangerous reptiles whose nature it is to sting and communicate their deadly venom; he attaches himself to the other, esteems him, loves him, as he does those delicious fruits with whose rich maturity his palate is pleasantly gratified, with whose cooling juices he finds himself agreeably refreshed: he sees the wicked without anger—he cherishes the good with pleasure—he delights in the bountiful: he knows full well that the tree which is languishing without culture in the arid, sandy desert, that is stunted for want of attention, leafless for want of moisture, that has grown crooked from neglect, become barren from want of loam, whose tender bark is gnawed by rapacious beasts of prey, pierced by innumerable insects, would perhaps have expanded far and wide its verdant boughs from a straight and stately stem, have brought forth delectable fruit, have afforded from its luxuriant foliage under its lambent leaves an umbrageous refreshing retreat from the scorching rays of a meridian sun, have offered beneath its swelling branches, under its matted tufts a shelter from the pitiless storm, it its seed had been fortunately sown in a more fertile soil, placed in a more congenial climate, had experienced the fostering cares of a skilful cultivator.

Let it not then be said, that it is degrading man reduce his functions to a pure mechanism; that it is shamefully to undervalue him, scandalously to abuse him, to compare him to a tree; to an abject vegetation. The philosopher devoid of prejudice does not understand this language, invented by those who are ignorant of what constitutes the true dignity of man. A tree is an object which, in its station, joins the useful with the agreeable; it merits our approbation when it produces sweet and pleasant fruit; when it affords a favourable shade. All machines are precious, when they are truly useful, when they faithfully perform the functions for which they are designed. Yes, I speak it with courage, reiterate it with pleasure, the honest man, when he has talents, when he possesses virtue, is, for the beings of his species, a tree that furnishes them with delicious fruit, that affords them refreshing shelter: the honest man is a machine of which the springs are adapted to fulfil its functions in a manner that must gratify the expectation of all his fellows. No, I should not blush, I should not feel degraded, to be a machine of this sort; and my heart would leap with joy, if I could foresee that the fruit of my reflections would one day be useful to my race, consoling to my fellow-man.

Is not Nature herself a vast machine, of which the human species is but a very feeble spring? I see nothing contemptible either in her or her productions; all the beings who come out of her hands are good, are noble, are sublime, whenever they co-operate to the production of another, to the maintenance of harmony in the sphere where they must act. Of whatever nature the soul may be, whether it is made mortal, or whether it be supposed immortal; whether it is regarded as a spirit, or whether it be looked upon as a portion of the body; it will be found noble, it will be estimated great, it will be ranked good, it will be considered sublime, in a Socrates, in an Aristides, in a Cato: it will be thought abject, it will be viewed as despicable, it will be called corrupt, in a Claudius, in a Sejanus, in a Nero: its energies will be admired, we shall be delighted with its manner, fascinated with its efforts, in a Shakespeare, in a Corneille, in a Newton, in a Montesquieu: its baseness will be lamented, when we behold mean, contemptible men, who flatter tyranny, or who servilely cringe at the foot of superstition.

All that has been said in the course of this work, proves clearly that every thing is necessary; that every thing is always in order, relatively to Nature; where all beings do nothing more than follow the laws that are imposed on their respective classes. It is part of her plan, that certain portions of the earth shall bring forth delicious fruits, shall blossom beauteous flowers; whilst others shall only furnish brambles, shall yield nothing but noxious vegetables: she has been willing that some societies should produce wise men, great heroes; that others should only give birth to abject souls, contemptible men, without energy, destitute of virtue. Passions, winds, tempests, hurricanes, volcanoes, wars, plagues, famines, diseases, death, are as necessary to her eternal march as the beneficent heat of the sun, the serenity of the atmosphere, the gentle showers of spring, plentiful years, peace, health, harmony, life: vice and virtue, darkness and light, and science are equally necessary; the one are not benefits, the other are not evils, except for those beings whose happiness they influence by either favouring or deranging their peculiar mode of existence. *The whole cannot be miserable, but it may contain unhappy individuals.*

Nature, then, distributes with the same hand that which is called *order*, and that which is called *disorder*; that which is called *pleasure*, and that which is called *pain*: in short, she diffuses by the necessity of her existence, good and evil in the world we inhabit. Let not man, therefore, either arraign her bounty, or tax her with malice; let him not imagine that his feeble cries, his weak supplications, can never arrest her colossal power, always acting after immutable laws; let him submit silently to his condition; and when he suffers, let him not seek a remedy by recurring to chimeras that his own distempered imagination has created; let him draw from the stores of Nature herself, the remedies which she offers for the evil she brings upon him: if she sends him diseases, let him search in her bosom for those salutary productions to which she has given birth, which will cure them: if she gives him errors, she also furnishes him with experience to counteract them; in truth, she supplies him with an antidote suitable to destroy their fatal effects. If she permits man to groan under the pressure of his vices, beneath the load of his follies, she also shews him in virtue, a sure remedy for his infirmities: if the evils that some societies experience are necessary, when they shall have become too incommodious they will be irresistibly obliged to search for those remedies which Nature will always point out to them. If this Nature has rendered existence insupportable, to some unfortunate beings, whom she appears to have selected for her victims, still death, is a door that will surely be opened to them—that will deliver them from their misfortunes, although in their puny, imbecile, wayward judgment, they may be deemed impossible of cure.

Let not man, then, accuse Nature with being inexorable to him, since there does not exist in her whole circle an evil for which she has not furnished the remedy, to those who have the courage to seek it, who have the fortitude to apply it. Nature follows general and necessary laws in all her operations; physical calamity and moral evil are not to be ascribed to her want of kindness, but to the necessity of things. Physical calamity is the derangement produced in man's organs by physical causes which he sees act: moral evil is the derangement produced in him by physical causes of which the action is to him a secret. These causes always terminate by producing sensible effects, which are capable of striking his senses; neither the thoughts nor the will of man ever shew themselves, but by the marked effects they produce either in himself or upon those beings whom Nature has rendered susceptible of feeling their impulse. He suffers, because it is of the essence of some beings to derange the economy of his machine; he enjoys, because the properties of some beings are analogous to his own mode of existence; he is born, because it is of the nature of some matter to combine itself under a determinate form; he lives, he acts, he thinks, because it is of the essence of certain combinations to maintain themselves in existence by given means for a season; at length he dies, because a necessary law prescribes that all the combinations which are formed, shall either be destroyed or dissolve themselves. From all this it results, that Nature is impartial to all its productions; she submits man, like all other beings, to those eternal laws from which she has not even exempted herself; if she was to suspend these laws, even for an instant, from that moment disorder would reign in her, system; her harmony would be disturbed.

Those who wish to study Nature, must take experience for their guide; this, and this only, can enable them to dive into her secrets, to unravel by degrees, the frequently imperceptible woof of those slender causes, of which she avails herself to operate the greatest phenomena: by the aid of experience, man often discovers in her properties, perceives modes of action entirely unknown to the ages which have preceded him; those effects which his grandfathers contemplated as marvellous, which they regarded as supernatural efforts, looked upon as miracles, have become familiar to him in the present day, and are at this moment contemplated as simple and natural consequences, of which he comprehends the mechanism—of which he understands the cause—of which he can unfold the manner of action. Man, in fathoming Nature, has arrived at discovering the true causes of earthquakes; of the periodical motion of the sea; of subterraneous conflagrations; of meteors; of the electrical fluid, the whole of which were considered by his ancestors, and are still so by the ignorant, by the uninformed, as indubitable signs of heaven's wrath. His posterity, in following up, in rectifying the experience already made, will perhaps go further, and discover those causes which are totally veiled from present eyes. The united efforts of the human species will one day perhaps penetrate even into the sanctuary of Nature, and throw into light many of those mysteries which up to the present time she seems to have refused to all his researches.

In contemplating man under his true aspect; in quitting authority to follow experience; in laying aside error to consult reason; in submitting every thing to physical laws, from which his imagination has vainly exerted its utmost power to withdraw them; it will be found that the phenomena of the moral world follow exactly the same general rules as those of the physical; that the greater part of those astonishing effects, which ignorance, aided by his prejudices, make him consider as inexplicable, and regard as wonderful, are natural consequences flowing from simple causes. He will find that the eruption of a volcano and the birth of a Tamerlane are to Nature the same thing; in recurring to the primitive causes of those striking events which he beholds with consternation, which he contemplates with fearful alarm, in falling back to the sources of those terrible revolutions, those frightful convulsions, those dreadful explosions that distract mankind, lay waste the fairest works of Nature, ravage nations, and tear up society by the roots; he will find the wills that compassed the most surprising changes, that operated the most extensive alterations in the state of things, that brought about the most unlooked-for events, were moved by physical causes, whose exility made him treat them as contemptible; whose want of consequence in his own purblind eyes led him to believe them utterly incapable to give birth to the phenomena whose magnitude strikes him with such awe, whose stupendous range fills him with such amazement.

If man was to judge of causes by their effects, there would be no small causes in the universe. In a Nature where every thing is connected, where every thing acts and re-acts, moves and changes, composes and decomposes, forms and destroys, there is not an atom which does not play an important part—that does not occupy a necessary station; there is not an imperceptible particle, however minute, which, placed in convenient circumstances, does not operate the most prodigious effects. If man was in a capacity to follow the eternal chain, to pursue the concatenated links, that connect with their causes all the effects he witnesses, without losing sight of any one of its rings,—if he could unravel the ends of those insensible threads that give impulse to the thoughts, decision to the will, direction to the passions of those men who are called mighty, according to their actions, he would find, they are true atoms which Nature employs to move the moral world; that it is the unexpected but necessary function of these indiscernible particles of matter, it is their aggregation, their combination, their proportion, their fermentation, which modifying the individual by degrees, in despite of himself, frequently without his own knowledge, make him think, will, and act, in a determinate, but necessary mode. If, then, the will and the actions of this individual have an influence over a great number of other men, here is the moral world in a state of the greatest combustion, and those consequences ensue which man contemplates with fearful wonder. Too much acrimony in the bile of a fanatic—blood too much inflamed in the heart of a conqueror—a painful indigestion in the stomach of a monarch—a whim that passes in the mind of a woman—are sometimes causes sufficient to bring on war—to send millions of men to the slaughter—to root out an entire people—to overthrow walls—to reduce cities into ashes—to plunge nations into slavery—to put a whole people into mourning—to breed famine in a land—to engender pestilence—to propagate calamity—to extend misery—to spread desolation far and wide upon the surface of our globe, through a long series of ages.

The dominant passion of an individual of the human species, when it disposes of the passions of many others, arrives at combining their will, at uniting their efforts, and thus decides the condition of man. It is after this manner that an ambitious, crafty, and voluptuous Arab, gave to his countrymen an impulse of which the effect was the subjugation and desolation of vast countries in Asia, in Africa, and in Europe; whose consequences were sufficiently potential to erect a new, extensive, but slavish empire; to give a novel system of religion to millions of human beings; to overturn the altars of their former gods; in short, to alter the opinions, to change the customs of a considerable portion of the population of the earth. But in examining the primitive sources of this strange revolution, what were the concealed causes that had an influence over this man—that excited his peculiar passions, and modified his temperament? What was the matter from the combination of which resulted a crafty, ambitious, enthusiastic, and eloquent man; in short, a personage competent to impose on his fellow-creatures—capable of making them concur in his most extravagant views. They were, undoubtedly, the insensible particles of his blood; the imperceptible texture of his fibres; the salts, more or less acrid, that stimulated his nerves; the proportion of igneous fluid that circulated in his system. From whence came these elements? It was from the womb of his mother; from the aliments which nourished him; from the climate in which he had his birth; from the ideas he received; from the air which he respired; without reckoning a thousand inappreciable, a thousand transitory causes, that in the instance given had modified, had determined the passions of this important being, who had thereby acquired the capacity to change the face of this mundane sphere.

To causes so weak in their principles, if in the origin the slightest obstacle had been opposed, these wonderful events, which have astounded man, would never have been produced. The fit of an ague, the consequence of bile a little too much inflamed, had sufficed, perhaps, to have rendered abortive all the vast projects, of the legislator of the Mussulmen. Spare diet, a glass of water, a sanguinary evacuation, would sometimes have been sufficient to have saved kingdoms.

It will be seen, then, that the condition of the human species, as well as that of each of its individuals, every instant depends on insensible causes, to which circumstances, frequently fugitive, give birth; that opportunity developes, that convenience puts in action: man attributes their effects to chance, whilst these causes operate necessarily, act according to fixed rules: he has frequently neither the sagacity nor the honesty to recur to their true principles; he regards such feeble motives with contempt, because he has been taught to consider them as incapable of producing such stupendous events. They are, however, these motives, weak as they may appear to be, these springs, so pitiful in his eyes, is which according to her necessary laws, suffice in the hands of Nature to move the universe. The conquests of a Gengis-Khan have nothing in them that is more strange to the eye of a philosopher than the explosion of a mine, caused in its principle by a feeble spark, which commences with setting fire to a single grain of powder; this presently communicates itself to many millions of other contiguous grains, of which the united force, the multiplied powers, terminate by blowing up mountains, overthrowing fortifications, or converting populous, well-built cities, into heaps of ruins.

Thus, imperceptible causes, concealed in the bosom of Nature, until the moment their action is displayed, frequently decide the fate of man. The happiness or the wretchedness, the prosperity or the misery of each individual, as well as that of whole nations, are attached to powers which it is impossible for him to foresee, which he cannot appreciate, of which he is incapable to arrest the action. Perhaps at this moment atoms are amassing, insensible particles are combining, of which the assemblage shall form a sovereign, who will be either the scourge or the saviour of a mighty empire. Man cannot answer for his own destiny one single instant; he has no cognizance of what is passing within himself; he is ignorant of the causes which act in the interior of his machine; he knows nothing of the circumstances that will give them activity: he is unacquainted with what may develope their energy; it is, nevertheless, on these causes, impossible to be unravelled by him, that depends his condition in life. Frequently, an unforeseen rencontre gives birth to a passion in his soul, of which the consequences shall, necessarily, have an influence over his felicity. It is thus that the most virtuous man, by a whimsical combination of unlooked-for circumstances, may become in an instant the most criminal of his species.

This truth, without doubt, will be found frightful—this fact will unquestionably appear terrible: but at bottom, what has it more revolting than that which teaches him that an infinity of accidents, as irremediable as they are unforeseen, may every instant wrest from him that life to which he is so strongly attached? Fatalism reconciles the good man easily to death: it makes him contemplate it as a certain means of withdrawing himself from wickedness; this system shews death, even to the happy man himself, as a medium between him and those misfortunes which frequently terminate by poisoning his happiness; that end with embittering the most fortunate existence.

Let man, then, submit to necessity: in despite of himself it will always hurry him forward: let him resign himself to Nature, let him accept the good with which she presents him: let him oppose to the necessary evil which she makes him experience, those necessary remedies which she consents to afford him; let him not disturb his mind with useless inquietude; let him enjoy with moderation, because he will find that pain is the necessary companion of excess: let him follow the paths of virtue, because every thing will prove to him, even in this world of perverseness, that it is absolutely necessary to render him estimable in the eyes of others, to make him contented with himself.

Feeble, vain mortal, thou pretendest to be a free agent. Alas! dost thou not see all the threads which enchain thee? Dost thou not perceive that they are atoms which form thee; that they are atoms which move thee; that they are circumstances independent of thyself, that modify thy being; that they are circumstances over which thou hast not any controul, that rule thy destiny? In the puissant Nature that environs thee, shalt thou pretend to be the only being who is able to resist her power? Dost thou really believe that thy weak prayers will induce her to stop in her eternal march; that thy sickly desires can oblige her to change her everlasting course?

CHAP. XIII.

Of the Immortality of the Soul;—of the Doctrine of a future State;—of the Fear of Death.

The reflections presented to the reader in this work, tend to shew what ought to be thought of the human soul, as well as of its operations and faculties: every thing proves, in the most convincing manner, that it acts, that it moves according to laws similar to those prescribed to the other beings of Nature; that it cannot be distinguished from the body; that it is born with it; that it grows up with it; that it is modified in the same progression; in short, every thing ought to make man conclude that it perishes with it. This soul, as well as the body, passes through a state of weakness and infancy; it is in this stage of its existence, that it is assailed by a multitude of modifications; that it is stored with an infinity of ideas, which it receives from exterior objects through the medium of the organs; that it amasses facts, that it collects experience, whether true or false, that it forms to itself a system of conduct, according to which it thinks, in conformity with which it acts, from whence results either its happiness or its misery, its reason or its delirium, its virtues or its vices; arrived with the body at its full powers, having in conjunction with it reached maturity, it does not cease for a single instant to partake in common of its sensations, whether these are agreeable or disagreeable; it participates in all its pleasures; it shares in all its pains; in consequence it conjointly approves or disapproves its state; like it, it is either sound or diseased; active or languishing; awake or asleep. In old age man extinguishes entirely, his fibres become rigid, his nerves loose their elasticity, his senses are obtunded, his sight grows dim, his ears lose their quickness, his ideas become unconnected, his memory fails, his imagination cools: what then becomes of his soul? Alas! it sinks down with the body; it gets benumbed as this loses its feeling; becomes sluggish as this decays in activity; like it, when enfeebled by years it fulfils its functions with pain; this substance, which is deemed spiritual, which is considered immaterial, which it is endeavoured to distinguish from matter, undergoes the same revolutions, experiences the same vicissitudes, submits to the same modifications, as does the body itself.

In despite of this proof of the materiality of the soul, of its identity with the body, so convincing to the unprejudiced, some thinkers have supposed, that although the latter is perishable, the former does not perish: that this portion of man enjoys the especial privilege of *immortality*; that it is exempt from dissolution: free from those changes of form all the beings in Nature undergo: in consequence of this, man has persuaded himself, that this privileged soul does not die: its immortality, above all, appears indubitable to those who suppose it spiritual: after having made it a simple being, without extent, devoid of parts, totally different from any thing of which he has a knowledge, he pretended that it was not subjected to the laws of decomposition common to all beings, of which experience shews him the continual operation.

Man, feeling within himself a concealed force, that insensibly produced action, that imperceptibly gave direction to the motion of his machine, believed that the entire of Nature, of whose energies he is ignorant, with whose modes of acting he is unacquainted, owed its motion to an agent analogous to his own soul; who acted upon the great macrocosm, in the same manner that this soul acted upon his body. Man, having supposed himself double, made Nature double also: he distinguished her from her own peculiar energy; he separated her from her mover, which by degrees he made spiritual. Thus Nature, distinguished from herself, was regarded as the soul of the world; and the soul of man was considered as opinions emanating from this universal soul. This notion upon the origin of the soul is of very remote antiquity. It was that of the Egyptians, of the Chaldeans, of the Hebrews, of the greater number of the *wise men of the east.* It should appear that Moses believed with the Egyptians the divine emanation of souls: according to him, *"God formed man of the dust of the ground, and breathed into his nostrils the breath of life; and man became a living soul:"* nevertheless, the Catholic, at this day, rejects this system of *divine emanation,* seeing that it supposes the Divinity divisible: which would have, been inconvenient to the Romish idea of purgatory, or to the system of everlasting punishment. Although Moses, in the above quotation, seems to indicate that the soul was a portion of the Divinity, it does not appear that the doctrine of the *immortality of the soul* was established in any one of the books attributed to him. It was during the Babylonish captivity, that the Jews learned the doctrine of future rewards and punishments, taught by Zoroaster to the Persians, but which the Hebrew legislator did not understand, or, at least, he left his people ignorant on the subject. It was in those schools, that Pherecydes, Pythagoras, and Plato, drew up a doctrine so flattering to the vanity of human nature—so gratifying to the imagination of mortals. Man thus believed himself a portion of the Divinity; immortal, like the Godhead, in one part of himself: nevertheless, subsequent religions have renounced these advantages, which they judged incompatible with the other parts of their systems; they held forth that the Sovereign of Nature, or her contriver was not the soul of man, but, that, in virtue of his omnipotence, he created human souls, in proportion as he produced the bodies which they must animate; and they taught, that these souls once produced, by an effect of the same omnipotence, enjoyed immortality.

However it may be with these variations upon the origin of souls, those who supposed them emanating from the Divinity, believed that after the death of the body, which served them for an envelope, they returned, by refunding to their first source. Those who, without adopting the opinion of divine emanation, admired the spirituality, believed the immortality of the soul, were under the necessity to suppose a region, to find out an abode for these souls, which their imagination painted to them, each according to his fears, his hopes, his desires, and his prejudices.

Nothing is more popular than the doctrine of the *immortality of the soul;* nothing is more universally diffused than the expectation of another life. Nature having inspired man with the most ardent love for his existence, the desire of preserving himself for ever was a necessary consequence; this desire was presently converted into certainty: from that desire of existing eternally which Nature has implanted in him, he made an argument, to prove that man would never cease to exist. Abady says, "our soul has no useless desires, it naturally desires an eternal life;" and by a very strange logic, he concludes that this desire could not fail to be fulfilled. Cicero, before Abady, had declared the immortality of the soul to be an innate idea in man; yet, strange to tell, in another part of his works he considers Pherecydes as the inventor of the doctrine. However this may be, man, thus disposed, listened with avidity to those who announced to him systems so conformable to his wishes. Nevertheless, he ought not to regard as supernatural the desire of existing, which always was, and always will be, of the essence man; it ought not to excite surprise, if he received with eagerness an hypothesis that flattered his hopes, by promising that his desire would one day be gratified; but let him beware how he concludes that this desire itself is an indubitable proof of the reality of this future life, with which at present he seems to be so much occupied. The passion for existence is in man only a natural consequence of the tendency of a sensible being, whose essence it is to be willing to conserve himself: in the human being it follows the energy of his soul—keeps pace with the force of his imagination—always ready to realize that which he strongly desires. He desires the life of the body, nevertheless this desire is frustrated; wherefore should not the desire for the life of the soul be frustrated like the other? The partizans of the doctrine of the immortality of the soul reason thus: "All men desire to live for ever, therefore they will live for ever." Suppose the argument retorted on them; would it be believed? If it was asserted, "All men naturally desire to be rich; therefore all men will one day be rich," how many partizans would this doctrine find?

The most simple reflection upon the nature of his soul, ought to convince man that the idea of its immortality is only an illusion of the brain. Indeed what is his soul, save the principle of sensibility? What is it, to think, to enjoy, to suffer; is it not to feel? What is life, except it be the assemblage of modifications, the congregation of motion, peculiar to an organized being? Thus, as soon as the body ceases to live, its sensibility can no longer exercise itself; when its sensibility is no more, it can no longer have ideas, nor in consequence thoughts. Ideas, as we have proved, can only reach man through his senses; now, how will they have it, that once deprived of his senses, he is yet capable of receiving sensations, of having perceptions, of forming ideas? As they have made the soul of man a being separated from the animated body, wherefore have they not made life a being distinguished from the living body? Life in a body is the totality of this motion; feeling and thought make a part of this motion: thus it is reasonable to suppose, that in the dead man these motions will cease, like all the others.

Indeed, by what reasoning will it be proved, that this soul, which cannot feel, think, will, or act, but by aid of man's organs, can suffer pain, be susceptible of pleasure, or even have a consciousness of its own existence, when the organs which should warn it of their presence are decomposed or destroyed? Is it not evident, that the soul depends on the arrangement of the various parts of the body; on the order with which these parts conspire to perform their functions; on the combined motion of the whole? Thus the organic structure once destroyed, can it be reasonably doubted the soul will be destroyed also? Is it not seen, that during the whole course of human life this soul is stimulated, changed, deranged, disturbed, by all the changes man's organs experience? And yet it will be insisted, that this soul acts, thinks, subsists, when these same organs have entirely disappeared!

An organized being may be compared to a clock, which once broken, is no longer suitable to the use for which it was designed. To say, that the soul shall feel, shall think, shall enjoy, shall suffer after the death of the body; is to pretend that a clock, shivered into a thousand pieces, will continue to strike the hour; shall yet have the faculty of marking the progress of time. Those who say, that the soul of man is able to subsist, notwithstanding the destruction of the body, evidently support the position, that the modification of a body will be enabled to conserve itself after the subject is destroyed: this on any other occasion would be considered as completely absurd.

It will be said that the conservation of the soul after the death of the body, is an effect of the Divine Omnipotence: but this is supporting an absurdity by a gratuitous hypothesis. It surely is not meant by Divine Omnipotence, of whatever nature it may be supposed, that a thing shall exist and not exist at the same time: unless this be granted, it will be rather difficult to prove, that a soul shall feel and think without the intermediates necessary to thought.

Let them then, at least, forbear asserting, that reason is not wounded by the doctrine of the immortality of the soul; or by the expectation of a future life. These notions, formed to flatter man, to disturb the imagination of the uninformed, who do not reason, cannot appear either convincing or probable to enlightened minds. Reason, exempted from the illusions of prejudice, is, without doubt, wounded by the supposition of a soul, that feels, that thinks, that is afflicted, that rejoices, that has ideas, without having organs; that is to say, destitute of the only known medium, wanting all the natural means, by which, according to what we can understand, it is possible for it to feel sensations, have perceptions, or form ideas. If it be replied, other means are able to exist, which are *supernatural* or *unknown*, it may be answered, that these means of transmitting ideas to the soul, separated from the body, are not better known to, or more within the reach of, those who suppose it, that they are of other men. It is, at least, very certain, it cannot admit even of a controversy, that all those who reject the system of innate ideas, cannot, without contradicting their own principles, admit the doctrine of the immortality of the soul.

In defiance of the consolation that so many persons pretend to find in the notion of an eternal existence; in despite of that firm persuasion which such numbers of men assure us they have, that their souls will survive their bodies, they seem so very much alarmed at the dissolution of this body, that they do not contemplate their end, which they ought to desire as the period of so many miseries, but with the greatest inquietude; so true it is, that the real, the present, even accompanied with pain, has much more influence over mankind, than the most beautiful chimeras of the future; which he never views but through the clouds of uncertainty. Indeed the most religious men, notwithstanding the conviction they express of a blessed eternity, do not find these flattering hopes sufficiently consoling to repress their fears; to prevent their trembling, when they think on the necessary dissolution of their bodies. Death was always, for mortals, the most frightful point of view; they regard it as a strange phenomenon, contrary to the order of things, opposed to Nature; in a word, as an effect of the celestial vengeance, as the *wages of sin*. Although every thing proves to man that death is inevitable, he is never able to familiarize himself with its idea; he never thinks on it without shuddering; the assurance of possessing an immortal soul but feebly indemnifies him for the grief he feels in the deprivation of his perishable body. Two causes contribute to strengthen his fears, to nourish his alarm; the one is, that this death, commonly accompanied with pain, wrests from him an existence that pleases him— with which he is acquainted—to which he is accustomed; the other is the uncertainty of the state that must succeed his actual existence.

The illustrious Bacon has said, that "men fear death for the same reason that children dread being alone in darkness." Man naturally challenges every thing with which he is unacquainted; he is desirous to see clearly to the end, that he may guarantee himself against those objects which may menace his safety; that he may also be enabled to procure for himself those which may be useful to him; the man who exists cannot form to himself any idea of non-existence; as this circumstance disturbs him, for want of experience, his imagination sets to work; this points out to him, either well or ill, this uncertain state: accustomed to think, to feel, to be stimulated into activity, to enjoy society, he contemplates as the greatest misfortune, a dissolution that will strip him of these objects, that will deprive him of those sensations which his present nature has rendered necessary to him; he views with dismay a situation that will prevent his being warned of his own existence—that shall bereave him of his pleasures—to plunge him into nothing. In supposing it even exempt from pain, he always looks upon this nothing as an afflicting solitude—as an heap of profound darkness; he sees himself in a state of general desolation; destitute of all assistance; and he feels keenly all the rigour of this frightful situation. But does not a profound sleep help to give him a true idea of this nothing? Does not that deprive him of every thing? Does it not appear to annihilate the universe to him, and him to the universe? Is death any thing more than a profound, a permanent steep? It is for want of being able to form an idea of death that man dreads it; if he could figure to himself a true image of this state of annihilation, he would from thence cease to fear it; but he is not able to conceive a state in which there is no feeling; he therefore believes, that when he shall no longer exist, he will have the same feelings, the same consciousness of things, which, during his existence, appear so sad to his mind; which his fancy paints in such gloomy colours. Imagination pictures to him his funeral pomp—the grave they are digging for him—the lamentations that will accompany him to his last abode-the epicedium that surviving friendship may dictate; he persuades himself that these melancholy objects will affect him as painfully even after his decease, as they do in his present condition, in which he is in full possession of his senses.

Mortal, led astray by fear! after thy death thine eyes will see no more; thine ears will hear no longer; in the depth of thy grave thou wilt no more be witness to this scene, which thine imagination, at present, represents to thee under such dismal colours; thou wilt no longer take part in what shall be done in the world; thou wilt no more be occupied with what may befal thine inanimate remains, than thou wast able to be the day previous to that which ranked thee among the beings of thy species. To die is to cease to think; to lack feeling; no longer to enjoy; to find a period to suffering; thine ideas will perish with thee; thy sorrows will not follow thee to the silent tomb. Think of death, not to feed thy fears—not to nourish thy melancholy—but to accustom thyself to look upon it with a peaceable eye; to cheer thee up against those false terrors with which the enemies to thy repose labour to inspire thee! The fears of death are vain illusions, that must disappear as soon as we learn to contemplate this necessary event under its true point of view. A great man has defined philosophy to be *a meditation on death;* he is not desirous by that to have it understood that man ought to occupy himself sorrowfully with his end, with a view to nourish his fears; on the contrary, he wishes to invite him to familiarize himself with an object that Nature has rendered necessary to him; to accustom himself to expect it with a serene countenance. If life is a benefit, if it be necessary to love it, it is no less necessary to quit it; reason ought to teach him a calm resignation to the decrees of fate: his welfare exacts that he should contract the habit of contemplating with placidity, of viewing without alarm, an event that his essence has rendered inevitable: his interest demands that he should not brood gloomily over his misfortune; that he should not, by continual dread, embitter his life; the charms of which he must inevitably destroy, if he can never view its termination but with trepidation. Reason and his interest then, concur to assure him against those vague terrors with which his imagination inspires him, in this respect. If he was to call them to his assistance, they would reconcile him to an object that only startles him, because he has no knowledge of it; because it is only shewn to him with those hideous accompaniments with which it is clothed by superstition. Let him then, endeavour to despoil death of these vain illusions, and he will perceive that it is only the sleep of life; that this sleep will not be disturbed with disagreeable dreams; that an unpleasant awakening is never likely to follow it. To die is to sleep; it is to enter into that state of insensibility in which he was previous to his birth; before he had senses; before he was conscious of his actual existence. Laws, as necessary as those which gave him birth, will make him return into the bosom of Nature, from whence he was drawn, in order to reproduce him afterwards under some new form, which it would be useless for him to know: without consulting him, Nature places him for a season in the order of organized beings; without his consent, she will oblige him to quit it, to occupy some other order.

Let him not complain then, that Nature is callous; she only makes him undergo a law from which she does not exempt any one being she contains. Man complains of the short duration of life—of the rapidity with which time flies away; yet the greater number of men do not know how to employ either time or life. If all are born and perish—if every thing is changed and destroyed—if the birth of a being is never more than the first step towards its end; how is it possible to expect that man, whose machine is so frail, of which the parts are so complicated, the whole of which possesses such extreme mobility, should be exempted from the common law; which decrees, that even the solid earth he inhabits shall experience change—shall undergo alteration—perhaps be destroyed! Feeble, frail mortal! Thou pretendest to exist for ever; whit thou, then, that for thee alone eternal Nature shall change her undeviating course? Dost thou not behold in those eccentric comets with which thine eyes are sometimes astonished, that the planets themselves are subject to death? Live then in peace for the season that Nature permits thee; if thy mind be enlightened by reason thou wilt die without terror!

Notwithstanding the simplicity of these reflections; nothing is more rare than the sight of men truly fortified against the fears of death: the wise man himself turns pale at its approach; he has occasion to collect the whole force of his mind, to expect it with serenity. It cannot then, furnish matter for surprise, if the idea of death is so revolting to the generality of mortals; it terrifies the young—it redoubles the chagrin of the middle-aged—it even augments the sorrow of the old, who are worn down with infirmity: indeed the aged, although enfeebled by time, dread it much more than the young, who are in the full vigour of life; the man of many lustres is more accustomed to live years as they roll over his head, confirm his attachment to existence; nevertheless, long unwearied exertions weaken the powers of his mind; labour, sickness, and pain, waste his animal strength; he has less energy; his volition becomes faint, superstitious terrors easily appal him; at length disease consumes him; sometimes with excruciating tortures: the unhappy wretch, thus plunged into misfortune, has, notwithstanding, scarcely ever dared to contemplate death; which he ought to consider as the period to all his anguish.

If the source of this pusillanimity be sought, it will be found in his nature, which attaches him to life; in that deficiency of energy in his soul, which hardly any thing tends to corroborate, but which every thing strives to enfeeble: which superstition, instead of strengthening, contributes to bruise. Almost all human institutions, nearly all the opinions of man, conspire to augment his fears; to render his ideas of death more terrible; to make them more revolting to his feelings. Indeed, superstition pleases itself with exhibiting death under the most frightful traits: it represents it to man under the most disgusting colours; as a dreadful moment, which not only puts an end to his pleasures, but gives him up without defence to the strange rigour of a pitiless decree, which nothing can soften. According to this superstition, the most virtuous man has reason to tremble for the severity of his fate; is never certain of being happy; the most dreadful torments, endless punishments, await the victim to involuntary weakness; to the necessary faults of a short-lived existence; his infirmities, his momentary offences, the propensities that have been planted in his heart, the errors of his mind, the opinions he has imbibed, even in the society in which he was born without his own consent, the ideas he has formed, the passions he has indulged above all, his not being able to comprehend all the extravagant dogmas offered to his acceptance, are to be implacably avenged with the most severe and never-ending penalties. Ixion is for ever fastened to his wheel; Sisyphus must to all eternity roll his stone without ever being able to reach the apex of his mountain; the vulture must perpetually prey on the liver of the unfortunate Prometheus: those who dare to think for themselves—those who have refused to listen to their enthusiastic guides—those who have not reverenced the oracles—those who have had the audacity to consult their reason—those who have boldly ventured to detect impostors—those who have doubted the divine mission of the Phythonissa—those who believe that Jupiter violated decency in his visit to Danae—those who look upon Apollo as no better than a strolling musician—those who think that Mahomet was an arch knave—are to smart everlastingly in flaming oceans of burning sulpher; are to float to all eternity in the most excruciating agonies on seas of liquid brimstone, wailing and gnashing their teeth: what wonder, then, if man dreads to be cast into these hideous gulfs; if his mind loathes the horrific picture; if he wishes to defer for a season these dreadful punishments; if he clings to an existence, painful as it may be, rather than encounter such revolting cruelties.

Such, then, are the afflicting objects with which superstition occupies its unhappy, its credulous disciples; such are the fears which the tyrant of human thoughts points out to them as salutary. In defiance Of the exility of the effect which these notions produce oil the greater number, even of those who say they are, or who believe themselves persuaded, they are held forth as the most powerful rampart that can be opposed to the irregularities of man. Nevertheless, as will be seen presently, it will be found that these systems, or rather these chimeras, so terrible to behold, operate little or nothing on the larger portion of mankind, who dream of them but seldom, never in the moment that passion, interest, pleasure, or example, hurries them along. If these fears act, it is commonly on those, who have but little occasion to abstain from evil; they make honest hearts tremble, but fail of effect on the perverse. They torment sensible souls, but leave those that are hardened in repose; they disturb tractable, gentle minds, but cause no trouble to rebellious spirits: thus they alarm none but those who are already sufficiently alarmed; they coerce only those who are already restrained.

These notions, then, impress nothing on the wicked; when by accident they do act on them, it is only to redouble the wickedness of their natural character—to justify them in their own eyes—to furnish them with pretexts to exercise it without fear—to follow it without scruple. Indeed, the experience of a great number of ages has shewn to what excess of wickedness, to what lengths, the passions of man have carried him, when they have been authorized by the priesthood—when they have been unchained by superstition—or, at least, when he has been enabled to cover himself with its mantle. Man has never been more ambitious, never more covetous, never more crafty, never more cruel, never more seditious, than when he has persuaded himself that superstition permitted or commanded him to be so: thus, superstition did nothing more than lend an invincible force to his natural passions, which under its sacred auspices he could exercise with impunity, indulge without remorse; still more, the greatest villains, in giving free vent to the detestable propensities of their natural wickedness, have under its influence believed, that, by displaying an over-heated zeal, they merited well of heaven; that they exempted themselves by new crimes, from that chastisement which they thought their anterior conduct had richly merited.

These, then, are the effects which what are called the *salutary* notions of superstition, produce on mortals. These reflections will furnish an answer to those who say that, "If heaven was promised equally to the wicked as to the righteous, there would be found none incredulous of another life." We reply, that, in point of fact, superstition does accord heaven to the wicked, since it frequently places in this happy abode the most useless, the most depraved of men. Is not Mahomet himself enthroned in the empyrean by this superstition? If the calendar of the Romish saints was examined, would it be found to contain none but righteous, none but good men? Does not Mahometanism cut off from all chance of future existence, consequently from all hope of reaching heaven, the female part of mankind? Have the Jews exalted no one to the celestial regions, save the virtuous? When the Jew is condemned to the devouring flames, do not the men who thus torture an unhappy wretch, whose only crime is adherence to the religion of his forefathers, expect to be rewarded for the deed with everlasting happiness? Are they not promised eternal salvation for their orthodoxy? Was Constantine, was St. Cyril, was St. Athanasius, was St. Dominic, worthy beatification? Were Jupiter, Thor, Mercury, Woden, and a thousand others, deserving of celestial diadems? Is erring, feeble man, with all his imbecilities, competent to form a judgment of the heavenly deserts of his fellows? Can be, with his dim optics, with his limited vision, fathom the human heart? Can he sound its depths, trace its meanderings, dive into its recesses, with sufficient precision, to determine who amongst his race is or is not possessed of the requisite merit to enjoy a blessed eternity? Thus wicked men are held up as models by superstition, which as we shall see, sharpens the passions of evil-disposed men, by legitimating those crimes, at which, without this sanction, they would shudder; which they would fear to commit; or for which, at least, they would feel shame; for which they would experience remorse. In short, the ministers of superstition furnish to the most profligate men the power of indulging their inflamed passions, and then hold forth to them means of diverting from their own heads the thunderbolt that should strike their crimes, by spreading before them fresh incentives to intolerant persecution, with the promise of a never-fading happiness.

With respect to the incredulous, without doubt, there may be amongst them wicked men, as well as amongst the most credulous; but incredulity no more supposes wickedness, than credulity supposes righteousness. On the contrary, the man who thinks, who meditates, knows far better the true motives to goodness, than he who suffers himself to be blindly guided by uncertain motives, or by the interest of others. Sensible men have the greatest advantage in examining opinions, which it is pretended must have an influence over their eternal happiness: if these are found false, if they appear injurious to their present life, they will not therefore conclude, that they have not another life either to fear or to hope; that they are permitted to deliver themselves up with impunity to vice, which would do an injury to themselves, that would draw upon them the contempt of their neighbour, which would subject them to the anger of society: the man who does not expect another life, is only more interested in prolonging his existence in this; in rendering himself dear to his fellows, by cultivating virtue; by performing all his duties with more strictness, in the only life of which he has any knowledge: he has made a great stride towards felicity, in disengaging himself from those terrors which afflict others, which frequently prevent their acting. Such a man has nothing to fear, but every thing to hope; if, contrary to what he is able to judge, there should be an hereafter existence, will not his actions have been so regulated by virtue, will he not have so comported himself in his present existence, as to stand a fair chance of enjoying in their fullest extent those felicities prepared for his species?

Superstition, in fact, takes a pride in rendering man slothful, in moulding him to credulity, in making him pusillanimous. It is its principle to afflict him without intermission; to redouble in him the horrors of death: ever ingenious in tormenting him, it has extended his inquietudes beyond even his own existence; its ministers, the more securely to dispose of him in this world, invented, in future regions, a variety of rewards and punishments, reserving to themselves the privilege of awarding these heavenly recompences to those who yielded most implicitly to their arbitrary laws; of decreeing punishment to those refractory beings who rebelled against their power: thus, according to them, Tantalus for divulging their secrets, must eternally fear, engulphed in burning sulphur, the stone ready to fall on his devoted head; whilst Romulus was beatified and worshipped as a god under the name of Quirinus. The same system of superstition caused the philosopher Callisthenes to be put to death, for opposing the worship of

Alexander; and elevated the monk Athanasius to be a saint in heaven. Far from holding forth consolation to mortals, far from cultivating man's reason, far from teaching him to yield under the hands of necessity, superstition, in a great many countries, strives to render death still more bitter to him; to make its yoke sit heavy; to fill up its retinue with a multitude of hideous phantoms; to paint it in the most frightful colours; to render its approach terrible: by this means it has crowded the world with enthusiasts, whom it seduces by vague promises; with contemptible slaves, whom it coerces with the fear of imaginary evils: it has at length persuaded man, that his actual existence is only a journey, by which he will arrive at a more important life: this doctrine, whether it be rational or irrational, prevents him from occupying himself with his true happiness; from even dreaming of ameliorating his institutions, of improving his laws, of advancing the progress of science, of perfectioning his morals. Vain and gloomy ideas have absorbed his attention: he consents to groan under fanatical tyranny—to writhe under political inflictions—to live in error—to languish in misfortune—in the hope, when he shall be no more, of being one day happier; in the firm confidence, that after he has disappeared, his calamities, his patience, will conduct him to a never-ending felicity: he has believed himself submitted to cruel priests, who are willing to make him purchase his future welfare at the expence of every thing most dear to his peace, most valuable to his existence here below: they have pictured heaven as irritated against him, as disposed to appease itself by punishing him eternally, for any efforts he should make to withdraw himself from, their power. It is thus the doctrine of a future life has been made fatal to the human species: it plunged whole nations into sloth, made them languid, filled them with indifference to their present welfare, or else precipitated them, into the most furious enthusiasm, which hurried them on to such lengths that they tore each other in pieces in order to merit the promised heaven.

It will be asked, perhaps, by what road has man been conducted to form to himself these gratuitous ideas of another world? I reply, that it is a truth man has no idea of a future life, they are the ideas of the past and the present that furnish his imagination with the materials of which he constructs the edifice of the regions of futurity. Hobbes says, "We believe that, that which is will always be, and that the same causes will have the same effects." Man in his actual state, has two modes of feeling, one that he approves, another that he disapproves: thus, persuaded that these two modes of feeling must accompany him, even beyond his present existence, he placed in the regions of eternity two distinguished abodes, one destined to felicity, the other to misery: the one must contain those who obey the calls of superstition, who believe in its dogmas; the other is a prison, destined to avenge the cause of heaven, on all those who shall not faithfully believe the doctrines promulgated by the ministers of a vast variety of superstitions. Has sufficient attention been paid to the fact that results as a necessary consequence from this reasoning; which on examination will be found to have rendered the first place entirely useless, seeing, that by the number and contradiction of these various systems, let man believe which ever he may, let him follow it in the most faithful manner, still he must be ranked as an infidel, as a rebel to the Divinity, because he cannot believe in all; and those from which he dissents, by a consequence of their own creed, condemn him to the prison-house?

Such is the origin of the ideas upon a future life, so diffused among mankind. Every where may be seen an Elysium and a Tartarus; a Paradise and a Hell; in a word, two distinguished abodes, constructed according to the imagination of the enthusiasts who have invented them, who have accommodated them to their own peculiar prejudices, to the hopes, to the fears, of the people who believe in them. The Indian figures the first of these abodes as one of in-action, of permanent repose, because, being the inhabitant of a hot climate, he has learned to contemplate rest as the extreme of felicity: the Mussulman promises himself corporeal pleasures, similar to those that actually constitute the object of his research in this life: each figures to himself, that on which he has learned to set the greatest value.

Of whatever nature these pleasures may be, man apprehended that a body was needful, in order that his soul might be enabled to enjoy the pleasures, or to experience the pains in reserve for him: from hence the doctrine of the *resurrection*; but as he beheld this body putrify, as he saw it dissolve, as he witnessed its decomposition, after death, he was at a loss how to form anew what he conceived so necessary to his system he therefore had recourse to the Divine Omnipotence, by whose interposition he now believes it will be effected. This opinion, so incomprehensible, is said to have originated in Persia, among the Magi, and finds a great number of adherents, who have never given it a serious examination: but the doctrine of the resurrection appears perfectly useless to all those, who believe in the existence of a soul that feels, thinks, suffers, and enjoys, after a separation from the body: indeed, there are already sects who begin to maintain, that the body is not necessary; that therefore it will not be resurrected. Like Berkeley, they conceive that "the soul has need neither of body nor any exterior being, either to experience sensations, or to have ideas:" the Malebranchists, in particular, must suppose that the rejected souls will see every thing in the Divinity; will feel themselves burn, without having occasion for bodies for that purpose. Others, incapable of elevating themselves to these sublime notions, believed, that under divers forms, man animated successively different animals of various species; that he never ceased to be an inhabitant of the earth; such was the opinion of those who adopted the doctrine of Metempsychosis.

As for the miserable abode of souls, the imagination of fanatics, who were desirous of governing the people, strove to assemble the most frightful images, to render it still more terrible: fire is of all beings that which produces in man the most pungent sensation; not finding any thing more cruel, the enemies to the several dogmas were to be everlastingly punished with this torturing element: fire, therefore, was the point at which their imagination was obliged to stop. The ministers of the various systems agreed pretty generally, that fire would one day avenge their offended divinities: thus they painted the victims to the anger of the gods, or rather those who questioned their own creeds, as confined in fiery dungeons, as perpetually rolling in a vortex of bituminous flames, as plunged in unfathomable gulphs of liquid sulphur, making the infernal caverns resound with their useless groanings, with their unavailing gnashing of teeth.

But it will, perhaps, be enquired, how could man reconcile himself to the belief of an existence accompanied with eternal torments; above all, as many according to their own superstitions had reason to fear it for themselves? Many causes have concurred to make him adopt so revolting an opinion: in the first place, very few thinking men have ever believed such an absurdity, when they have deigned to make use of their reason; or, when they have accredited it, this notion was always counterbalanced by the idea of the goodness, by a reliance on the mercy, which they attributed to their respective divinities: in the second place, those who were blinded by their fears, never rendered to themselves any account of these strange doctrines, which they either received with awe from their legislators, or which were transmitted to them by their fathers: in the third place, each sees the object of his terrors only at a favourable distance: moreover, superstition promises him the means of escaping the tortures he believes he has merited. At length, like those sick people whom we see cling with fondness, even to the most painful life, man preferred the idea of an unhappy, though unknown existence, to that of non-existence, which he looked upon as the most frightful evil that could befal him; either because he could form no idea of it, or because his imagination painted to him this non-existence this nothing, as the confused assemblage of all evils. A known evil, of whatever magnitude, alarmed him less (above all, when there remained the hope of being able to avoid it), than an evil of which he knew nothing, upon which, consequently, his imagination was painfully employed, but to which he knew not how to oppose a remedy.

It will be seen, then, that *superstition*, far from consoling man upon the necessity of death, only redoubles his terrors, by the evils with which it pretends his decease will be followed; these terrors are so strong, that the miserable wretches who believe strictly in these formidable doctrines, pass their days in affliction, bathed in the most bitter tears. What shall be said of an opinion so destructive to society, yet adopted by so many nations, which announces to them, that a severe fate may at each instant take them unprovided; that at each moment they are liable to pass under the most rigorous judgment? What idea can be better suited to terrify man—what more likely to discourage him—what more calculated to damp the desire of ameliorating his condition—than the afflicting prospect of a world always on the brink of dissolution; of a Divinity seated upon the ruins of Nature, ready to pass judgment on the human species? Such are, nevertheless, the fatal opinions with which the mind of nations has been fed for thousands of years: they are so dangerous, that if by a happy want of just inference, he did not derogate in his conduct from these afflicting ideas, he would fall into the most abject stupidity. How could man occupy himself with a perishable world, ready every moment to crumble into atoms? How dream of rendering himself happy on earth, when it is only the porch to an eternal kingdom? Is it then, surprising, that the superstitions to which similar doctrines serve for a basis, have prescribed to their disciples a total detachment from things below—an entire renunciation of the most innocent pleasures; have given birth to a sluggishness, to a pusillanimity, to an abjection of soul, to an insociability, that renders him useless to himself, dangerous to others? If necessity did not oblige man to depart in his practice from these irrational systems—if his wants did not bring him back to reason, in despite of these superstitious doctrines—the whole world would presently become a vast desert, inhabited by some few isolated savages, who would not even have courage to multiply themselves. What are these, but notions which he must necessarily put aside, in order that human association may subsist?

Nevertheless, the doctrine of a future life, accompanied with rewards and punishments, has been regarded for a great number of ages as the most powerful, or even as the only motive capable of coercing the passions of man; as the sole means that can oblige him to be virtuous: by degrees, this doctrine has become the basis of almost all religions and political systems, so much so, that at this day it is said, this prejudice cannot be attacked without absolutely rending asunder the bonds of society. The founders of superstition have made use of it to attach their credulous disciples; legislators have looked upon it as the curb best calculated to keep mankind under discipline; religion considers it necessary to his happiness; many philosophers themselves have believed with sincerity, that this doctrine was requisite to terrify man, was the only means to divert him from crime: notwithstanding, when the doctrine of the immortality of the soul first came out of the school of Plato; when it first diffused itself among the Greeks, it caused the greatest ravages; it determined a multitude of men, who were discontented with their condition, to terminate their existence: Ptolemy Philadelphus, king of Egypt, seeing the effect this doctrine, which at the present day is looked upon as so salutary, produced on the brains of his subjects, prohibited the teaching of it under the penalty of death.

It must, indeed, be allowed that this doctrine has been of the greatest utility to those who have given superstitions to nations, who at the same time made themselves its ministers; it was the foundation of their power, the source of their wealth, the permanent cause of that blindness, the solid basis of those terrors, which it was their interest to nourish in the human race. It was by this doctrine the priest became first the rival, then the master of kings: it is by this dogma that nations are filled with enthusiasts inebriated with superstition, always more disposed to listen to its menaces, than to the counsels of reasons, to the orders of the sovereign, to the cries of Nature, or to the laws of society. Politics itself was enslaved to the caprice of the priest; the temporal monarch was obliged to bend under the yoke of the monarch of superstition; the one only disposed of this perishable world, the other extended his power into the world to come; much more important for man than the earth, on which he is only a pilgrim, a mere passenger. Thus the doctrine of another life placed the government itself in a state of dependance upon the priest; the monarch was nothing more than his first subject; he was never obeyed, but when the two were in accord. Nature in vain cried out to man, to be careful of his present happiness; the priest ordered him to be unhappy, in the expectation of future felicity; reason in vain exhorted him to be peaceable; the priest breathed forth fanaticism, fulminated fury, obliged him to disturb the public tranquillity, every time there was a question of the supposed interests of the invisible monarch of another life, and the real interests of his ministers in this.

Such is the fruit that politics has gathered from the doctrine of a future life; the regions of the world to come have enabled the priesthood to conquer the present world. The expectation of celestial happiness, and the dread of future tortures, only served to prevent man from seeking after the means to render himself happy here below. Thus error, under whatever aspect it is considered, will never be more than a source of evil for mankind. The doctrine of another life, in presenting to mortals an ideal happiness, will render them enthusiasts; in overwhelming them with fears, it will make useless beings; generate cowards; form atrabilarious or furious men; who will lose sight of their present abode, to occupy themselves with the pictured regions of a world to come, with those dreadful evils which they must fear after their death.

If it be insisted that the doctrine of future rewards and punishments is the most powerful curb to restrain the passions of man, we shall reply by calling in daily experience. If we only cast our eyes around, if for a moment we examine what passes in review before us, we shall see this assertion contradicted; we shall find that these marvellous speculations do not in any manner diminish the number of the wicked, because they are incapable of changing the temperament of man, of annihilating those passions which the vices of society engender in his heart. In those nations who appear the most thoroughly convinced of this future punishment, may be seen assassins, thieves, crafty knaves, oppressors, adulterers, voluptuaries; all these pretend they are firmly persuaded of the reality of an hereafter; yet in the whirlwind of dissipation, in the vortex of pleasure, in the fury of their passions, they no longer behold this formidable future existence, which in those moments has no kind of influence over their earthly conduct.

In short, in many of those countries where the doctrine of another life is so firmly established, that each individual irritates himself against whoever may have the temerity to combat the opinion, or even to doubt it, we see that it is utterly incapable of impressing any thing on rulers who are unjust, who are negligent of the welfare of their people, who are, debauched, on courtezans who are lewd in their habits, on covetous misers, on flinty extortioners who fatten on the substance of a nation, on women without modesty, on a vast multitude of drunken, intemperate, vicious men, on great numbers even amongst those priests, whose function it is to preach this future state, who are paid to announce the vengeance of heaven, against vices which they themselves encourage by their example. If it be enquired of them, how they dare to give themselves up to such scandalous actions, which they ought to know are certain to draw upon them eternal punishment? They will reply, that the madness of their passions, the force of their habits, the contagion of example, or even the power of circumstances, have hurried them along; have made them forget the dreadful consequences in which their conduct is likely to involve them; besides, they will say, that the treasures of the divine mercy are infinite; that repentance suffices to efface the foulest transgressions; to cleanse the blackest guilt; to blot out the most enormous crimes: in this multitude of wretched beings, who each after his own manner desolates society with his criminal pursuits, you will find only a small number who are sufficiently intimidated by the fears of the miserable hereafter, to resist their evil propensities. What did I say? These propensities are in themselves too weak to carry them forward without the aid of the doctrine of another life; without this, the law and the fear of censure would have been motives sufficient to prevent them from rendering themselves criminal.

It is indeed, fearful, timorous souls, upon whom the terrors of another life make a profound impression; human beings of this sort come into the world with moderate passions, are of a weakly organization, possess a cool imagination; it is not therefore surprising, that in such men, who are already restrained by their nature, the fear of future punishment counterbalances the weak efforts of their feeble passions; but it is by no means the same with those determined sinners, with those hardened criminals, with those men who are habitually vicious, whose unseemly excesses nothing can arrest, who in their violence shut their eyes to the fear of the laws of this world, despising still more those of the other. Nevertheless, how many persons say they are, and even believe themselves, restrained by the fears of the life to come? But, either they deceive us, or they impose upon themselves, by attributing to these fears, that which is only the effect of motives much nearer at hand; such as the feebleness of their machine, the mildness of their temperament, the slender energy of their souls, their natural timidity, the ideas imbibed in their education, the fear of consequences immediately resulting from criminal actions, the physical evils attendant on unbridled irregularities: these are the true motives that restrain them; not the notions of a future life: which men, who say they are most firmly persuaded of its existence, forget whenever a powerful interest solicits them to sin. If for a time man would pay attention to what passes before his eyes, he would perceive that he ascribes to the fear of the gods that which is in reality only the effect of peculiar weakness, of pusillanimity, of the small interest found to commit evil: these men would not act otherwise than they do, if they had not this fear before them; if, therefore he reflected, he would feel that it is always necessity that makes men act as they do.

Man cannot be restrained, when he does not find within himself motives sufficiently powerful to conduct him back to reason. There is nothing, either in this world or in the other, that can render him virtuous, when an untoward organization—a mind badly cultivated—a violent imagination—inveterate habits—fatal examples—powerful interests—invite him from every quarter to the commission of crime. No speculations are capable of restraining the man who braves public opinion, who despises the law, who is careless of its censure, who turns a deaf ear to the cries of conscience, whose power in this world places him out of the reach of punishment; in the violence of his transports, he will fear still less a distant futurity, of which the idea always recedes before that which he believes necessary to his immediate interests, consistent with his present happiness. All lively passions blind man to every thing that is not its immediate object; the terrors of a future life, of which his passions always possess the secret to diminish to him the probability, can effect nothing upon the wicked man, who does not fear even the much nearer punishment of the law; who sets at nought the assured hatred of those by whom he is surrounded. Man, when he delivers himself up to crime, sees nothing certain except the supposed advantage which attends it; the rest always appear to him either false or problematical.

If man would but open his eyes, even for a moment, he would clearly perceive, that to effect any thing upon hearts hardened by crime, he must not reckon upon the chastisement of an avenging Divinity, which the self-love natural to man always shews him as pacified in the long run. He who has arrived at persuading himself he cannot be happy without crime, will always readily deliver himself up to it, notwithstanding the menaces of religion. Whoever is sufficiently blind not to read his infamy in his own heart, to see his own vileness in the countenances of his associates, his own condemnation in the anger of his fellow-men, his own unworthiness in the indignation of the judges established to punish the offences he may commit: such a man, I say, will never feel the impression his crimes shall make on the features of a judge, that is either hidden from his view, or that he only contemplates at a distance. The tyrant who with dry eyes can hear the cries of the distressed, who with callous heart can behold the tears of a whole people, of whose misery he is the cause, will not see the angry countenance of a more powerful master: like another Menippus, he may indeed destroy himself from desperation, to avoid reiterated reproach; which only proves, that when a haughty, arrogant despot pretends to be accountable for his actions to the Divinity alone, it is because he fears his nation more than he does his God.

On the other hand, does not superstition itself, does not even religion, annihilate the effects of those fears which it announces as salutary? Does it not furnish its disciples with the means of extricating themselves from the punishments with which it has so frequently menaced them? Does it not tell them, that a steril repentance will, even at the moment of death, disarm the celestial wrath; that it will purify the filthy souls of sinners? Do not even the priests, in some superstitions, arrogate to themselves the right of remitting to the dying the punishment due to the crimes committed during the course of a disorderly life? In short, do not the most perverse men, encouraged in iniquity, countenanced in debauchery, upheld in crime, reckon, even to the last moment, either upon the assistance of superstition, or upon the aid of religion, that promises them the infallible means of reconciling themselves to the Divinity, whom they have irritated; of avoiding the rigorous punishments pronounced against their enormities?

In consequence of these notions, so favourable to the wicked, so suitable to tranquillize their fears, we see that the hope of an easy expiation, far from correcting man, engages him to persist, until death, in the most crying disorders. Indeed, in despite of the numberless advantages which he is assured flows from the doctrine of a life to come, in defiance of its pretended efficacy to repress the passions of men, do not the priests themselves, although so interested in the maintenance of this system, every day complain of its insufficiency? They acknowledge, that mortals, who from their infancy they have imbued with these ideas, are not less hurried forward by their evil propensities—less sunk in the vortex of dissipation—less the slaves to their pleasures—less captivated by bad habits—less driven along by the torrent of the world—less seduced by their present interest—which make them forget equally the recompense and the chastisement of a future existence. In a word, the interpreters of superstition, the ministers of religion themselves, allow that their disciples, for the greater part, conduct themselves in this world as if they had nothing either to hope or fear in another.

In short, let it be supposed for a moment, that the doctrine of eternal punishments was of some utility; that it really restrained a small number of individuals; what are these feeble advantages compared to the numberless evils that flow from it? Against one timid man whom this idea restrains, there are thousands upon whom it operates nothing; there are thousands whom it makes irrational; whom it renders savage persecutors; whom it converts into fanatics; there are thousands whose mind it disturbs; whom it diverts from their duties towards society; there are an infinity whom it grievously afflicts, whom it troubles without producing any real good for their associates.

Notwithstanding so many are inclined to consider those who do not fall in with this doctrine as the enemies of society; it will be found on examination that the wisest the most enlightened men of antiquity, as well as many of the moderns, have believed not only that the soul is material and perishes with the body, but also that they have attacked without subterfuge the opinion of future everlasting punishments; it will also be found that many of the systems, set up to establish the immortality of the soul, are in themselves the best evidence that can be adduced of the futility of this doctrine; if for a moment we only follow up the natural the just inferences that are to be drawn from them. This sentiment was far from being, as some have supposed, peculiar to the Epicureans, it has been adopted by philosophers of all sects, by Pythagoreans, by Stoics, by Peripatetics, by Academics; in short by the most godly the most virtuous men of Greece and of Rome.

Pythagoras, according to Ovid, speaks strongly to the fact. Timaeus of Locris, who was a Pythagorean, admits that the doctrine of future punishments was fabulous, solely destined for the imbecility of the uninformed; but little calculated for those who cultivate their reason.

Aristotle expressly says, that "man has neither good to hope nor evil to fear after death."

Zeno, according to Cicero, supposed the soul to be an igneous substance, from whence he concluded it destroyed itself.

Cicero, the philosophical orator, who was of the sect of Academics, although he is not on all occasions, in accord with himself, treats openly as fables the torments of Hell; and looks upon death as the end of every thing for man.

Seneca, the philosopher, is filled with passages which contemplate death as a state of total annihilation, particularly in speaking of it to his brother: and nothing can be more decisive of his holding this opinion, than what he writes to Marcia, to console him.

Seneca, the tragedian, explains himself in the same manner as the philosopher.

The Platonists, who made the soul immortal, could not have an idea of future punishments, because the soul according to them was a portion of the divinity which after the dissolution of the body it returned to rejoin.

Epictetus has the same idea. In a passage reported by Arrian, he says, "but where are you going? It cannot be to a place of suffering: you will only return to the place from whence you came; you are about to be again peaceably associated with the elements from which you are derived. That which in your composition, is of the nature of fire, will return to the element of fire; that which is of the nature of earth, will rejoin itself to the earth; that which is air, will re-unite itself with air; that which is water, will resolve itself into water; there is no Hell, no Acheron, no Cocytus, no Phlegethon."

In another place he says, "the hour of death approaches; but do not aggravate your evil, nor render things worse than they are: represent them to yourself under their true point of view. The time is come when the materials of which you are composed, go to resolve themselves into the elements from whence they were originally borrowed. What is there that is terrible or grievous in that? Is there any thing in the world that perishes totally?"

The sage and pious Antoninus says, "he who fears death, either fears to be deprived of all feeling, or dreads to experience different sensations. If you lose all feeling, you will no longer be subject either to pain or to misery. If you are provided with other senses of a different nature, you will become a creature of a different species." This great emperor further says, "that we must expect death with tranquillity, seeing, that it is only a dissolution of the elements of which each animal is composed."

To the evidence of so many great men of *Pagan antiquity*, may be joined, that of the author of Ecclesiastes, who speaks of death, and of the condition of the human soul, like an *epicurean*; he says, "for that which befalleth the sons of men, befalleth beasts; even one thing befalleth them: as the one dieth, so dieth the other; yea, they have all one breath: so that a man hath no pre-eminence above a beast; for all is vanity. All go unto one place; all are of the dust, and all turn to dust again." And further, "wherefore I perceive that there is nothing better than that a man should rejoice in his own works; for that is his portion: for who shall bring him to see what shall be after him."

In short, how can the utility or the necessity of this doctrine be reconciled with the fact, that the great *legislator of the Jews*, who is supposed to have been inspired by the Divinity, should have remained silent on a subject, that is said to be of so much importance? In the third chapter of Genesis it, is said, "In the sweat of thy face shalt thou eat bread, till thou return unto the ground; for out of it wast thou taken: for dust thou art, and unto dust shalt thou return."

CHAP. XIV.

Education, Morals, and the Laws suffice to restrain Man.—Of the desire of Immortality.—Of Suicide.

It is not then in an ideal world, existing no where perhaps, but in the imagination of man, that he must seek to collect motives calculated to make him act properly in this; it is in the visible world that will be found incitements to divert him from crime; to rouse him to virtue. It is in Nature,—in experience,—in truth, that he must search out remedies for the evils of his species; for motives suitable to infuse into the human heart, propensities truely useful to society; calculated to promote its advantage; to conduce to the end for which it was designed.

If attention has been paid to what has been said In the course of this work, it will be seen that above all it is *education* that will best furnish the true means of rectifying the errors, of recalling the wanderings of mankind. It is this that should scatter the Seeds in his heart; cultivate the tender shoots; make a profitable use of his dispositions; turn to account those faculties, which depend on his organization: which should cherish the fire of his imagination, kindle it for useful objects; damp it, or extinguish it for others; in short, it is this which should make sensible souls contract habits which are advantageous for society and beneficial to the individual. Brought up in this manner, man would not have occasion for celestial punishments, to teach him the value of virtue; he would not need to behold burning gulphs of brimstone under his feet, to induce him to feel horror for crime; Nature without these fables, would teach much better what he owes to himself; the law would point out what he owes to the body politic, of which he is a member. It is thus, that education grounded upon utility, would form valuable citizens to the state; the depositaries of power would distinguish those whom education should have thus formed, by reason of the advantages which they would procure for their country; they would punish those who should be found injurious to it; it would make the citizens see, that the promises of reward which education held forth, the punishments denounced by morals, are by no means vain; that in a state well constituted, *virtue* is the true, the only road to happiness; *talents* the way to gain respect; that *inutility* conducts to misfortune: that *crime* leads to contempt.

A just, enlightened, virtuous, and vigilant government, who should honestly propose the public good, would have no occasion either for fables or for falsehoods, to govern reasonable subjects; it would blush to make use of imposture, to deceive its citizens; who, instructed in their duties, would find their interest in submitting to equitable laws; who would be capable of feeling the benefit these have the power of conferring on them; it would feel, that habit is sufficient to inspire them with horror, even for those concealed crimes that escape the eyes of society; it would understand that the visible punishments of this world impose much more on the generality of men, than those of an uncertain and distant futurity: in short, it would ascertain that the sensible benefits within the compass of the sovereign power to distribute, touch the imagination of mortals more keenly, than those vague recompences which are held forth to them in a future existence: above all, it would discover that those on whom these distant advantages do operate, would be still more attached to virtue by receiving their reward both here and hereafter.

Man is almost every where so wicked, so corrupt, so rebellious to reason, only because he is not governed according to his Nature, nor properly instructed in her necessary laws: he is almost in every climate fed with superstitious chimeras; submitted to masters who neglect his instruction or who seek to deceive him. On the face of this globe, may be frequently witnessed unjust sovereigns, who, enervated by luxury, corrupted by flattery, depraved by licentiousness, made wicked by impunity, devoid of talents, without morals, destitute of virtue, are incapable of exerting any energy for the benefit of the states they govern; they are consequently but little occupied with the welfare of their people; indifferent to their duties; of which indeed they are often ignorant. Such governors suffer their whole attention to be absorbed by frivolous amusement; stimulated by the desire of continually finding means to feed their insatiable ambition they engage in useless depopulating wars; and never occupy their mind with those objects which are the most important to the happiness of their nation: yet these weak men feel interested in maintaining the received prejudices, and visit with severity those who consider the means of curing them: in short themselves deprived of that understanding, which teaches man that it is his interest to be kind, just, and virtuous; they ordinarily reward only those crimes which their imbecility makes them imagine as useful to them; they generally punish those virtues which are opposed to their own imprudent passions, but which reason would point out as truly beneficial to their interests. Under such masters is it surprising that society should be ravaged; that weak beings should be willing to imitate them; that perverse men should emulate each other in oppressing its members; in sacrificing its dearest interests; in despoiling its happiness? The state of society in such countries, is a state of hostility of the sovereign against the whole, of each of its members the one against the other. Man is wicked, not because he is born so, but because he is rendered so; the great, the powerful, crush with impunity the indigent and the unhappy; these, at the risk of their lives seek to retaliate, to render back the evil they have received: they attack either openly or in secret a country, who to them is a step-mother, who gives all to some of her children, and deprives the others of every thing: they punish it for its partiality, and clearly shew that the motives borrowed from a life hereafter are impotent against the fury of those passions to which a corrupt administration has given birth; that the terror of the punishments in this world are too feeble against necessity; against criminal habits; against dangerous organization uncorrected by education.

In many countries the morals of the people are neglected; the government is occupied only with rendering them timid; with making them miserable. Man is almost every where a slave; it must then follow of necessity, that he is base, interested, dissimulating, without honour, in a word that he has the vices of the state of which he is a citizen. Almost every where he is deceived; encouraged in ignorance; prevented from cultivating his reason; of course he must be stupid, irrational, and wicked almost every where he sees vice applauded, and crime honoured; thence he concludes vice to be a good; virtue, only a useless sacrifice of himself: almost every where he is miserable, therefore he injures his fellow-men in a fruitless attempt to relieve his own anguish: it is in vain to shew him heaven in order to restrain him; his views presently descend again to earth; he is willing to be happy at any price; therefore, the laws which have neither provided for his instruction, for his morals, nor his happiness, menace him uselessly; he plunges on in his pursuits, and these ultimately punish him, for the unjust negligence of his legislators. If politics more enlightened, did seriously occupy itself with the instruction, with the welfare of the people; if laws were more equitable; if each society, less partial, bestowed on its members the care, the education, and the assistance which they have a right to expect; if governments less covetous, and more vigilant, were sedulous to render their subjects more happy, there would not be seen such numbers of malefactors, of robbers, of murderers, who every where infest society; they would not be obliged to destroy life, in order to punish wickedness; which is commonly ascribable to the vices of their own institutions: it would be unnecessary to seek in another life for fanciful chimeras, which always prove abortive against the infuriate passions; against the real wants of man. In short, if the people were instructed, they would be more happy; politics would no longer be reduced to the exigency of deceiving them, in order to restrain them; nor to destroy so many unfortunates, for having procured necessaries, at the expence of their hard-hearted fellow-citizens.

When it shall be desired to enlighten man, let him always have truth laid before him. Instead of kindling his imagination by the idea of those punishments that a future state has in reserve for him, let him be solaced—let him be succoured; or, at least, let him be permitted to enjoy the fruit of his labour—let not his substance be ravished from him by cruel imposts—

let him not be discouraged from work, by finding all his labour inadequate to support his existence; let him not be driven into that idleness, that will surely lead him on to crime: let him consider his present existence, without carrying his views to that which may attend him after his death; let his industry be excited—let his talents be rewarded—let him be rendered active, laborious, beneficent, and virtuous, in the world he inhabits; let it be shewn to him, that his actions are capable of having an influence over his fellow-men. Let him not be menaced with the tortures of a future existence when he shall be no more; let him behold society armed against those who disturb its repose; let him see the consequence of the hatred of his associates; let him learn to feel the value of their affection; let him be taught to esteem himself; let him understand, that to obtain it, he must have virtue; above all, that the virtuous man in society has nothing to fear, but every thing to hope.

If it be desired to form honest, courageous, industrious citizens, who may be useful to their country, let them beware of inspiring man from his infancy with an ill-founded dread of death; of amusing his imagination with marvellous fables; of occupying his mind with his destiny in a future life, quite useless to be known, which has nothing in common with his real felicity. Let them speak of immortality to intrepid, noble souls; let them shew it as the price of their labours to energetic minds, who are solely occupied with virtue; who springing forward beyond the boundaries of their actual existence—who, little satisfied with eliciting the admiration, with gaining the love of their contemporaries, are will also to wrest the homage, to secure the affection of future races. Indeed, this is an immortality to which genius, talents, above all virtue, has a just right to pretend; do not therefore let them censure—do not let them endeavour to stifle so noble a passion in man; which is founded upon his nature; which is so calculated to render him happy; from which society gather the most advantageous fruits.

The idea of being buried in total oblivion, of having nothing in common after his death with the beings of his species; of losing all possibility of again having any influence over them, is a thought extremely painful to man; it is above all afflicting to those who possess an ardent imagination. The *desire of immortality*, or of living in the memory of his fellow men, was always the passion of great souls; it was the motive to the actions of all those who have played a great part on the earth. *Heroes* whether virtuous or criminal, *philosophers* as well as *conquerors*, *men of genius* and *men of talents*, those sublime personages who have done honor to their species, as well as those illustrious villains who have debased and ravaged it, have had an eye to posterity in all their enterprises; have flattered themselves with the hope of acting upon the souls of men, even when they themselves should no longer exist. If man in general does not carry his views so far, he is at least sensible to the idea of seeing himself regenerated in his children; whom he knows are destined to survive him; to transmit his name; to preserve his memory; to represent him in society; it is for them that he rebuilds his cottage; it is for them that he plants the tree which his eyes will never behold in its vigour; it is that they may be happy that he labours. The sorrow which embitters the life of those rich men, frequently so useless to the world, when they have lost the hope of continuing their race, has its source in the fear of being entirely forgotten: they feel that the useless man dies entirely. The idea that his name will be in the mouths of men, the thought that it will be pronounced with tenderness, that it will be recollected with kindness, that it will excite in their hearts favourable sentiments, is an illusion that is useful; is a vision suitable to flatter even those who know that nothing will result from it. Man pleases himself with dreaming that he shall have power, that he shall pass for something in the universe, even after the term of his human existence; he partakes by imagination in the projects, in the actions, in the discussions of future ages, and would be extremely unhappy if he believed himself entirely excluded from their society. The laws in all countries have entered into these views; they have so far been willing to console their citizens for the necessity of dying, by giving them the means of exercising their will, even for a long time after their death: this condescension goes to that length, that the dead frequently regulate the condition of the living during a long series of years.

Every thing serves to prove the desire in man of surviving himself. *Pyramids, mausoleums, monuments, epitaphs,* all shew that he is willing to prolong his existence even beyond his decease. He, is not insensible to the judgment of posterity; it is for him the philosopher writes; it is to astonish him that the monarch erects sumptuous edifices, gorgeous palaces; it is his praises, it is his commendations, that the great man already hears echo in his ears; it is to him that the virtuous citizen appeals from unjust laws; from prejudiced contemporaries—happy chimera! generous illusion! mild vision! its power is so consoling, so bland, that it realizes itself to ardent imaginations; it is calculated to give birth, to sustain, to nurture, to mature enthusiasm of genius, constancy of courage, grandeur of soul, transcendency of talent; its force is so gentle, its influence so pleasing, that it is sometimes able to repress the vices, to restrain the excesses of the most powerful men; who are, as experience has shewn, frequently very much disquieted for the judgment of their posterity; from a conviction that this will sooner or later avenge the living of the foul injustice which they may be inclined to make them suffer.

No man, therefore, can consent to be entirely effaced from the remembrance of his fellows; some men have not the temerity to place themselves above the judgment of the future human species, to degrade themselves in his eyes. Where is the being who is insensible to the pleasure of exciting the tears of those who shall survive him; of again acting upon their souls; of once more occupying their thoughts; of exercising upon them his power even from the bottom of his grave? Let then eternal silence be imposed upon those superstitious beings, upon those melancholy men, upon those furious bigots, who censure a sentiment from which society derives so many real advantages; let not mankind listen to those passionless philosophers who are willing to smother this great, this noble spring of his soul; let him not be seduced by the sarcasms of those voluptuaries, who pretend to despise an immortality, towards which they lack the power to set forward; the desire of pleasing posterity, of rendering his name agreeable to generations yet to come, is a respectable, a laudable motive, when it causes him to undertake those things, of which the utility may be felt, of which the advantages may have an influence not only over his contemporaries, but also over nations who have not yet an existence. Let him not treat as irrational, the enthusiasm of those beneficent beings, of those mighty geniuses, of those stupendous talents, whose keen, whose penetrating regards, have foreseen him even in their day; who have occupied themselves for him; for his welfare; for his happiness; who have desired his suffrage; who have written for him; who have enriched him by their discoveries; who have cured him of some of his errors. Let him render them the homage which they have expected at his hands; let him, at least, reverence their memory for the benefits he has derived from them; let him treat their mouldering remains with respect, for the pleasure he receives from their labours; let him pay to their ashes a tribute of grateful recollection, for the happiness they have been sedulous to procure for him. Let him sprinkle with his tears, let him hallow with his remembrance, let him consecrate with his finest sensibilities, the urns of Socrates, of Phocion; of Archimedes; of Anaxarchus; let him wash out the stain that their punishment has made on the human species; let him expiate by his regret the Athenian ingratitude, the savage barbarity of Nicocreon; let him learn by their example to dread superstitious fanaticism; to hold political intolerance in abhorrence; let him fear to harrass merit; let him be cautious how he insults virtue, in persecuting those who may happen to differ from him in his prejudices.

Let him strew flowers over the tombs of an Homer—of a Tasso—of a Shakespeare—of a Milton—of a Goldsmith; let him revere the immortal shades of those happy geniuses, whose songs yet vibrate on his ears; whose harmonious lays excite in his soul the most tender sentiments; let him bless the memory of all those benefactors to the people, who were the delight of the human race; let him adore the virtues Of a Titus—of a Trajan—of an Antoninus—of a Julian: let him merit in his sphere, the eulogies of future ages; let him always remember, that to carry with him to the grave the regret of his fellow man, he must display talents; evince integrity; practice virtue. The funeral ceremonies of the most powerful monarchs, have rarely been wetted with the tears of the people, they have commonly drained them while living. The names of tyrants excite the horror of those who bear them pronounced. Tremble then cruel kings! ye who plunge your subjects into misery; who bathe them with bitter tears—who ravage nations—who deluge the land with the vital stream—who change the fruitful earth into a barren cemetery; tremble for the sanguinary traits under which the future historian will paint you, to generations yet unborn: neither your splendid monuments—your imposing victories—your innumerable armies, nor your sycophant courtiers, can prevent posterity from avenging their grandfathers; from insulting your odious manes; from treating your execrable memories with scorn; from showering their contempt on your transcendant crimes.

Not only man sees his dissolution with pain, but again, he wishes his death may be an interesting event for others. But, as we have already said, he must have talents—he must have beneficence—he must have virtue, in order, that those who surround him, may interest themselves in his condition; that those who survive him, may give regret to his ashes. Is it, then, surprising if the greater number of men, occupied entirely with themselves, completely absorbed by their own vanity, devoted to their own puerile objects, for ever busied with the care of gratifying their vile passions, at the expence, perhaps, of their family happiness, unheedful of the wants of a wife, unmindful of the necessity of their children, careless of the calls of friendship, regardless of their duty to society, do not by their death excite the sensibilities of their survivors; or that they should be presently forgotten? There is an infinity of monarchs of which history does not tell us any thing, save that they have lived. In despite of the inutility in which men for the most part pass their existence, maugre the little care they bestow, to render themselves dear to the beings who environ them; notwithstanding the numerous actions they commit to displease their associates; the self love of each individual, persuades him, that his death must be an interesting occurrence: few men but think themselves an Euryalus in friendship, all expect to find a Nisus, thus man's over-weening philauty shews him to say thus the order of things are overturned at his decease. O mortal! feeble and vain! Dost thou not know the Sesostris's, the Alexanders, the Caesars are dead? Yet the course of the universe is not arrested; the demise of those famous conquerors, afflicting to some few favoured slaves, was a subject of delight for the whole human race. Dost thou then foolishly believe that thy talents ought to interest thy species, that they are of sufficient extent to put it into mourning at thy decease? Alas! The Corneilles, the Lockes, the Newtons, the Boyles, the Harveys, the Montesquieus, the Sheridans are no more! Regretted by a small number of friends, who have presently consoled themselves by their necessary avocations, their death was indifferent to the greater number of their fellow citizens. Darest thou then flatter thyself, that thy reputation, thy titles, thy riches, thy sumptuous repasts, thy diversified pleasures, will make thy funeral a melancholy event! It will be spoken of by some few for two days, and do not be at all surprised: learn that there have died in former ages, in Babylon, in Sardis, in Carthage, in Athens, in Rome, millions of citizens more illustrious, more powerful, more opulent, more voluptuous, than thou art; of whom, however, no one has taken care to transmit to thee even the names. Be then virtuous, O man! in whatever station thy destiny assigns thee, and thou shalt be happy in thy life time; do thou good and thou shalt be cherished; acquire talents and thou shalt be respected; posterity shall admire thee, if those talents, by becoming beneficial to their interests, shall bring them acquainted with the name under which they formerly designated thy annihilated being. But the universe will not be disturbed by thy loss; and when thou comest to die, whilst thy wife, thy children, thy friends, fondly leaning over thy sickly couch, shall be occupied with the melancholy task of closing thine eyes, thy nearest neighbour shall perhaps be exulting with joy!

Let not then man occupy himself with his condition that may be to come, but let him sedulously endeavour to make himself useful, to those with whom he lives; let him for his own peculiar happiness render himself dutiful to his parents—faithful to his wife—attentive to his children—kind to his relations——true to his friends—lenient to his servants; let him strive to become estimable in the eyes of his fellow citizens; let him faithfully serve a country which assures to him his welfare; let the desire of pleasing posterity, of meriting its applause, excite him to those labours that shall elicit their eulogies: let a legitimate self-love, when he shall be worthy of it, make him taste in advance those commendations which he is willing to deserve; let him learn to love himself—to esteem himself; but never let him consent that concealed vices, that sacred crimes, shall degrade him in his own eyes; shall oblige him to be ashamed of his own conduct.

Thus disposed, let him contemplate his own decease with the same indifference, that it will be looked upon by the greater number of his fellows; let him expect death with constancy; wait for it with calm resignation; let him learn to shake off those vain terrors with which superstition, would overwhelm him; let him leave to the enthusiast his vague hopes; to the fanatic his mad-brained speculations; to the bigot those fears with which he ministers to his own melancholy; but let his heart, fortified by reason, corroborated by a love of virtue, no longer dread a dissolution that will destroy all feeling.

Whatever may be the attachment man has to life, whatever may be his fear of death, it is every day witnessed, that habit, that opinion, that prejudice, are motives sufficiently powerful to annihilate these passions in his breast; to make him brave danger; to cause him to hazard his existence. Ambition, pride, jealousy, love, vanity, avarice, the desire of glory, that deference of opinion which is decorated with the sounding title of *a point of honour*, have the efficacy to make him shut his eyes to danger; to laugh at peril; to push him on to death: vexation, anxiety of mind, disgrace, want of success, softens to him its hard features; makes him regard it as a door that will afford him shelter from the injustice of mankind: indigence, trouble, adversity, familiarizes him with this death, so terrible to the happy. The poor man, condemned to labour, inured to privations, deprived of the comforts of life, views its approach with indifference: the unfortunate, when he is unhappy, when he is without resource, embraces it in despair; the wretched accelerates its march as soon as he sees that happiness is no longer within his grasp.

Man in different ages, in different countries, has formed opinions extremely various upon the conduct of those, who have had the temerity to put an end to their own existence. His ideas upon this subject, as upon all others, have taken their tone from his religion, have been governed by his superstitious systems, have been modified by his political institutions. The Greeks, the Romans, and other nations, which every thing conspired to make intrepid, to render courageous, to lead to magnanimity, regarded as heroes, contemplated as Gods, those who voluntarily cut the thread of life. In Hindoostan, the Brahmin yet knows how to inspire even women with sufficient fortitude to burn themselves upon the dead bodies of their husbands. The Japanese, upon the most trifling occasion, takes no kind of difficulty in plunging a dagger into his bosom.

Among the people of our own country, religion renders man less prodigal of life; it teaches that it is offensive to the Deity that he should destroy himself. Some moralists, abstracting the height of religious ideas, have held that it is never permitted to man to break the conditions of the covenant that he has made with society. Others have looked upon suicide as cowardice; they have thought that it was weakness, that it displayed pusillanimity, to suffer, himself to be overwhelmed with the shafts of his destiny; and have held that there would be much more courage, more elevation of soul, in supporting his afflictions, in resisting the blows of fate.

If nature be consulted upon this point, it will be found that all the actions of man, that feeble plaything in the hands of necessity, are indispensable; that they depend on causes which move him in despite of himself—that without his knowledge, make him accomplish at each moment of his existence some one of its decrees. If the same power that obliges all intelligent beings to cherish their existence, renders that of man so painful, so cruel, that he finds it insupportable he quits his species; order is destroyed for him, he accomplishes a decree of Nature, that wills he shall no longer exist. This Nature has laboured during thousands of years, to form in the bowels of the earth the iron that must number his days.

If the relation of man with Nature be examined, it will be found that his engagement was neither voluntary on his part, nor reciprocal on the part of Nature. The volition of his will had no share in his birth; it is commonly against his will that he is obliged to finish life; his actions are, as we have proved, only the necessary effects of unknown causes which determine his will. He is, in the hands of Nature, that which a sword is in his own hands; he can fall upon it without its being able to accuse him with breaking his engagements; or of stamping with ingratitude the hand that holds it: man can only love his existence on condition of being happy; as soon as the entire of nature refuses him this happiness; as soon as all that surrounds him becomes incommodious to him, as soon as his melancholy ideas offer nothing but afflicting pictures to his imagination; he already exists no longer; he is suspended in the void; he quits a rank which no longer suits him; in which he finds no one interest; which offers him no protection; which overwhelms him with calamity; in which he can no more be useful either to himself or to others.

If the covenant which unites man to society be considered, it will be obvious that every contract is conditional, must be reciprocal; that is to say, supposes mutual advantages between the contracting parties. The citizen cannot be bound to his country, to his associates, but by the bonds of happiness. Are these bonds cut asunder? He is restored to liberty. Society, or those who represent it, do they use him with harshness, do they treat him with injustice, do they render his existence painful? Does disgrace hold him out to the finger of scorn; does indigence menace him in an obdurate world? Perfidious friends, do they forsake him in adversity? An unfaithful wife, does she outrage his heart? Rebellious, ungrateful children, do they afflict his old age? Has he placed his happiness exclusively on some object which it is impossible for him to procure? Chagrin, remorse, melancholy, and despair, have they disfigured to him the spectacle of the universe? In short, for whatever cause it may be: if he is not able to support his evils, he quits a world, which from henceforth, is for him only a frightful desert he removes himself for ever from a country he thinks no longer willing to reckon him amongst the number of her children—he quits a house that to his mind is ready to bury him under its ruins—he renounces a society, to the happiness of which he can no longer contribute; which his own peculiar felicity alone can render dear to him: and could the man be blamed, who, finding himself useless; who being without resources, in the town where destiny gave him birth, should quit it in chagrin, to plunge himself in solitude? Death appears to the wretched the only remedy for despair; it is then the sword seems the only friend, the only comfort that is left to the unhappy: as long as hope remains the tenant of his bosom—as long as his evils appear to him at all supportable—as long as he flatters himself with seeing them brought to a termination—as long as he finds some comfort in existence, however slender, he will not consent to deprive himself of life: but when nothing any longer sustains in him the love of this existence, then to live, is to him the greatest of evils; to die, the only mode by which he can avoid the excess of despair. This has been the opinion of many great men: Seneca, the moralist, whom Lactantius calls the divine Pagan, who has been praised equally by St. Austin and St. Augustine, endeavours by every kind of argument to make death a matter of indifference to man. Cato has always been commended, because he would not survive the cause of liberty; for that he would not live a slave. Curtius, who rode voluntarily into the gap, to save his country, has always been held forth as a model of heroic virtue. Is it not evident, that those martyrs who have delivered themselves up to punishment, have preferred quitting the world to living in it contrary to their own ideals of happiness? When Samson wished to be revenged on the Philistines, did he not consent to die with them as the only means? If our country is attacked, do we not voluntarily sacrifice our lives in its defence?

That society who has not the ability, or who is not willing to procure man any one benefit, loses all its rights over him; Nature, when it has rendered his existence completely miserable, has in fact, ordered him to quit it: in dying he does no more than fulfil one of her decrees, as he did when he first drew his breath. To him who is fearless of death, there is no evil without a remedy; for him who refuses to die, there yet exists benefits which attach him to the world; in this case let him rally his powers—let him oppose courage to a destiny that oppresses him—let him call forth those resources with which Nature yet furnishes him; she cannot have totally abandoned him, while she yet leaves him the sensation of pleasure; the hopes of seeing a period to his pains.

Man regulates his judgment on his fellows, only by his own peculiar mode of feeling; he deems as folly, he calls delirium all those violent actions which he believes but little commensurate with their causes; or which appear to him calculated to deprive him of that happiness, towards which he supposes a being in the enjoyment of his senses, cannot cease to have a tendency: he treats his associate as a weak creature, when he sees him affected with that which touches him but lightly; or when he is incapable of supporting those evils, which his self-love flatters him, he would himself be able to endure with more fortitude. He accuses with madness whoever deprives himself of life, for objects that he thinks unworthy so dear a sacrifice; he taxes him with phrenzy, because he has himself learned to regard this life as the greatest blessing. It is thus that he always erects himself into a judge of the happiness of others—of their mode of seeing—of their manner of feeling: a miser who destroys himself after the loss of his treasure, appears a fool in the eyes of him who is less attached to riches; he does not feel, that without money, life to this miser is only a continued torture; that nothing in the world is capable of diverting him from his painful sensations: he will proudly tell you, that in his place he had not done so much; but to be exactly in the place of another man, it is needful to have his organization—his temperament—his passions—his ideas; it is in fact needful to be that other; to be placed exactly in the same circumstances; to be moved by the same causes; and in this case all men, like the miser, would sacrifice their life, after being deprived of the only source of their happiness.

He who deprives himself of his existence, does not adopt this extremity, so repugnant to his natural tendency; but when nothing in this world has the faculty of rejoicing him; when no means are left of diverting his affliction; when reason no longer acts; his misfortune whatever it may be, for him is real; his organization, be it strong, or be it weak, is his own, not that of another: a man who is sick only in imagination, really suffers considerably; even troublesome dreams place him in a very uncomfortable situation. Thus when a man kills himself, it ought to be concluded, that life, in the room of being a benefit, had become a very great evil to him; that existence had lost all its charms in his eyes; that the entire of nature was to him destitute of attraction; that it no longer contained any thing that could seduce him; that after the comparison which his disturbed imagination had made of existence with non-existence, the latter appeared to him preferable to the first.

Many will consider these maxims as dangerous; they certainly account why the unhappy cut the thread of life, in a manner not corresponding with the received prejudices; but, nevertheless, it is a temperament soured by chagrin, a bilious constitution, a melancholy habit, a defect in the organization, a derangement in the mind; it is in fact necessity and not reasonable speculations, that breed in man the design of destroying himself. Nothing invites him to this step so long as reason remains with him; or whilst he yet possesses hope, that sovereign balm for every evil: as for the unfortunate, who cannot lose sight of his sorrows—who cannot forget his pains—who has his evils always present to his mind; he is obliged to take counsel from these alone: besides, what assistance, what advantage can society promise to himself, from a miserable wretch reduced to despair; from a misanthrope overwhelmed with grief; from a wretch tormented with remorse, who has no longer any motive to render himself useful to others—who has abandoned himself—who finds no more interest in preserving his life? Frequently, those who destroy themselves are such, that had they lived, the offended laws must have ultimately been obliged to remove them from a society which they disgraced; from a country which they had injured.

As life is commonly the greatest blessing for man, it is to be presumed that he who deprives himself of it, is compelled to it by an invincible force. It is the excess of misery, the height of despair, the derangement of his brain, caused by melancholy, that urges man on to destroy himself. Agitated by contrary impulsions, he is, as we have before said, obliged to follow a middle course that conducts him to his death; if man be not a free-agent, in any one instant of his life, he is again much less so in the act by which it is terminated.

It will be seen then, that he who kills himself, does not, as it is pretended, commit an outrage on nature. He follows an impulse which has deprived him of reason; adopts the only means left him to quit his anguish; he goes out of a door which she leaves open to him; he cannot offend in accomplishing a law of necessity: the iron hand of this having broken the spring that renders life desirable to him; which urged him to self-conservation, shews him he ought to quit a rank or system where he finds himself too miserable to have the desire of remaining. His country or his family have no right to complain of a member, whom it has no means of rendering happy; from whom consequently they have nothing more to hope: to be useful to either, it is necessary he should cherish his own peculiar existence; that he should have an interest in conserving himself—that he should love the bonds by which he is united to others—that he should be capable of occupying himself with their felicity—that he should have a sound mind. That the suicide should repent of his precipitancy, he should outlive himself, he should carry with him into his future residence, his organs, his senses, his memory, his ideas, his actual mode of existing, his determinate manner of thinking.

In short, nothing is more useful for society, than to inspire man with a contempt for death; to banish from his mind the false ideas he has of its consequences. The fear of death can never do more than make cowards; the fear of its consequences will make nothing but fanatics or melancholy beings, who are useless to themselves, unprofitable to others. Death is a resource that ought not by any means to be taken away from oppressed virtue; which the injustice of man frequently reduces to despair. If man feared death less, he would neither be a slave nor superstitious; truth would find defenders more zealous; the rights of mankind would be more hardily sustained; virtue would be intrepidly upheld: error would be more powerfully opposed; tyranny would be banished from nations: cowardice nourishes it, fear perpetuates it. In fact, *man can neither be contented nor happy whilst his opinions shall oblige him to tremble.*

CHAP. XV.

Of Man's true Interest, or of the Ideas he forms to himself of Happiness.—Man cannot be happy without Virtue.

Utility, as has been before observed, ought to be the only standard of the judgment of man. To be useful, is to contribute to the happiness of his fellow creatures; to be prejudicial, is to further their misery. This granted, let us examine if the principles we have hitherto established be prejudicial or advantageous, useful or useless, to the human race. If man unceasingly seeks after his happiness, he can only approve of that which procures for him his object, or furnishes him the means by which it is to be obtained.

What has been already said will serve in fixing our ideas upon what constitutes this happiness: it has been already shewn that it is only continued pleasure: but in order that an object may please, it is necessary that the impressions it makes, the perceptions it gives, the ideas which it leaves, in short, that the motion it excites in man should be analogous to his organization; conformable to his temperament; assimilated to his individual nature:—modified as it is by habit, determined as it is by an infinity of circumstances, it is necessary that the action of the object by which he is moved, or of which the idea remains with him, far from enfeebling him, far from annihilating his feelings, should tend to strengthen him; it is necessary, that without fatiguing his mind, exhausting his faculties, or deranging his organs, this object should impart to his machine that degree of activity for which it continually has occasion. What is the object that unites all these qualities? Where is the man whose organs are susceptible of continual agitation without being fatigued; without experiencing a painful sensation; without sinking? Man is always willing to be warned of his existence in the most lively manner, as long as he can be so without pain. What do I say? He consents frequently to suffer, rather than not feel. He accustoms himself to a thousand things which at first must have affected him in a disagreeable manner; but which frequently end either by converting themselves into wants, or by no longer affecting him any way: of this truth tobacco, coffee, and above all brandy furnish examples: this is the reason he runs to see tragedies; that he witnesses the execution of criminals. In short, the desire of feeling, of being powerfully moved, appears to be the principle of curiosity; of that avidity with which man seizes on the marvellous; of that earnestness with which he clings to the supernatural; of the disposition he evinces for the incomprehensible. Where, indeed, can he always find objects in nature capable of continually supplying the stimulus requisite to keep him in activity, that shall be ever proportioned to the state of his own organization; which his extreme mobility renders subject to perpetual variation? The most lively pleasures are always the least durable, seeing they are those which exhaust him most.

That man should be uninterruptedly happy, it would be requisite that his powers were infinite; it would require that to his mobility he joined a vigor, attached a solidity, which nothing could change; or else it is necessary that the objects from which he receives impulse, should either acquire or lose properties, according to the different states through which his machine is successively obliged to pass; it would need that the essences of beings should be changed in the same proportion as his dispositions; should be submitted to the continual influence of a thousand causes, which modify him without his knowledge, and in despite of himself. If, at each moment, his machine undergoes changes more or less marked, which are ascribable to the different degrees of elasticity, of density, of serenity of the atmosphere; to the portion of igneous fluid circulating through his blood; to the harmony of his organs; to the order that exists between the various parts of his body; if, at every period of his existence, his nerves have not the same tensions, his fibres the same elasticity, his mind the same activity, his imagination the same ardour, &c. it is evident that the same causes in preserving to him only the same qualities, cannot always affect him in the same manner. Here is the reason why those objects that please him in one season displease him in another: these objects have not themselves sensibly changed; but his organs, his dispositions, his ideas, his mode of seeing, his manner of feeling, have changed:—such is the source of man's inconstancy.

If the same objects are not constantly in that state competent to form the happiness of the same individual, it is easy to perceive that they are yet less in a capacity to please all men; or that the same happiness cannot be suitable to all. Beings already various by their temperament, unlike in their faculties, diversified in their organization, different in their imagination, dissimilar in their ideas, of distinct opinions, of contrary habits, which an infinity of circumstances, whether physical or moral, have variously modified, must necessarily form very different notions of happiness. Those of a MISER cannot be the same as those of a PRODIGAL; those of a VOLUPTUARY, the same as those of one who is PHLEGMATIC; those of an intemperate, the same as those of a rational man, who husbands his health. The happiness of each, is in consequence composed of his natural organization, and of those circumstances, of those habits, of those ideas, whether true or false, that have modified him: this organization and these circumstances, never being the same in any two men, it follows, that what is the object of one man's views, must be indifferent, or even displeasing to another; thus, as we have before said, no one can be capable of judging of that which may contribute to the felicity of his fellow man.

Interest is the object to which each individual according to his temperament and his own peculiar ideas, attaches his welfare; from which it will be perceived that this interest is never more than that which each contemplates as necessary to his happiness. It must, therefore, be concluded, that no man is totally without interest. That of the miser to amass wealth; that of the prodigal to dissipate it: the interest of the ambitious is to obtain power; that of the modest philosopher to enjoy tranquillity; the interest of the debauchee is to give himself up, without reserve, to all sorts of pleasure; that of the prudent man, to abstain from those which may injure him: the interest of the wicked is to gratify his passions at any price: that of the virtuous to merit by his conduct the love, to elicit by his actions the approbation of others; to do nothing that can degrade himself in his own eyes.

Thus, when it is said that *Interest is the only motive of human actions;* it is meant to indicate that each man labours after his own manner, to his own peculiar happiness; that he places it in some object either visible or concealed; either real or imaginary; that the whole system of his conduct is directed to its attainment. This granted, no man can be called disinterested; this appellation is only applied to those of whose motives we are ignorant; or whose interest we approve. Thus the man who finds a greater pleasure in assisting his friends in misfortune than preserving in his coffers useless treasure, is called generous, faithful, and disinterested; in like manner all men are denominated disinterested, who feel their glory far more precious than their fortune. In short, all men are designated disinterested who place their happiness in making sacrifices which man considers costly, because he does not attach the same value to the object for which the sacrifice is made.

Man frequently judges very erroneously of the interest of others, either because the motives that animate them are too complicated for him to unravel; or because to be enabled to judge of them fairly, it is needful to have the same eyes, the same organs the same passions, the same opinions: nevertheless, obliged to form his judgment of the actions of mankind, by their effect on himself, he approves the interest that actuates them whenever the result is advantageous for his species: thus, he admires valour, generosity, the love of liberty, great talents, virtue, &c. he then only approves of the objects in which the beings he applauds have placed their happiness; he approves these dispositions even when he is not in a capacity to feel their effects; but in this judgment he is not himself disinterested; experience, reflection, habit, reason, have given him a taste for morals, and he finds as much pleasure in being witness to a great and generous action, as the man of *virtu* finds in the sight of a fine picture of which he is not the proprietor. He who has formed to himself a habit of practising virtue, is a man who has unceasingly before his eyes the interest that he has in meriting the affection, in deserving the esteem, in securing the assistance of others, as well as to love and esteem himself: impressed with these ideas which have become habitual to him, he abstains even from concealed crimes, since these would degrade him in his own eyes: he resembles a man who having from his infancy contracted the habit of cleanliness, would be painfully affected at seeing himself dirty, even when no one should witness it. The honest man is he to whom truth has shewn his interest or his happiness in a mode of acting that others are obliged to love, are under the necessity to approve for their own peculiar interest.

These principles, duly developed, are the true basis of morals; nothing is more chimerical than those which are founded upon imaginary motives placed out of nature; or upon innate sentiments; which some speculators have regarded as anterior to man's experience; as wholly independant of those advantages which result to him from its use: it is the essence of man to love himself; to tend to his own conservation; to seek to render his existence happy: thus interest, or the desire of happiness, is the only real motive of all his actions; this interest depends upon his natural organization, rests itself upon his wants, is bottomed upon his acquired ideas, springs from the habits he has contracted: he is without doubt in error, when either a vitiated organization or false opinions shew him his welfare in objects either useless or injurious to himself, as well as to others; he marches steadily in the paths of virtue when true ideas have made him rest his happiness on a conduct useful to his species; in that which is approved by others; which renders him an interesting object to his associates. *Morals* would be a vain science if it did not incontestibly prove to man that *his interest consists in being virtuous*. Obligation of whatever kind, can only be founded upon the probability or the certitude of either obtaining a good or avoiding an evil.

Indeed, in no one instant of his duration, can a sensible, an intelligent being, either lose sight of his own preservation or forget his own welfare; he owes happiness to himself; but experience quickly proves to him, that bereaved of assistance, quite alone, left entirely to himself, he cannot procure all those objects which are requisite to his felicity: he lives with sensible, with intelligent beings, occupied like himself with their own peculiar happiness; but capable of assisting him, in obtaining those objects he most desires; he discovers that these beings will not be favorable to his views, but when they find their interest involved; from which he concludes, that his own happiness demands, that his own wants render it necessary he should conduct himself at all times in a manner suitable to conciliate the attachment, to obtain the approbation, to elicit the esteem, to secure the assistance of those beings who are most capacitated to further his designs. He perceives, that it is man who is most necessary to the welfare of man:

that to induce him to join in his interests, he ought to make him find real advantages in recording his projects: but to procure real advantages to the beings of the human species, is to have virtue; the reasonable man, therefore, is obliged to feel that it is his interest to be virtuous. *Virtue is only the art of rendering himself happy, by the felicity of others.* The virtuous man is he who communicates happiness to those beings who are capable of rendering his own condition happy; who are necessary to his conservation; who have the ability to procure him a felicitous existence.

Such, then, is the true foundation of all morals; merit and virtue are founded upon the nature of man; have their dependance upon his wants. It is virtue alone that can render him truly happy: without virtue society can neither be useful nor indeed subsist; it can only have real utility when it assembles beings animated with the desire of pleasing each other, and disposed to labour to their reciprocal advantage: there exists no comfort in those families whose members are not in the happy disposition to lend each other mutual succours; who have not a reciprocity of feeling that stimulates them to assist one another; that induces them to cling to each other, to support the sorrows of life; to unite their efforts, to put away those evils to which nature has subjected them; the conjugal bonds, are sweet only in proportion as they identify the interest of two beings, united by the want of legitimate pleasure; from whence results the maintenance of political society, and the means of furnishing it with citizens. Friendship has charms only when it more particularly associates two virtuous beings; that is to say, animated with the sincere desire of conspiring to their reciprocal happiness. In short, it is only by displaying virtue, that man can merit the benevolence, can win the confidence, can gain the esteem, of all those with whom he has relation; in a word, no man can be independently happy.

Indeed, the happiness of each human individual depends on those sentiments to which he gives birth, on those feelings which he nourishes in the beings amongst whom his destiny has placed him; grandeur may dazzle them; power may wrest from them an involuntary homage; force may compel an unwilling obedience; opulence may seduce mean, may attract venal souls; but it is humanity, it is benevolence, it is compassion, it is equity, that unassisted by these, can without efforts obtain for him, from those by whom he is surrounded, those delicious sentiments of attachments, those soothing feelings of tenderness, those sweet ideas of esteem, of which all reasonable men feel the necessity. To be virtuous then, is to place his interest in that which accords with the interest of others; it is to enjoy those benefits, to partake of that pleasure which he himself diffuses over his fellows. He whom, his nature, his education, his reflections, his habits, have rendered susceptible of these dispositions, and to whom his circumstances have given him the faculty of gratifying them, becomes an interesting object to all those who approach him: he enjoys every instant, he reads with satisfaction the contentment, he contemplates with pleasure the joy which he has diffused over all countenances: his wife, his children, his friends, his servants greet him with gay, serene faces, indicative of that content, harbingers of that peace, which he recognizes for his own work: every thing that environs him is ready to partake his pleasures; to share his pains; cherished, respected, looked up to by others, every thing conducts him to agreeable reflections; he knows the rights he has acquired over their hearts; he applauds himself for being the source of a felicity that captivates all the world; his own condition, his sentiments of self-love, become an hundred times more delicious when he sees them participated by all those with whom his destiny has connected him. The habit of virtue creates for him no wants but those which virtue itself suffices to satisfy; it is thus that *virtue is always its own peculiar reward*, that it remunerates itself with all the advantages which it incessantly procures for others.

It will be said, and perhaps even proved, that under the present constitution of things, virtue far from procuring the welfare of those who practice it frequently plunges man into misfortune; often places continual obstacles to his felicity; that almost every where it is without recompence. What do I say? A thousand examples could be adduced as evidence, that in almost every country it is hated, persecuted, obliged to lament the ingratitude of human nature. I reply with avowing, that by a necessary consequence of the errors of his race, virtue rarely conducts man to those objects in which the uninformed make their happiness consist. The greater number of societies, too frequently ruled by those whose ignorance makes them abuse their power,—whose prejudices render them enemies of virtue,—who flattered by sycophants, secure in the impunity their actions enjoy, commonly lavish their esteem, bestow their kindness, on none but the most unworthy objects; reward only the most frivolous, recompence none but the most prejudicial qualities; and hardly ever accord that justice to merit which is unquestionably its due. But the truly honest man, is neither ambitious of renumeration, nor sedulous of the suffrages of a society thus badly constituted: contented with domestic happiness, he seeks not to augment relations, which would do no more than increase his danger; he knows that a vitiated community is a whirlwind, with which an honest man cannot co-order himself: he therefore steps aside; quits the beaten path, by continuing in which he would infallibly be crushed. He does all the good of which he is capable in his sphere; he leaves the road free to the wicked, who are willing to wade through its mire; he laments the heavy strokes they inflict on themselves; he applauds mediocrity that affords him security: he pities those nations made miserable by their errors,—rendered unhappy by those passions which are the fatal but necessary consequence; he sees they contain nothing but wretched citizens, who far from cultivating their true interest, far from labouring to their mutual felicity, far from feeling the real value of virtue, unconscious how dear it ought to be to them, do nothing but either openly attack, or secretly injure it; in short, who detests a quality which would restrain their disorderly propensities.

In saying that virtue is its own peculiar reward, it is simply meant to announce, that in a society whose views were guided by truth, trained by experience, conducted by reason, each individual would be acquainted with his real interests; would understand the true end of association; would have sound motives to perform his duties; find real advantages in fulfilling them; in fact, it would be convinced, that to render himself solidly happy, he should occupy his actions with the welfare of his fellows; by their utility merit their esteem, elicit their kindness, and secure their assistance. In a well-constituted society, the government, the laws, education, example, would all conspire to prove to the citizen, that the nation of which he forms a part, is a whole that cannot be happy, that cannot subsist without virtue; experience would, at each step, convince him that the welfare of its parts can only result from that of the whole body corporate; justice would make him feel, that no society, can be advantageous to its members, where the volition of wills in those who act, is not so conformable to the interests of the whole, as to produce an advantageous re-action.

But, alas! by the confusion which the errors of man have carried into his ideas: virtue disgraced, banished, and persecuted, finds not one of those advantages it has a right to expect: man is indeed shewn those rewards for it in a future life, of which he is almost always deprived in his actual existence. It is thought necessary to deceive, considered proper to seduce, right to intimidate him, in order to induce him to follow that virtue which every thing renders incommodious to him; he is fed with distant hopes, in order to solicit him to practice virtue, while contemplation of the world makes it hateful to him; he is alarmed by remote terrors, to deter him from committing evil, which his associates paint as amiable; which all conspires to render necessary. It is thus that politics, thus that superstition, by the formation of chimeras, by the creation of fictitious interests pretend to supply those true, those real motives which nature furnishes,—which experience would point out,—which an enlightened government should hold forth,—which the law ought to enforce,—which instruction should sanction,—which example should encourage,-which rational opinions would render pleasant. Man, blinded by his passions, not less dangerous than necessary, led away by precedent, authorised by custom, enslaved by habit, pays no attention to these uncertain promises, is regardless of the menaces held out; the actual interests of his immediate pleasures, the force of his passions, the inveteracy of his habits, always rise superior to the distant interests pointed out in his future welfare, or the remote evils with which he is threatened; which always appear doubtful, whenever he compares them with present advantages.

Thus *superstition, far from making man virtuous by principle, does nothing more than impose upon him a yoke as severe as it is useless*; it is borne by none but enthusiasts, or by the pusillanimous; who, without becoming better, tremblingly champ the feeble bit put into their mouth; who are either rendered unhappy by their opinions, or dangerous by their tenets; indeed, experience, that faithful monitor, incontestibly proves, that superstition is a dyke inadequate to resist the torrent of corruption, to which so many accumulated causes give an irresistible force: nay more, does not this superstition itself augment the public disorder, by the dangerous passions which it lets loose, by the conduct which it sanctions, by the actions which it consecrates? Virtue, in almost every climate, is confined to some few rational souls, who have sufficient strength of mind to resist the stream of prejudice; who are contented by remunerating themselves with the benefits they difuse over society: whose temperate dispositions are gratified with the suffrages of a small number of virtuous approvers; in short, who are detached from those frivolous advantages which the injustice of society but too commonly accords only to baseness, which it rarely bestows, except to intrigue, with which in general it rewards nothing but crime.

In despite of the injustice that reigns in the world, there are, however, some virtuous men in the bosom even of the most degenerate nations; notwithstanding the general depravity, there are some benevolent beings, still enamoured of virtue; who are fully acquainted with its true value; who are sufficiently enlightened to know that it exacts homage even from its enemies; who to use the language of ECCLESIASTES, "*rejoice in their own works*;" who are, at least, happy in possessing contented minds, who are satisfied with concealed pleasures, those internal recompences of which no earthly power is competent to deprive them. The honest man acquires a right to the esteem, has a just claim to the veneration, wins the confidence, gains the love, even of those whose conduct is exposed by a contrast with his own. In short, vice is obliged to cede to virtue; of which it blushingly, though unwillingly, acknowledges the superiority. Independent of this ascendancy so gentle, of this superiority so grand, of this pre-eminence so infallible, when even the whole universe should be unjust to him, when even every tongue should cover him with venom, when even every arm should menace him with hostility, there yet remains to the honest man the sublime advantage of loving his own conduct; the ineffable pleasure of esteeming himself; the unalloyed gratification of diving with satisfaction into the recesses of his own heart; the tranquil delight of contemplating his own actions with that delicious complacency that others ought to do, if they were not hood-winked, No power is adequate to ravish from him the merited esteem of himself; no authority is sufficiently potent to give it to him when he deserves it not; the mightiest monarch cannot lend stability to this esteem, when it is not well founded; it is then a ridiculous sentiment: it ought to be considered, it really is "*vanity and vexation of spirit*," it is not wisdom, but folly in the extreme; it ought to be censured when it displays itself in a mode that is mortifying to its neighbour, in a manner that is troublesome to others; it is then called ARROGANCE; it is called VANITY; but when it cannot be condemned, when it is known for legitimate when it is discovered to have a solid foundation, when it bottoms itself upon talents, when it rises upon great actions that are useful to the community, when it erects its edifice upon virtue; even though society should not set these merits at their just price, it is NOBLE PRIDE, ELEVATION OF MIND, and GRANDEUR OF SOUL.

Of what consequence then, is it to listen to those superstitious beings, those enemies to man's happiness, who have been desirous of destroying it, even in the inmost recesses of his heart; who have prescribed to him hatred of his follower; who have filled him with contempt for himself; who pretend to wrest from the honest man that self-respect which is frequently the only reward that remains to virtue, in a perverse world. To annihilate in him this sentiment, so full in justice, this love of himself, is to break the most powerful spring, to weaken the most efficacious stimulus, that urges him to act right; that spurs him on to do good to his fellow mortals. What motive, indeed, except it be this, remains for him in the greater part of human societies? Is not virtue discouraged? Is not honesty contemned? Is not audacious crime encouraged? Is not subtle intrigue eulogized? Is not cunning vice rewarded? Is not love of the public weal taxed as folly; exactitude in fulfilling duties looked upon as a bubble? Is not compassion laughed to scorn? ARE NOT TRAITORS DISTINGUISHED BY PUBLIC HONORS? Is not negligence of morals applauded,—sensibility derided,—tenderness scoffed,—conjugal fidelity jeered,—sincerity despised,—enviolable friendship treated with ridicule: while seduction, adultery, hard-heartedness, punic faith, avarice, and fraud, stalk forth unabashed, decked in gorgeous array, lauded by the world? Man must have motives for action: he neither acts well nor ill, but with a view to his own happiness: that which he judges will conduce to this "*consummation so devoutly to be wished*," he thinks his interest; he does nothing gratuitously; when reward for useful actions is withheld from him, he is reduced either to become as abandoned as others, or else to remunerate himself with his own applause.

This granted; the honest man can never be completely unhappy; he can never be entirely deprived of the recompence which is his due; virtue is competent to repay him for all the benefits he may bestow on others; can amply make up to him all the happiness denied him by public opinion; *but nothing can compensate to him the want of virtue.* It does not follow that the honest man will be exempted from afflictions: like, the wicked, he is subject to physical evils; he may pine in indigence; he may be deprived of friendship; he may be worn down with disease; he may frequently be the subject of calumny; he may be the victim to injustice; he may be treated with ingratitude; he may be exposed to hatred; but in the midst of all his misfortunes, in the very bosom of his sorrows, in the extremity of his vexation, he finds support in himself; he is contented with his own conduct; he respects himself; he feels his own dignity; he knows the equity of his rights; he consoles himself with the confidence inspired by the justness of his cause; he cheers himself amidst the most sullen circumstances. These supports are not calculated for the wicked; they avail him nothing: equally liable with the honest man to infirmities, equally submitted to the caprices of his destiny, equally the sport of a fluctuating world, he finds the recesses of his own heart filled with dreadful alarms; diseased with care; cankered with solitude; corroded with regret; gnawed by remorse; he dies within himself; his conscience sustains him not but loads him with reproach; his mind, overwhelmed, sinks beneath its own turpitude; his reflection is the bitter dregs of hemlock; maddening anguish holds him to the mirror that shews him his own deformity; that recalls unhallowed deeds; gloomy thoughts rush on his too faithful memory; despondence benumbs him; his body, simultaneously assailed on all sides, bends under the storm of—his own unruly passions; at last despair grapples him to her filthy bosom, he flies from himself. The honest man is not an insensible Stoic; virtue does not procure impassibility; honesty gives no exemption from misfortune, but it enables him to bear cheerly up against it; to cast off despair, to keep his own company: if he is infirm, if he is worn with disease, he has less to complain of than the vicious being who is oppressed with sickness, who is enfeebled by years; if he is indigent, he is less unhappy in his poverty; if he is in disgrace, he can endure it with fortitude, he is not overwhelmed by its pressure, like the wretched slave to crime.

Thus the happiness of each individual depends on the cultivation of his temperament; nature makes both the happy and the unhappy; it is culture that gives value to the soil nature has formed; it is instruction that makes the fruit it produces palatable; It is reflection that makes it useful. For man to be happily born, is to have received from nature a sound body, organs that act with precision—a just mind, a heart whose passions are analogous, whose desires are conformable to the circumstances in which his destiny has placed him: nature, then, has done every thing for him, when she has joined to these faculties the quantum of vigour, the portion of energy, sufficient to enable him to obtain those Proper things, which his station, his mode of thinking, his temperament, have rendered desirable. Nature has made him a fatal present, when she has filled his sanguinary vessels with an over-heated fluid; when she has given him an imagination too active; when she has infused into him desires too impetuous; when he has a hankering after objects either impossible or improper to be obtained under his circumstances; or which at least he cannot procure without those incredible efforts, that either place his own welfare in danger or disturb the repose of society. The most happy man, is commonly he who possesses a peaceful soul; who only desires those things which he can procure by labour, suitable to maintain his activity; which he can obtain without causing those shocks, that are either too violent for society, or troublesome to his associates. A philosopher whose wants are easily satisfied, who is a stranger, to ambition, who is contented with the limited circle of a small number of friends, is, without doubt a being much more happily constituted than an ambitious conqueror, whose greedy imagination is reduced to despair by having only one world to ravage. He who is happily born, or whom nature has rendered susceptible of being conveniently modified, is not a being injurious to society: it is generally disturbed by men who are unhappily born, whose organization renders them turbulent; who are discontented with their destiny; who are inebriated with their own licentious passions; who are infatuated with their own vile schemes; who are smitten with difficult enterprises; who set the world in combustion, to gather imaginary benefits in order to attain which they must inflict he heaviest curses on mankind, but in which they make their own happiness consist. An ALEXANDER requires the destruction of empires, nations to be deluged with blood, cities to be laid in ashes, its inhabitants to be exterminated, to content that passion for glory, of which he has formed to himself a false idea; but which his too ardent imagination, his too vehement mind anxiously thirsts after: for a DIOGENES there needs only a tub with the liberty of appearing whimsical; a SOCRATES wants nothing but the pleasure of forming disciples to virtue.

Man by his organization is a being to whom motion is always necessary; he must therefore always desire it: this is the reason why too much facility In procuring the objects of his search, renders them quickly insipid. To feel happiness, it is necessary to make efforts to obtain it; to find charms in its enjoyment, it is necessary that the desire should be whetted by obstacles; he is presently disgusted with those benefits which have cost him but little pains. The expectation of happiness, the labour requisite to procure it, the varied prospects it holds forth, the multiplied pictures which his imagination forms to him, supply his brain with that motion for which it has occasion; this gives impulse to his organs, puts his whole machine into activity, exercises his faculties, sets all his springs in play, in a word, puts him into that agreeable activity, for the want of which the enjoyment of happiness itself cannot compensate him. Action is the true element of the human mind; as soon as it ceases to act, it falls into disgust, sinks into lassitude. His soul has the same occasion for ideas, his stomach has for aliment.

Thus the impulse given him by desire, is itself a great benefit; it is to the mind what exercise is to the body; without it he would not derive any pleasure in the aliments presented to him; it is thirst that renders the pleasure of drinking so agreeable; life is a perpetual circle of regenerated desires and wants satisfied: repose is only a pleasure to him who labours; it is a source of weariness, the cause of sorrow, the spring of vice to him who has nothing to do. To enjoy without interruption is not to enjoy any thing: the man who has nothing to desire is certainly more unhappy than he who suffers.

These reflections, grounded upon experience, drawn from the fountain of truth, ought to prove to man, that good as well as evil depends on the essence of things. Happiness to be felt cannot be continued. Labour is necessary, to make intervals between his pleasures; his body has occasion for exercise, to co-order him with the beings who surround him; his heart must have desires; trouble alone can give him the right relish of his welfare; it is this which puts in the shadows, this which furnishes the true perspective to the picture of human life. By an irrevocable law of his destiny, man is obliged to be discontented with his present condition; to make efforts to change it; to reciprocally envy that felicity which no individual enjoys perfectly. Thus the poor man envies the opulence of his richer neighbour, although this is frequently more unhappy than his needy maligner; thus the rich man views with pain the advantages of a poverty, which he sees active, healthy, and frequently jocund, even in the bosom of penury.

If man was perfectly contented, there would no longer be any activity in the world; it is necessary that he should desire; it is requisite that he should act; it is incumbent he should labour, in order that he may be happy: such is the course of nature of which the life consists in action. Human societies can only subsist, by the continual exchange of those things in which man places his happiness. The poor man is obliged to desire, he is necessitated to labour, that he may procure what he knows is requisite to the preservation of his existence; the primary wants given to him by nature, are to nourish himself, clothe himself, lodge himself, and propagate his species; has he satisfied these? He is quickly obliged to create others entirely new; or rather, his imagination only refines upon the first; he seeks to diversify them; he is willing to give them fresh zest; arrived at opulence, when he has run over the whole circle of wants, when he has completely exhausted their combinations, he falls into disgust. Dispensed from labour, his body amasses humours; destitute of desires, his heart feels a languor; deprived of activity, he is obliged to participate his riches, with beings more active, more laborious than himself: these, following their own peculiar interests, take upon themselves the task of labouring for his advantage; of procuring for him means to satisfy his want; of ministering to his caprices, in order to remove the languor that oppresses him. It is thus the great, the rich excite the energies, give play to the activity, rouse the faculties, spur on the industry of the indigent; these labour to their own peculiar welfare by working for others: thus the desire of ameliorating his condition, renders man necessary to his fellow man; thus wants, always regenerating, never satisfied, are the principles of life,—the soul of activity,—the source of health,—the basis of society. If each individual was competent to the supply of his own exigencies, there would be no occasion for him to congregate in society; but it is his wants, his desires, his whims, that place him in a state of dependence on others: these are the causes that each individual, in order to further his own peculiar interest, is obliged to be useful to those, who have the capability of procuring for him the objects which he himself has not. A nation is nothing more than the union of a great number of individuals, connected with each other by the reciprocity of their wants; by their mutual desire of pleasure. The most happy man is he who has the fewest wants, and who has the most numerous means of satisfying them. The man who would be truly rich, has no need to increase his fortune, it suffices he should diminish his wants.

In the individuals of the human species, as well as in political society, the progression of wants, is a thing absolutely necessary; it is founded upon the essence of man, it is requisite that the natural wants once satisfied, should be replaced by those which he calls *Imaginary, or wants of the Fancy:* these become as necessary to his happiness as the first. Custom, which permits the native American to go quite naked, obliges the more civilized inhabitant of Europe to clothe himself; the poor man contents himself with very simple attire, which equally serve him for winter and for summer, for autumn and for spring; the rich man desires to have garments suitable to each mutation of these seasons; he would experience pain if he had not the convenience of changing his raiment with every variation of his climate; he would be wretched if he was obliged to wear the same habiliments in the heat of summer, which he uses in the winter; in short, he would be unhappy if the expence and variety of his costume did not display to the surrounding multitude his opulence, mark his rank, announce his superiority. It is thus habit multiplies, the wants of the wealthy; it is thus that vanity itself becomes a want which sets a thousand hands in, motion, a thousand heads to work, who are all eager to gratify its cravings; in short, this very vanity procures for the necessitous man, the means of subsisting at the expense of his opulent neighbours He who is accustomed to pomp, who is used to ostentatious splendour, whose habits are luxurious, whenever he is deprived of these insignia of opulence, to which he has attached the idea of happiness, finds himself just as unhappy as the needy wretch who has not wherewith to cover his nakedness. The civilized nations of the present day were in their origin savages composed of erratic tribes,—mere wanderers who were occupied with war; employed in, the chace; painfully obliged to seek precarious subsistence by hunting in those woods which the industry of their successors has cleared; which their labour has covered with yellow waving ears of nutritious corn; in time they have become stationary: they first applied themselves to Agriculture, afterwards to commerce: by degrees they have refined on their primitive wants, extended their sphere of action, given birth to a thousand new wants, imagined a thousand new means to satisfy them; this is the natural course, the necessary progression, the regular march of active beings, who cannot live without feeling; who to be happy, must of necessity diversify their sensations. In proportion as man's wants multiply the means to satisfy them becomes more difficult, he is obliged to depend on a greater number of his fellow creatures; his interest obliges him to rouse their activity; to engage them to concur with his views; consequently he is obliged to procure for them those objects by which they can be excited; he is under the necessity of contenting their desires, which increase like his own, by the very food that satisfies them. The savage needs only put forth his hand to gather the fruit that offers itself spontaneously to his reach: this he finds sufficient for his nourishment. The opulent citizen of a flourishing society is obliged to set innumerable hands to work to produce the sumptuous repast; the four quarters of the globe are ransacked to procure the far-fetched viands become necessary to revive his languid appetite; the merchant, the sailor, the mechanic, leave nothing unattempted to flatter his inordinate vanity. From this it will appear, that in the same proportion the wants of man are multiplied, he is obliged to augment the means to satisfy them. Riches are nothing more than the measure of a convention, by the assistance of which man is enabled to make a great number of his fellows concur in the gratification of his desires; by which he is capacitated to invite them, for their own peculiar interests, to contribute to his pleasures. What, in fact, does the rich man do, except announce to the needy, that he can furnish him with the means of subsistence if he consents to lend himself to his will? What does the man in power, except shew to others, that he is in a state to supply the requisites to render them happy? Sovereigns, nobles, men of wealth, appear to be happy, only because they possess the ability, are masters of the motives sufficient to determine a great number of individuals to occupy themselves with their respective felicity.

The more things are considered the more man will be convinced that his false opinion are the true source of his misery; the clearer it will appear to him that happiness is so rare, only because he attaches it to objects either indifferent or useless to his welfare; which, when enjoyed, convert themselves into real evils; which afflict him; which become the cause of his misfortune.

Riches are indifferent in themselves, it is only by their application, by the purposes they compass, that they either become objects of utility to man, or are rendered prejudicial to his welfare.

Money, useless to the savage who understands not its value, is amassed by the miser, for fear it should be employed uselessly; lest it should be squandered by the prodigal; or dissipated by the voluptuary; who make no other use of it than to purchase infirmities; to buy regret.

Pleasures are nothing for the man who is incapable of feeling them; they become real evils when they are too freely indulged, when they are destructive to his health,—when they derange the economy of his machine,—when they entail diseases on himself and on his posterity,—when they make him neglect his duties,—when they render him despicable in the eyes of others.

Power is nothing in itself, it is useless to man if he does not avail himself of it to promote his own peculiar felicity, by augmenting the happiness of his species; it becomes fatal to him as soon as he abuses it; it becomes odious whenever he employs it to render others miserable; it is always the cause of his own misery whenever he stretches it beyond the due bounds prescribed by nature.

For want of being enlightened on his true interest, the man who enjoys all the means of rendering himself completely happy, scarcely ever discovers the secret of making those means truly subservient to his own peculiar felicity: the art of enjoying, is that which of all others is least understood; man should learn this art before he begins to desire; the earth is covered with individuals who only occupy themselves with the care of procuring the means without ever being acquainted with the end. All the world desire fortune, solicit power, seek after pleasure, yet very few, indeed, are those whom objects render truly happy.

It is quite natural in man, it is extremely reasonable, it is absolutely necessary, to desire those things which can contribute to augment the sum of his felicity. *Pleasure, riches, power,* are objects worthy his ambition, deserving his most strenuous efforts, when he has learned how to employ them; when he has acquired the faculty of making them render his existence really more agreeable. It is impossible to censure him who desires them, to despise him who commands them, but when to obtain them he employs odious means; or when after he has obtained them he makes a pernicious use of them, injurious to himself, prejudicial to others; let him wish for power, let him seek after grandeur, let him be ambitious of reputation, when he can shew just pretensions to them; when he can obtain them, without making the purchase at the expence of his own repose, or that of the beings with whom he lives: let him desire riches, when he knows how to make a use of them that is truly advantageous for himself, really beneficial for others; but never let him employ those means to procure them of which he may be ashamed; with which he may be obliged to reproach himself; which may draw upon him the hatred of his associates; or which may render him obnoxious to the castigation of society: let him always recollect, that his solid happiness should rest its foundations upon its own esteem,—upon the advantages he procures for others; above all, never let him for a moment forget, that of all the objects to which his ambition may point, the most impracticable for a being who lives in society, is that of *attempting to render himself exclusively happy.*

CHAP. XVI

The Errors of Man,—upon what constitutes Happiness.—the true Source of his Evil.—Remedies that may be applied.

Reason by no means forbids man from forming capacious desires; ambition is a passion useful to his species when it has for, its object the happiness of his race. Great minds, elevated souls, are desirous of acting on an extended sphere; geniuses who are powerful, beings who are enlightened, men who are beneficent, distribute very widely their benign influence; they must necessarily, in order to promote their own peculiar felicity, render great numbers happy. So many princes fail to enjoy true happiness only, because their feeble, narrow souls, are obliged to act in a sphere too extensive for their energies: it is thus that by the supineness, the indolence, the incapacity of their chiefs, nations frequently pine in misery; are often submitted to masters, whose exility of mind is as little calculated to promote their own immediate happiness, as it is to further that of their miserable subjects. On the other hand, souls too vehement, too much inflamed, too active, are themselves tormented by the narrow sphere that confines them; their ardour misplaced, becomes the scourge of the human race. Alexander was a monarch who was equally injurious to the earth, equally discontented with his condition, as the indolent despot whom he dethroned. The souls of neither were by any means commensurate with their sphere of action.

The happiness of man will never be more than the result of the harmony that subsists between his desires and his circumstances. The sovereign power to him who knows not how to apply it to the advantage of his citizens, is as nothing; it cannot even conduce to his own peculiar happiness. If it renders him miserable, it is a real evil; if it produces the misfortune of a portion of the human race, it is a detestable abuse. The most powerful princes are ordinarily such strangers to happiness, their subjects are commonly so unfortunate, only because the first possess all the means of rendering themselves happy without ever giving them activity; or because the only knowledge they have of them, is their abuse. A wise man seated on a throne, would be the most happy of mortals. A monarch is a man for whom his power, let it be of whatever extent, cannot procure other organs, other modes of feeling, than the meanest of his subjects; if he has an advantage over them, it is by the grandeur, the variety, the multiplicity of the objects with which he can occupy himself; which by giving perpetual activity to his mind, can prevent it from decay; from falling into sloth. If his soul is virtuous, if his mind is expansive, his ambition finds continual food in the contemplation of the power he possesses, to unite by gentleness, to consolidate by kindness, the will of his subjects with his own; to interest them in his own conservation, to merit their affections,—to draw forth the respect of strangers,—to render luminous the page of history—to elicit the eulogies of all nations—to clothe the orphan,—to dry the widow's tears. Such are the conquests that reason proposes to all those whose destiny it is to govern the fate of empires; they are sufficiently grand to satisfy the most ardent imagination, of a sublimity to gratify the most capacious ambition: for a monarch they are paramount duties.—KINGS are the most happy of men, only because they have the power of making others happy; because they possess the means of multiplying the causes of legitimate content with themselves.

The advantages of the sovereign power are participated by all those who contribute to the government of states. Thus grandeur, rank, reputation, are desirable, are legitimate objects for all who are acquainted with the means of rendering them subservient to their own peculiar felicity; they are useless, they are illegitimate to those ordinary men who have neither the energy nor the capacity to employ them in a mode advantageous to themselves; they are detestable whenever to obtain them man compromises his own happiness, when he implicates the welfare of society: this society itself is in an error every time it respects men who only employ to its destruction, a power, the exercise of which it ought never to approve but when it reaps from it substantial benefits.

Riches, useless to the miser, who is no more than their miserable gaoler; prejudicial to the debauchee, for whom they only procure infirmities; injurious to the voluptuary, to whom they only bring disgust—whom they oppress with satiety; can in the hands of the honest man produce unnumbered means of augmenting the sum of his happiness; but before man covets wealth it is proper he should know how to employ it; money is only a token, a representative of happiness; to enjoy it is so to use it as to make others happy: this is the great secret, this is the talisman, this is the reality. Money, according to the compact of man, procures for him all those benefits he can desire; there is only one, which it will not procure, that is, *the knowledge how to apply it properly*. For man to have money, without the true secret how to enjoy it, is to possess the key of a commodious palace to which he is interdicted entrance; to lavish it, prodigally, is to throw the key into the river; to make a bad use of it, is only to make it the means of wounding himself. Give the most ample treasures to the enlightened man, he will not be overwhelmed with them; if he has a capacious mind, if he has a noble soul, he will only extend more widely his benevolence; he will deserve the affection of a greater number of his fellow men; he will attract the love, he will secure the homage, of all those who surround him; he will restrain himself in his pleasures, in order that he may be enabled truly to enjoy them; he will know that money cannot re-establish a soul worn out with enjoyment; cannot give fresh elasticity to organs enfeebled by excess; cannot give fresh tension to nerves grown flaccid by abuse; cannot invigorate a body enervated by debauchery; cannot corroborate a machine, from thenceforth become incapable of sustaining him, except by the necessity of privations; he will know that the licentiousness of the voluptuary stifles pleasure in its source; that all the treasure in the world cannot renew his senses.

From this, it will be obvious, that nothing is more frivolous than the declamations of a gloomy philosophy against the desire of power; nothing more absurd than the rant of superstition against the pursuit of grandeur; nothing more inconsistent than homilies against the acquisition of riches; nothing more unreasonable than dogmas that forbid the enjoyment of pleasure. These objects are desirable for man, whenever his situation allows him to make pretensions to them; they are useful to society, conducive to public happiness, whenever he has acquired the knowledge of making them turn to his own real advantage; reason cannot censure him, virtue cannot despise him, when in order to obtain them, he never travels out of the road of truth; when in their acquisition, he wounds no one's interest; when he pursues only legitimate means: his associates will applaud him; his contemporaries will esteem him: he will respect himself, when he only employs their agency to secure his own happiness, and that of his fellows. Pleasure is a benefit, it is of the essence of man to love, it is even rational when it renders his existence really valuable to himself—when it does not injure him in his own esteem; when its consequences are not grievous to others. *Riches* are the symbols of the great majority of the benefits of this life; they become a reality in the hands of the man who has the clew to their just application. *Power* is the most sterling of all benefits, when he who is its depositary has received from nature a soul sufficiently noble, a mind sufficiently elevated, a heart sufficiently benevolent, faculties sufficiently energetic, above all, when he has derived from education a true regard for virtue, that sacred love for truth which enables him to extend his happy influence over whole nations; which by this means he places in, a state of legitimate dependence on his will; *man only acquires the right of commanding men, when he renders them happy.*

The right of man over his fellow man can only be founded either upon the actual happiness he secures to him, or that which he gives him reason to hope he will procure for him; without this, the power he exercises would be violence, usurpation, manifest tyranny; it is only upon the faculty of rendering him happy, that legitimate authority builds its structure; without this it is the *"baseless fabric of a vision."* No man derives from nature the right of *commanding another*, but it is voluntarily accorded to those, from whom he expects his welfare. *Government* is the right of commanding, conferred on the sovereign only for the advantage of those who are governed. Sovereigns are the defenders of the persons, the guardians of the property, the protectors of the liberty of their subjects: this is the price of their obedience; it is only on this condition these consent to obey; government would not be better than a robbery whenever it availed itself of the powers confided to it, to render society unhappy. *The empire of religion* is founded on the opinion man entertains of its having power to render nations happy; government and religion are reasonable institutions; but only so, inasmuch as they equally contribute to the felicity of man: it would be folly in him to submit himself to a yoke from which there resulted nothing but evil. It would be folly to expect that man should bind himself to misery; it would be rank injustice to oblige him to renounce his rights without some corresponding advantage!

The authority which a father exercises over his family is only founded on the advantages which he is supposed to procure for it. Rank, in political society, has only for its basis the real or imaginary utility of some citizens for which the others are willing to distinguish them—agree to respect them—consent to obey them. The rich acquire rights over the indigent, the wealthy claim the homage of the needy, only by virtue of the welfare they are conditioned to procure them. Genius, talents, science, arts, have rights over man, only in consequence of their utility; of the delight they confer; of the advantages they procure for society. In a word, it is happiness, it is the expectation of happiness, it is its image that man cherishes—that he esteems—that he unceasingly adores. Monarchs, the rich, the great, may easily impose on him, may dazzle him, may intimidate him, but they will never be able to obtain the voluntary submission of his heart, which alone can confer upon them legitimate rights, without they make him experience real benefits—without they display virtue. Utility is nothing more than true happiness; to be useful is to be virtuous; to be virtuous is to make others happy.

The happiness which man derives from them is the invariable, the necessary standard of his sentiments, for the beings of his species; for the objects he desires; for the opinions he embrases; for those actions on which he decides. He is the dupe of his prejudices every time he ceases to avail himself of this standard to regulate his judgment. He will never run the risk of deceiving himself, when he shall examine strictly what is the real utility resulting to his species from the religion, from the superstition, from the laws, from the institutions, from the inventions, from the various actions of all mankind.

A superficial view may sometimes seduce him; but experience, aided by reflection, will reconduct him to reason, which is incapable of deceiving him. This teaches him that pleasure is a momentary happiness, which frequently becomes an evil; that evil is a fleeting trouble that frequently becomes a good: it makes him understand the true nature of objects, enables him to foresee the effects he may expect; it makes him distinguish those desires to which his welfare permits him to lend himself, from those to whose seduction he ought to make resistance. In short, it will always convince him that the true interest of intelligent beings, who love happiness, who desire to render their own existence felicitous, demands that they should root out all those phantoms, abolish all those chimerical ideas, destroy all those prejudices, which by traducing virtue, obstruct their felicity in this world.

If he consults experience, he will perceive that it is in illusions, in false opinions, rendered sacred by time, that he ought to search out the source of that multitude of evils which almost every where overwhelms mankind. From ignorance of natural causes, man has created imaginary causes; not knowing to what cause to attribute thunder, he ascribed it to an imaginary being whom he called JUPITER; imposture availing itself of this disposition, rendered these causes terrible to him; these fatal ideas haunted him without rendering him better; made him tremble without either benefit to himself or to others; filled his mind with chimeras that opposed themselves to the progress of his reason; that prevented him from really seeking after his happiness. His vain fears rendered him the slave of those who deceived him, under pretence of consulting his welfare; he committed evil, because they persuaded him his gods demanded sacrifices; he lived in misfortune, because they made him believe these gods condemned him to be miserable; the slave of beings, to which his own imagination had given birth, he never dared to disentangle himself from his chains; the artful ministers of these divinities gave him to understand that stupidity, the renunciation of reason, sloth of mind, abjection of soul, were the sure means of obtaining eternal felicity.

Prejudices, not less dangerous, have blinded man upon the true nature of government. Nations in general are ignorant of the true foundations of authority; they dare not demand happiness from those kings who are charged with the care of procuring it for them: some have believed their sovereigns were gods disguised, who received with their birth the right of commanding the rest of mankind; that they could at their pleasure dispose of the felicity of the people; that they were not accountable for the misery they engendered. By a necessary consequence of these erroneous opinions, politics have almost every where degenerated into the fatal art of sacrificing the interests of the many, either to the caprice of an individual, or to some few privileged irrational beings. In despite of the evils which assailed them, nations fell down in adoration before the idols they themselves had made: foolishly respected the instruments of their misery; had a stupid veneration for those who possessed the sovereign power of injuring them; obeyed their unjust will; lavished their blood; exhausted their treasure; sacrificed their lives, to glut the ambition, to feed the cupidity to minister to the regenerated phantasms, to gratify the never-ending caprices of these men; they bend the knee to established opinion, bowed to rank, yielded to title, to opulence, to pageantry, to ostentation: at length victims to their prejudices, they in vain expected their welfare at the hands of men who were themselves unhappy from their own vices; whose neglect of virtue, had rendered them incapable of enjoying true felicity; who are but little disposed to occupy themselves with their prosperity: under such chiefs their physical and moral happiness were equally neglected or even annihilated.

The same blindness may be perceived in the science of morals. Superstition, which never had any thing but ignorance for its basis, which never had more than a disordered imagination for its guide, did not found ethics upon man's nature; upon his relations with his fellows; upon those duties which necessarily flow from these relations; it preferred, as more in unison with itself, founding them upon imaginary relations which it pretended subsisted between him and those invisible powers it had so gratuitously imagined; that were delivered by oracles which their priests had the address to make him believe spoke the will of the Divinity: thus, TROPHONIUS, from his cave made affrightened mortals tremble; shook the stoutest nerves; made them turn pale with fear; his miserable, deluded supplicants, who were obliged to sacrifice to him, anointed their bodies with oil, bathed in certain rivers, and after they had offered their cake of honey and received their destiny, became so dejected, so wretchedly forlorn, that to this day their descendants, when they behold a malencholy man, exclaim, "*He has consulted the oracle of Trophonius.*" It was these invisible gods, which superstition always paints as furious tyrants, who were declared the arbiters of man's destiny; the models of his conduct: when he was willing to imitate them, when he was willing to conform himself to the lessons of their interpreters, he became wicked, was an unsociable creature, an useless being or else a turbulent maniac—a zealous fanatic. It was these alone who profited by superstition, who advantaged themselves by the darkness in which they contrived to involve the human mind; nations were ignorant of nature; they knew nothing of reason; they understood not truth; they had only a gloomy superstition, without one certain idea of either morals or virtue. When man committed evil against his fellow creature, he believed he had offended these gods; but he also believed himself forgiven, as soon as he had prostrated himself before them; as soon as he had by costly presents gained over the priest to his interest. Thus superstition, far from giving a sure, far from affording a natural, far from introducing a known basis to morals, only rested it on an unsteady foundation; made it consist in ideal duties impossible to be accurately understood. What did I say? It first corrupted him, and his expiations finished by ruining him. Thus when superstition was desirous to combat the unruly passions of man it attempted it in vain; always enthusiastic, ever deprived of experience, it knew nothing of the true remedies: those which it applied were disgusting, only suitable to make the sick revolt against them; it made them pass for divine, because they were not made of man; they were inefficacious, because chimeras could effectuate nothing against those substantive passions to which motives more real, impulsions more powerful, concurred to give birth, which every thing conspired, to flourish in his heart. The voice of superstition or of the gods, could not make itself heard amidst the tumult of society—where all was in confusion—where the priest cried out to man, that he could not render himself happy without injuring his fellow creatures, who happened to differ from him in opinion: these vain clamours only made virtue hateful to him, because they always represented it as the enemy to his happiness; as the bane of human pleasures: he consequently failed in the observation of his duties, because real motives were never held forth to induce him to make the requisite sacrifice; the present prevailed over the future; the visible over the invisible; the known over the unknown: man became wicked because every thing informed him he must be so, in order to obtain the happiness after which he sighed.

Thus the sum of human misery was never diminished; on the contrary, it was accumulating either by his superstition, by his government, by his education, by his opinions or by the institutions he adopted under the idea of rendering his condition more pleasant: it not unfrequently happened that the whole of these acted upon him simultaneously; he was then completely wretched. It cannot be too often repeated, *it is in error that man will find the true spring of those evils with which the human race is afflicted;* it is not nature that renders him miserable; it is not nature that makes him unhappy; it is not an irritated Divinity who is desirous he should live in tears; it is not hereditary depravation that has caused him to be wicked; it is to error, to long cherished, consecrated error, to error identified with his very existence, that these deplorable effects are to be ascribed.

The sovereign good, so much sought after by some philosophers, announced with so much emphasis by others, may be considered as a chimera, like unto that marvellous panacea which some adepts have been willing to pass upon mankind for an universal remedy. All men are diseased; the moment of their birth delivers them over to the contagion of error; but individuals are variously affected by it by a consequence of their natural organization; of their peculiar circumstances. If there is a sovereign remedy, which can be indiscriminately applied to the diseases of man, there is without doubt only ONE, this catholic balsam is TRUTH, Which he must draw from nature.

At the afflicting sight of those errors which blind the greater number of mortals—of those delusions which man is doomed to suck in with his mother's milk; viewing with painful sensations those irregular desires, those disgusting propensities, by which he is perpetually agitated; seeing the terrible effect of those licentious passions which torment him; of those lasting inquietudes which gnaw his repose; of those stupendous evils, as well physical as moral, which assail him on every side: the contemplator of humanity would be tempted to believe that happiness was not made for this world; that any effort to cure those minds which every thing unites to poison, would be a vain enterprize; that it was an Augean stable, requiring the strength of another Hercules. When he considers those numerous superstitions by which man is kept in a continual state of alarm—that divide him from his fellow—that render him vindictive, persecuting, and irrational; when he beholds the many despotic governments that oppress him; when he examines those multitudinous, unintelligible, contradictory laws that torture him; the manifold injustice under which he groans; when he turns his mind to the barbarous ignorance in which he is steeped, almost over the whole surface of the earth; when he witnesses those enormous crimes that debase society; when he unmasks those rooted vices that render it so hateful to almost every individual; he has great difficulty to prevent his mind from embracing the idea that misfortune is the only appendage of the human species; that this world is made solely to assemble the unhappy; that human felicity is a chimera, or at least a point so fugitive, that it is impossible it can be fixed.

Thus superstitious mortals, atrabilious men, beings nourished in melancholy, unceasingly see either nature or its author exasperated against the human race; they suppose that man is the constant object of heaven's wrath; that he irritates it even by his desires: that he renders himself criminal by seeking a felicity which is not made for him: struck with beholding that those objects which he covets in the most lively manner, are never competent to content his heart, they have decried them as abominations, as things prejudicial to his interest, as odious to his gods; they prescribe him abstinence from all search after them; that he should entirely shun them; they have endeavoured to put to the rout all his passions, without any distinction even of those which are the most useful to himself, the most beneficial to those beings with whom he lives: they have been willing that man should render himself insensible; should become his own enemy; that he should separate himself from his fellow creatures; that he should renounce all pleasure; that he should refuse happiness; in short, *that he should cease to be a man, that he should become unnatural.* "Mortals!" have they said, "ye were born to be unhappy; the author of your existence has destined ye for misfortune; enter then into his views, and render yourselves miserable. Combat those rebellious desires which have felicity for their object; renounce those pleasures which it is your essence to love; attach yourselves to nothing in this world; by a society that only serves to inflame your imagination, to make you sigh after benefits you ought not to enjoy; break up the spring of your souls; repress that activity that seeks to put a period to your sufferings; suffer, afflict yourselves, groan, be wretched; such is for you the true road to happiness."

Blind physicians! who have mistaken for a disease the natural state of man! they have not seen that his desires were necessary; that his passions were essential to him; that to defend him from loving legitimate pleasures; to interdict him from desiring them, is to deprive him of that activity which is the vital principle of society; that to tell him to hate, to desire him to despise himself, is to take from him the most substantive motive, that can conduct him to virtue. It is thus, by its supernatural remedies, by its wretched panacea, superstition, far from curing those evils which render man decrepid, which bend him almost to the earth, has only increased them; made them more desperate; in the room of calming his passions, it gives them inveteracy; makes them more dangerous; renders them more venomous; turns that into a curse which nature has given him for his preservation; to be the means of his own happiness. It is not by extinguishing the passions of man that he is to be rendered happier; it is by turning them into proper channels, by directing them towards useful objects, which by being truly advantageous to himself, must of necessity be beneficial to others.

In despite of the errors which blind the human race, in despite of the extravagance of man's superstition, maugre the imbecility of his political institutions, notwithstanding the complaints, in defiance of the murmurs he is continually breathing forth against his destiny, there are yet happy individuals on the earth. Man has sometimes the felicity to behold sovereigns animated by the noble passion to render nations flourishing; full of the laudable ambition to make their people happy; now and then he encounters an ANTONINUS, a TRAJAN, a JULIAN, an ALFRED, a WASHINGTON; he meets with elevated minds who place their glory in encouraging merit—who rest their happiness in succouring indigence—who think it honourable to lend a helping hand to oppressed virtue: he sees genius occupied with the desire of meriting the eulogies of posterity; of eliciting the admiration of his fellow-citizens by serving them usefully, satisfied with enjoying that happiness he procures for others.

Let it not be believed that the man of poverty himself is excluded from happiness: mediocrity and indigence frequently procure for him advantages that opulence and grandeur are obliged to acknowledge; which title and wealth are constrained to envy: the soul of the needy man, always in action, never ceases to form desires which his activity places within his reach; whilst the rich, the powerful, are frequently in the afflicting embarrassment, of either not knowing what to wish for, or else of desiring those objects which their listlessness renders it impossible for them to obtain. The poor man's body, habituated to labour, knows the sweets of repose; this repose of the body, is the most troublesome fatigue to him who is wearied with his idleness; exercise, and frugality, procure for the one vigour, health, and contentment; the intemperance and sloth of the other, furnish him only with disgust—load him with infirmities. Indigence sets all the springs of the soul to work; it is the mother of industry; from its bosom arises genius; it is the parent of talents, the hot-bed of that merit to which opulence is obliged to pay tribute; to which grandeur bows its homage. In short the blows of fate find in the poor man a flexible reed, who bends without breaking, whilst the storms of adversity tear the rich man like the sturdy oak in the forest, up by the very roots.

Thus Nature is not a step-mother to the greater number of her children. He whom fortune has placed in an obscure station is ignorant of that ambition which devours the courtier; knows nothing of the inquietude which deprives the intriguer of his rest; is a stranger to the remorse, an alien to the disgust, is unconscious of the weariness of the man, who, enriched with the spoils of a nation, does not know how to turn them to his profit. The more the body labours, the more the imagination reposes itself; it is the diversity of the objects man runs over that kindles it; it is the satiety of those objects that causes him disgust; the imagination of the indigent is circumscribed by necessity: he receives but few ideas: he is acquainted with but few objects: in consequence, he has but little to desire; he contents himself with that little: whilst the entire of nature with difficulty suffices to satisfy the insatiable desires, to gratify the imaginary wants of the man, plunged in luxury, who has run over and exhausted all common objects. Those, whom prejudice contemplates; as the most unhappy of men, frequently enjoy advantages more real, happiness much greater, than those who oppress them—who despise them—but who are nevertheless often reduced to the misery of envying them. Limited desires are a real benefit: the man of meaner condition, in his humble fortune, desires only bread: he obtains it by the sweat of his brow; he would eat it with pleasure if injustice did not sometimes render it bitter to him. By the delirium of some governments, those who roll in abundance, without for that reason being more happy, dispute with the cultivator even the fruits which the earth yields to the labour of his hands. *Princes* sometimes sacrifice their true happiness, as well as that of their states, to these passions—to those caprices which discourage the people; which plunge their provinces in misery: which make millions unhappy, without any advantage to themselves. *Tyrants* oblige the subjects to curse their existence; to abandon labour; take from them the courage of propagating a progeny who would be as unhappy as their fathers: the excess of oppression sometimes obliges them to revolt; makes them avenge themselves by wicked outrages of the injustice it has heaped on their devoted heads: injustice, by reducing indigence to despair, obliges it to seek in crime, resources, against its misery. An unjust government, produces discouragement in the soul: its vexations depopulate a country; under its influence, the earth remains without culture; from thence is bred frightful famine, which gives birth to contagion and plague. The misery of a people produce revolutions; soured by misfortunes, their minds get into a state of fermentation; the overthrow of an empire, is the necessary effect. It is thus that *physics* and *morals* are always connected, or rather are the *same thing*.

If the bad morals of chiefs do not always produce such marked effects, at least they generate slothfulness, of which their effect is to fill society with mendicants; to crowd it with malefactors; whose vicious course neither superstition nor the terror of the laws can arrest; which nothing can induce to remain the unhappy spectators of a welfare they are not permitted to participate. They seek a fleeting happiness at the expence even of their lives, when injustice has shut up to them the road of labour, those paths of industry which would have rendered them both useful and honest.

Let it not then be said that no government can render all its subjects happy; without doubt it cannot flatter itself with contenting the capricious humours of some idle citizens who are obliged to rack their imagination, to appease the disgust arising from lassitude: but it can, and it ought to occupy itself with ministering to the real wants of the multitude, with giving a useful activity to the whole body politic. A society enjoys all the happiness of which it is susceptible whenever the greater number of its members are wholesomely fed, decently cloathed, comfortably lodged—in short when they can without an excess of toil beyond their strength, procure wherewith to satisfy those wants which nature has made necessary to their existence. Their mind rests contented as soon as they are convinced no power can ravish from them the fruits of their industry; that they labour for themselves; that the sweat of their brow is for the immediate comfort of their own families. By a consequence of human folly in some regions, whole nations are obliged to toil incessantly, to waste their strength, to sweat under their burdens to undulate the air with their sighs, to drench the earth with their tears, in order to maintain the luxury, to gratify the whims, to support the corruption of a small number of irrational beings; of some few useless men to whom happiness has become impossible, because their bewildered imaginations no longer know any bounds. It is thus that superstitious, thus that political errors have changed the fair face of nature into a valley of tears.

For want of consulting reason, for want of knowing the value of virtue, for want of being instructed in their true interest, for want of being acquainted with what constitutes solid happiness, in what consists real felicity, the prince and the people, the rich and the poor, the great and the little, are unquestionably, frequently very far removed from content; nevertheless if an impartial eye be glanced over the human race, it will be found to comprise a greater number of benefits than of evils. No man is entirely happy, but he is so in detail; those who make the most bitter complaints of the rigour of their fate, are however, held in existence by threads frequently imperceptible; are prevented from the desire of quitting it by circumstances of which they are not aware. In short, habit lightens to man the burden of his troubles; grief suspended becomes true enjoyment; every want is a pleasure in the moment when it is satisfied; freedom from chagrin, the absence of disease, is a happy state which he enjoys secretly, without even perceiving it; hope, which rarely abandons him entirely, helps him to support the most cruel disasters. The PRISONER laughs in his irons. The wearied VILLAGER returns singing to his cottage. In short, the man who calls himself the most unfortunate, never sees death approach without dismay, at least, if despair has not totally disfigured nature in his eyes.

As long as man desires the continuation of his being, he has no right to call himself completely unhappy; whilst hope sustains him, he still enjoys a great benefit. If man was more just, in rendering to himself an account of his pleasures, in estimating his pains, he would acknowledge that the sum of the first exceeds by much the amount of the last; he would perceive that he keeps a very exact ledger of the evil, but a very unfaithful journal of the good: indeed he would avow, that there are but few days entirely unhappy during the whole course of his existence. His periodical wants procure for him the pleasure of satisfying them; his soul is perpetually moved by a thousand objects, of which, the variety, the multiplicity, the novelty, rejoices him, suspends his sorrows, diverts his chagrin. His physical evils, are they violent? They are not of long duration; they conduct him quickly to his end: the sorrows of his mind, when too powerful, conduct him to it equally. At the same time nature refuses him every happiness, she opens to him a door by which he quits life; does he refuse to enter it? It is that he yet finds pleasure in existence. Are nations reduced to despair? Are they completely miserable? They have recourse to arms; at the risque of perishing, they make the most violent efforts to terminate there sufferings.

Thus because he sees so many of his fellows cling to life, man ought to conclude they are not so unhappy as he thinks. Then let him not exaggerate the evils of the human race, but let him impose silence on that gloomy humour that persuades him these evils are without remedy; let him only diminish by degrees the number of his errors, his calamities will vanish in the same proportion; he is not to conclude himself infelicitous because his heart never ceases to form new desires, which he finds it difficult, sometimes impossible to gratify. Since his body daily requires nourishment, let him infer that it is sound, that it fulfils its functions. As long as he has desires, the proper deduction ought to be, that his mind is kept in the necessary activity; he should gather from all this that passions are essential to him, that they constitute the happiness of a being who feels; are indispensable to a man who thinks; are requisite to furnish him with ideas; that they are a vital principle with a creature who must necessarily love that which procures him comfort, who must equally desire that which promises him a mode of existence analogous to his natural energies. As long as he exists, as long as the spring of his soul maintains its elasticity, this soul desires; as long as it desires, he experiences the activity which is necessary to him; as long as he acts, so long he lives. Human life may be compared to a river, of which the waters succeed each other, drive each other forward, and flow on without interruption; these waters, obliged to roll over an unequal bed, encounter at intervals those obstacles which prevent their stagnation; they never cease to undulate; sometimes they recoil, then again rush forward, thus continuing to run with more or less velocity, until they are restored to *the ocean of nature*.

CHAP. XVII.

Those Ideas which are true, or founded upon Nature, are the only Remedies for the Evils of Man.—Recapitulation.—Conclusion of the first Part.

Whenever man ceases to take experience for his guide, he falls into error. His errors become yet more dangerous, assume a more determined inveteracy, when they are clothed with the sanction of superstition; it is then that he hardly ever consents to return into the paths of truth; he believes himself deeply interested in no longer seeing clearly that which lies before him; he fancies he has an essential advantage in no longer understanding himself; he supposes his happiness exacts that he should shut his eyes to truth. If the majority of moral philosophers have mistaken the human heart—if they have deceived themselves upon its diseases—if they have miscalculated the remedies that are suitable—if the remedies they have administered have been inefficacious or even dangerous—it is because they have abandoned nature—because they have resisted experience—because they have not had sufficient steadiness to consult their reason—because they have renounced the evidence of their senses—because they have only followed the caprices of an imagination either dazzled by enthusiasm or disturbed by fear; because they have preferred the illusions it has held forth to the realities of nature, *who never deceives.*

It is for want of having felt that an intelligent being cannot for an instant lose sight of his own peculiar conservation—of his particular interests, either real or fictitious—of his own welfare, whether permanent or transitory; in short, of his happiness, either true or false. It is for want of having considered that desires are natural, that passions are essential, that both the one and the other are motions necessary to the soul of man,—that the physicians of the, human mind have supposed supernatural causes for his wanderings; have only applied to his evils topical remedies, either useless or dangerous. Indeed, in desiring him to stifle his desires, to combat his propensities, to annihilate his passions, they have done no more than give him sterile precepts, at once vague and impracticable; these vain lessons have influenced no one; they have at most restrained some few mortals whom a quiet imagination but feebly solicited to evil; the terrors with which they have accompanied them have disturbed the tranquillity of those persons who were moderate by their nature, without ever arresting the ungovernable temperament of those who were inebriated by their passions, or hurried along; by the torrent of habit. In short, the promises of superstition, as well as the menaces it holds forth, have only formed fanatics, given birth to enthusiasts, who are either dangerous or useless to society, without ever making man truly virtuous; that is to say, useful to his fellow creatures.

These, empirics guided by a blind routine have, not seen that man as long as he exists, is obliged to feel, to desire, to have passions, to satisfy them in proportion to the energy which his organization has given him; they have not perceived that education planted these desires in his heart—that habit rooted them—that his government, frequently vicious, corroborated their growth—that public opinion stamped them with its approbation—that—experience render them necessary—that to tell men thus constituted to destroy their passions, was either to plunge them into despair or else to order them remedies too revolting for their temperament. In the actual state of opulent societies, to say to a man who knows by experience that riches procure every pleasure, that he must not desire them; that he must not make any efforts to obtain them; that he ought to detach himself from them: is to persuade him to render himself miserable. To tell an ambitious man not to desire grandeur, not to covet power, which every thing conspires to point out to him as the height of felicity, is to order him to overturn at one blow the habitual system of his ideas; it is to speak, to a deaf man. To tell a lover of an impetuous temperament to stifle his passions for the object that enchants him, is to make him understand, that he ought to renounce his happiness. To oppose superstition to such substantive, such puissant interests is to combat realities by chimerical speculations.

Indeed, if things were examined without prepossession, it would be found that the greater part of the precepts inculcated by superstition, which fanatical dogmas hold forth, which, supernatural mortals give to man, are as ridiculous as they are impossible to be put into practice. To interdict passion to man, is to desire of him not to be a human creature; to counsel an individual of a violent imagination to moderate his desires, is to advise him to change his temperament—is to request his blood to flow more sluggishly. To tell a man to renounce his habits, is to be willing that a citizen, accustomed to clothe himself, should consent to walk quite naked; it would avail as much, to desire him to change the lineament of his face, to destroy his configuration, to extinguish his imagination, to alter the course of his fluids, as to command him not to have passions which excite an activity analogous with his natural energy; or to lay aside those which confirmed habit has made him contract; which his circumstances, by a long succession of causes and effects, have converted into wants. Such are, however, the so much boasted remedies which the greater number of moral philosophers apply to human depravity. Is it, then surprising they do not produce the desired effect, or that they only reduce man to a state of despair by the effervescence that results from the continual conflict which they excite between the passions of his heart and these fanciful doctrines; between his vices and his virtues; between his habits and those chimerical fears with which superstition is at all times ready to overwhelm him? The vices of society, aided by the objects of which it avails itself to what the desires of man, the pleasures, the riches, the grandeur which his government holds forth to him as so many seductive magnets, the advantage which education, the benefits which example, the interests which public opinion render dear to him, attract him on one side; whilst a gloomy morality, founded upon superstitious illusions, vainly solicit him on the other; thus, superstition plunges him into misery; holds a violent struggle with his heart, without scarcely ever gaining the victory; when by accident it does prevail against so many united forces, it renders him unhappy; it completely destroys the spring of his soul.

Passions are the true counterpoise to passions; then let him not seek to destroy them; but let him endeavour to direct them; let him balance those which are prejudicial, by those which are useful to society. *Reason*, the fruit of experience, is only the art of choosing those passions to which for his own peculiar happiness he ought to listen. *Education* is the true art of disseminating the proper method of cultivating advantageous passions in the heart of man. *Legislation* is the art of restraining dangerous passions; of exciting those which may be conducive to the public welfare. *Superstition* is only the miserable art of planting the unproductive labour—of nourishing in the soul of man those chimeras, those illusions, those impostures, those incertitudes from whence spring passions fatal to himself as well as to others: it is only by bearing up with fortitude against these that he can securely place himself on the road to happiness. *True religion* is the art of advocating truth—of renouncing error—of contemplating reality—of drawing wisdom from experience—of cultivating man's nature to his own felicity, by teaching him to contribute to that of his associates; in short it is *reason, education,* and *legislation,* united to further the great end of human existence, by causing the passions of man to flow in a current genial to his own happiness.

Reason and *morals* cannot effect any thing on mankind if they do not point out to each individual that his true interest is attached to a conduct that is either useful to others or beneficial to himself; this conduct to be useful must conciliate for him the benevolence, gain for him the favor of these beings who are necessary to his happiness: it is then for the interest of mankind, for the happiness of the human race, it is for the esteem of himself, for the love of his fellows, for the advantages which ensue, that education in early life should kindle the imagination of the citizen; this is the true means of obtaining those happy results with which habit should familiarize him; which public opinion should render dear to his heart; for which example ought continually to rouse his faculties; after which he should be taught to search with unceasing attention. *Government* by the aid of recompences, ought to encourage him to follow this plan; by visiting crime with punishment it ought to deter those who are willing to interrupt it. Thus the hope of a true welfare, the fear of real evil, will be passions suitable to countervail those which by their impetuosity would injure society; these last will at least become very rare, if instead of feeding man's mind with unintelligible speculations, in lieu of vibrating on his ears words void of sense, he is only spoken to of realities, only shewn those interests which are in unison with truth.

Man is frequently so wicked, only, because he almost always feels himself interested in being so; let him be more enlightened, more familiarized with truth, more accustomed to virtue, he will be made more happy; he will necessarily become better. An equitable government, a vigilant administration, will presently fill the state with honest citizens; it will hold forth to them present reasons for benevolence; real advantages in truth; palpable motives to be virtuous; it will instruct them in their duties; it will foster them with its cares; it will allure them by the assurance of their own peculiar happiness; its promises faithfully fulfilled—its menaces regularly executed, will unquestionably have much more weight than those of a gloomy superstition, which never exhibits to their view other than illusory benefits, fallacious punishments, which the man hardened in wickedness will doubt every time he finds an interest in questioning them: present motives will tell more home to his heart than those which are distant and at best uncertain. The vicious and the wicked are so common upon the earth, so pertinacious in their evil courses, so attached to their irregularities, only because there are but few governments that make man feel the advantage of being just, the pleasure of being honest, the happiness of being benevolent on the contrary, there is hardly any place where the most powerful interests do not solicit him to crime, by favouring the propensities of a vicious organization; by countenancing those appetencies which nothing has attempted to rectify or lead towards virtue. A savage, who in his horde knows not the value of money, certainly would not commit a crime, if when transplanted into civilized society, he should presently learn to desire it, should make efforts to obtain it, and if he could without danger finish by stealing it; above all, if he had not been taught to respect the property of the beings who environ him. The savages and the child are precisely in the same state; it is the negligence of society, of those entrusted with their education, that renders both the one and the other wicked. The son of a noble, from his infancy learns to desire power, at a riper age he becomes ambitious; if he has the address to insinuate himself into favor, he perhaps becomes wicked, because in some societies he has been taught to know he may be so with impunity when he can command the ear of his sovereign. It is not therefore nature that makes man wicked, they are his institutions which determine him to vice. The infant brought up amongst robbers, can generally become nothing but a malefactor; if he had been reared with honest people, the chance is he would have been a virtuous man.

If the source be traced of that profound ignorance in which man is with respect to his morals, to the motives that can give volition to his will, it will be found in those false ideas which the greater number of speculators have formed to themselves, of human nature. The science of morals has become an enigma which it is impossible to unrevel; because man has made himself double; has distinguished his soul from his body; supposed it of a nature different from all known beings, with modes of action, with properties distinct from all other bodies, because he has emancipated this soul from physical laws, in order to submit it to capricious laws emanating from men who have pretended they are derived from imaginary regions, placed at very remote distances: metaphysicians seized upon these gratuitous suppositions, and by dint of subtilizing them, have rendered them completely unintelligible. These moralists have not perceived that motion is essential to the soul as well as to the living body; that both the one and the other are never moved but by material, by physical objects; that the want of each regenerate themselves unceasingly; that the wants of the soul, as well as those of the body are purely physical; that the most intimate, the most constant connection subsists between the soul and the body; or rather they have been unwilling to allow that they ate only the same thing considered under different points of view. Obstinate in their supernatural, unintelligible opinions, they have refused to open their eyes, which would have convinced them that the body in suffering rendered the soul miserable; that the soul afflicted undermined the body and brought it to decay; that both the pleasures and agonies of the mind have an influence over the body, either plunge it into sloth or give it activity: they have rather chosen to believe, that the soul draws its thoughts, whether pleasant or gloomy, from its own peculiar sources, while the fact is, that it derives its ideas only from material objects that strike on the physical organs; that it is neither determined to gaiety nor led on to sorrow, but by the actual state, whether permanent or transitory, in which the fluids and solids of the body are found. In short, they have been loath to acknowledge that the soul, purely passive, undergoes the same changes which the body experiences; is only moved by its intervention; acts only by its assistance, receives its sensations, its perceptions, forms its ideas, derives either its happiness or its misery from physical objects, through the medium of the organs of which the body is composed; frequently without its own cognizance, often in despite of itself.

By a consequence of these opinions, connected with marvellous systems, or systems invented to justify them, they have supposed the human soul to be a free agent; that is to say, that it has the faculty of moving itself; that it enjoys the privilege of acting independent of the impulse received from exterior objects, through the organs of the body; that regardless of these impulsions it can even resist them, and follow its own directions by its own energies; that it is not only different in its nature from all other beings, but has a separate mode of action; in other words, that it is an insolated point which is, not submitted to that uninterrupted chain of motion which bodies communicate to each other in a nature, whose parts are always in action. Smitten with their sublime notions, these speculators were not aware that in thus distinguishing the soul from the body and from all known beings, they rendered it an impossibility to form any true ideas of it, either to themselves or to others: they were unwilling to perceive the perfect analogy which is found between the manner of the soul's action and that by which the body is afflicted; they shut their eyes to the necessary and continual correspondence which is found between the soul and the body; they perhaps did not perceive that like the body it is subjected to the motion of attraction and repulsion; has an aptitude to be attracted, a disposition to repel, which is ascribable to qualities inherent in those physical subsistances, which give play to the organs of the body; that the volition of its will, the activity of its passions, the continual regeneration of its desires, are never more than consequences of that activity which is produced in the body by material objects which are not under its controul; that these objects render it either happy or miserable, active or languishing, contented or discontented, in despite of itself,—in defiance of all the efforts it is capable of making to render it otherwise; they have rather chosen to seek in the heavens for unknown powers to set it in motion; they have held forth to man distant, imaginary interests: under the pretext of procuring for him future happiness, he has been prevented from labouring to his present felicity, which has been studiously withheld from his knowledge: his regards have been fixed upon the heavens, that he might lose sight of the earth: truth has been concealed from him; and it has been pretended he would be rendered happy by dint of terrors, always at an immense distance; by means of shadows, with whose substances he could never come in contact; of chimeras formed by his own bewildered imagination, which changed nearly as often as the governments to which he was submitted. In short, hoodwinked by his fears, blinded by his own credulity, *he was only guided through the flexuous paths of life, by men blind as himself, where both the one and the other were frequently lost in the maze.*

CONCLUSION.

From every thing which has been hitherto said, it evidently results that all the errors of mankind, of whatever nature they may be, arise from man's having renounced reason, quitted experience, and refused the evidence of his senses that he might be guided by imagination, frequently deceitful; by authority, always suspicious. Man will ever mistake his true happiness as long as he neglects to study nature, to investigate her laws, to seek in her alone the remedies for those evils which are the consequence of his errors: he will be an enigma to himself, as long as he shall believe himself double; that he is moved by an inconceivable spiritual power, of the laws and nature of which he is ignorant; his intellectual, as well as his moral faculties, will remain unintelligible to him if he does not contemplate them with the same eyes as he does his corporeal qualities; if he does not view them as submitted in every thing to the same impulse, as governed by the same regulations. The system of his pretended free agency is without support; experience contradicts it every instant, and proves that he never ceases to be under the influence of necessity in all his actions; this truth, far from being dangerous to man, far from being destructive of his morals, furnishes him with their true basis by making him feel the necessity of those relations which subsists between sensible beings united in society: who have congregated with a view of uniting their common efforts for their reciprocal felicity. From the necessity of these relations, spring the necessity of his duties; these point out to him the sentiments of love, which he should accord to virtuous conduct; that aversion he should have for what is vicious; the horror he should feel for every thing criminal. From hence the true foundation of *Moral Obligation* will be obvious, which is only the necessity of talking means to obtain the end man proposes to himself by uniting in society; in which each individual for his own peculiar interest, his own particular happiness, his own personal security, is obliged to display dispositions requisite to conciliate the affections of his associates; to hold a conduct suitable to the preservation of the community; to contribute by his actions to the happiness of the whole. In a word, it is upon the necessary action and re-action of the human will upon the necessary attraction and repulsion of man's soul, that all his morals are bottomed: it is the unison of his will, the concert of his actions, that maintains society; it is rendered miserable by his discordance; it is dissolved by his want of union.

From what has been said, it may be concluded that the names under which man has designated the concealed causes acting in nature, and their various effects, are never more than *necessity* considered under different points of view, with the original cause of which—the great *cause of causes*—

he must ever remain ignorant. It will be found that what he calls *order*, is a necessary consequence of causes and effects, of which he sees, or believes he sees, the entire connection, the complete routine, which pleases him as a whole, when he finds it conformable to his existence. In like manner it will be seen that what he calls *confusion*, is a consequence of like necessary causes and effects, of which he loses the concatenation, which he therefore thinks unfavourable to himself, or but little suitable to his being. That he has designated by the names of—

Intelligence, those necessary causes that necessarily operate the chain of events which he comprises under the term *order*.

Divinity, those necessary but invisible causes which give play to nature, in which every thing acts according to immutable and necessary laws:

Destiny or *fatality*, the necessary connection of those unknown causes and, effects which he beholds in the world:

Chance, those effects which he is not able to foresee, or of which he is ignorant of the necessary connection, with their causes:

Intellectual and *moral faculties*, those effects and those modifications necessary to an organized being, whom he has supposed to be moved by an inconceivable agent; who he has believed distinguished from his body, of a nature totally different from it, and which he has designated by the word SOUL. In consequence, he has believed this agent immortal; not dissoluble like the body. It has been shewn that the marvellous doctrine of another life, is founded upon gratuitous suppositions, contradicted by reflections, unsupported by experience, that may or may not be, without man's knowing any thing on the subject. It has been proved, that the hypothesis is not only useless to man's morals, but again, that it is calculated to palsy his exertions; to divert him from actively pursuing the true road to his own happiness; to fill him with romantic caprices; to inebriate him with opinions prejudicial to his tranquillity; in short, to lull to slumber the vigilance of legislators; by dispensing them from giving to education, to the institutions, to the laws of society, all that attention, which it is the duty and for his interest they should bestow. It must have been felt, that *politics* has unaccountably rested itself upon wrong opinions; upon ideas little capable of satisfying those passions, which every thing conspires to kindle in the heart of man; who ceases to view the future, while the present seduces and hurries him along. It has been shewn, that contempt of death is an advantageous sentiment, calculated to inspire man's mind with courage; to render him intrepid; to induce him to undertake that which may be truly useful to society; in short, from what has preceded, it will be obvious, what is competent to conduct man to happiness, and also what are the obstacles that error opposes to his felicity.

Let us not then, be accused of demolishing prejudice, without edifying the mind; with combating error without substituting truth; with underrating the power of the great *cause of causes*; with sapping at one and the same time the foundations of superstition and of sound morals. The last is necessary to man; it is founded upon his nature; its duties are certain, they must last as long as the human race remains; it imposes obligations on him, because, without it, neither individuals nor society could be able to subsist, either obtain or enjoy those advantages which nature obliges them to desire.

Listen then, O man! to those morals which are established upon, experience; which are grounded upon the necessity of things; do not lend thine ear to those superstitions founded upon reveries; rested upon imposture; built upon the capricious whims of a disordered imagination. Follow the lessons of those humane, those gentle morals, which conduct man to virtue, by the voice of happiness: turn a deaf ear to the inefficacious cries of superstition, which renders man really unhappy; which can never make him reverence VIRTUE; which renders truth hateful; which paints veracity in hideous colours; in short, let him see if REASON, without the assistance of a rival, who prohibits its use, will not more surely conduct him towards that great end, which is the object of his research, which is the natural tendency of all his views.

Indeed, what benefit has the human race hitherto drawn from those sublime, those supernatural notions with which superstition has fed mortals during so many ages? All those phantoms conjured—up by ignorance—brooded by imagination; all those hypothesis, subtile as they are irrational; from which experience is banished, all those words devoid of meaning with which languages are crowded; all those fantastical hopes; those panic terrors which have been brought to operate on the will of man; what have they done? Has any or the whole of them rendered him better, more enlightened to his duties, more faithful in their performance? Have those marvellous systems, or those sophistical inventions, by which they have been supported, carried conviction to his mind, reason into his conduct, virtue into his heart? Have they led him to the least acquaintance with the great *Cause of Causes?* Alas! it is a lamentable fact, that cannot be too often exposed, that all these things have done nothing more than plunge the human understanding into that darkness from which it is difficult to be withdrawn; sown in man's heart the most dangerous errors; of which it is scarcely possible to divest him; given birth to those fatal passions, in which may be found the true source of those evils, with which his species is afflicted: but have never enlightened his mind with truth, nor led him to that right healthy worship, which man best pays by a rational enjoyment of the faculties with which he is gifted.

Cease then, O mortal! to let thyself he disturbed with chimeras, to let thy mind be troubled with phantoms which thine own imagination has created, or to which arch imposture has given birth. Renounce thy vague hopes, disengage thyself from thine overwhelming fears, follow without inquietude the necessary routine which nature has marked out for thee; strew the road with flowers if thy destiny permits; remove, if thou art able, the thorns scattered over it. Do not attempt to plunge thy views into an impenetrable futurity; its obscurity ought to be sufficient to prove to thee, that it is either useless or dangerous to fathom. Think of making thyself happy in that existence which is known to thee: if thou wouldst preserve thyself, be temperate, be moderate, be reasonable: if thou seekest to render thy existence durable, be not prodigal of pleasure; abstain from every thing that can be hurtful to thyself, injurious to others: be truly intelligent; that is to say, learn to esteem thyself, to preserve thy being, to fulfil that end which at each moment thou proposest to thyself. Be virtuous, to the end that thou mayest render thyself solidly happy, that thou mayest enjoy the affections, secure the esteem, partake of the assistance of those by whom thou art surrounded; of those beings whom nature has made necessary to thine own peculiar felicity. Even when they should be unjust, render thyself worthy of their applause, of thine own love, and thou shalt live content, thy serenity shall not be disturbed, the end of thy career shall not slander thy life; which will be exempted from remorse: death will be to thee the door to a new existence, a new order, in which thou wilt be submitted, as thou art at present, to the eternal laws of nature, which ordains, that to LIVE HAPPY HERE BELOW, THOU MUST MAKE OTHERS HAPPY. Suffer thyself then, to be drawn gently along thy journey, until thou shalt sleep peaceable on that bosom which has given thee birth: if contrary to thine expectation, there should be another life of eternal felicity, thou canst not fail being a partaker.

For thou, wicked unfortunate! who art found in continual contradiction with thyself; thou whose disorderly machine can neither accord with thine own peculiar nature, nor with that of thine associates, whatever may be thy crimes, whatever may be thy fears of punishment in another life, thou art at least already cruelly punished in this? Do not thy follies, thy shameful habits, thy debaucheries, damage thine health? Dost thou not linger out life in disgust, fatigued with thine own excesses? Does not listlessness punish thee for thy satiated passions? Has not thy vigour, thy gaiety, thy content, already yielded to feebleness, crouched under infirmities, given place to regret? Do not thy vices every day dig thy grave? Every time thou hast stained thyself with crime, hast thou dared without horror to return into thyself, to examine thine own conscience? Hast thou not found remorse, error, shame, established in thine heart? Hast thou not dreaded the scrutiny of thy fellow man? Hast thou not trembled when alone; unceasingly feared, that truth, so terrible for thee, should unveil thy dark transgressions, throw into light thine enormous iniquities? Do not then any longer fear to part with thine existence, it will at least put an end to those richly merited torments thou hast inflicted on thyself; *Death, in delivering the earth from an incommodious burthen, will also deliver thee from thy most cruel enemy, thyself.*

END OF PART I.